Kalecki and Kaleckian Economics

This book helps in pushing forward a Kaleckian research agenda that is even more urgent given the 2007–2009 financial crisis and the current post-COVID recovery. Michał Kalecki was a leading heterodox economist, whose influence in the field perhaps even surpasses that of Keynes. Kalecki's insights are even more relevant today, and scholars are encouraged to apply his conclusions to ensure the sustainability of our economic systems.

This edited volume, honouring the work of Michał Kalecki, includes chapters contributed by celebrated Kaleckian economists. In honour of the 50th anniversary of his demise, the *Review of Political Economy* (ROPE) and Edward Lipiński Foundation hosted a conference in September 2020 to celebrate his contribution to heterodox economics and his lasting legacy. These chapters, honouring the work of Michał Kalecki, span a panoply of topics and include a personal note from one of his former students and friend, and cover topics such as Kalecki's relationship with the Cantabrigians, labour economics, fiscal policy, income distribution, gender, finance, debt, and democracy.

The chapters in this book were originally published as a special issue of the journal *Review of Political Economy*.

Louis-Philippe Rochon is Full Professor of Economics at Laurentian University, Canada, where he has been teaching since 2004. He is the editor-in-chief of the *Review of Political Economy*. He is the founding editor (now emeritus) of the *Review of Keynesian Economics*. He is widely published in post-Keynesian economics, and monetary theory and policy. He has been a visiting professor in over a dozen universities around the world.

Marcin Czachor is Attorney-at-law, the founder of Heterodox Publishing House, and co-founder of the Edward Lipiński Foundation for promoting pluralism in economics.

Gracjan Robert Bachurewicz is President of the Edward Lipiński Foundation's Council. He is a PhD Candidate and teaching assistant at the Department of Banking and Financial Markets at the University of Warsaw.

Kalecki and Kaleckian Economics

Understanding the Economics of Michał Kalecki and His Legacy after 50 Years

Edited by
Louis-Philippe Rochon, Marcin Czachor and Gracjan Robert Bachurewicz

LONDON AND NEW YORK

First published 2022
by Routledge
2 Park Square, Milton Park, Abingdon, Oxon, OX14 4RN

and by Routledge
605 Third Avenue, New York, NY 10158

Routledge is an imprint of the Taylor & Francis Group, an informa business

© 2022 Taylor & Francis

British Library Cataloguing-in-Publication Data
A catalogue record for this book is available from the British Library

ISBN13: 978-1-032-13573-1 (hbk)
ISBN13: 978-1-032-13574-8 (pbk)
ISBN13: 978-1-003-22992-6 (ebk)

DOI: 10.4324/9781003229926

Typeset in Minion Pro
by codeMantra

Publisher's Note
The publisher accepts responsibility for any inconsistencies that may have arisen during the conversion of this book from journal articles to book chapters, namely the inclusion of journal terminology.

Disclaimer
Every effort has been made to contact copyright holders for their permission to reprint material in this book. The publishers would be grateful to hear from any copyright holder who is not here acknowledged and will undertake to rectify any errors or omissions in future editions of this book.

Contents

Citation Information

The chapters in this book were originally published in the journal *Review of Political Economy*, volume 32, issue 4 (2020). When citing this material, please use the original page numbering for each article, as follows:

For any permission-related enquiries please visit:
http://www.tandfonline.com/page/help/permissions

Notes on Contributors

Gracjan Bachurewicz, University of Warsaw, Poland.

Maria Cristina Barbieri Góes, Roma Tre University, Italy.

Amit Bhaduri, Jawaharlal Nehru University, New Delhi, India.

Marcin Czachor, Heterodox Economic Publishing House, Poland.

Joseph Halevi, International College of Turin, Italy.

Eckhard Hein, Institute for International Political Economy (IPE), Berlin School of Economics and Law (HWR Berlin), Germany.

Peter Kriesler, University of NSW, Sydney, Australia.

Marc Lavoie, University of Ottawa, Canada; University of Sorbonne Paris Nord (CEPN, France), Villetaneuse, France.

Maria Cristina Marcuzzo, Dipartimento di Scienze Statistiche, Sapienza, Università di Roma, Roma, Italy.

Judith Martschin, Institute for International Political Economy (IPE), Berlin School of Economics and Law (HWR Berlin), Berlin, Germany.

Won Jun Nah, Kyungpook National University, Daegu, Korea.

Jerzy Osiatyński, Institute of Economics, Polish Academy of Sciences, Warsaw, Poland.

Louis-Philippe Rochon, Laurentian University, Canada.

Malcolm Sawyer, University of Leeds, UK.

Jan Toporowski, SOAS University of London, UK.

Introduction: Kalecki and Kaleckian Economics

Louis-Philippe Rochon, Marcin Czachor and Gracjan Bachurewicz

2020 marks the 50th anniversary of the passing of Michał Kalecki (1899–1970). Born in Lodz, Poland on 22nd June 1899, Kalecki passed away on 18 April 1970. In his biography of the author, Feiwel (1975, p. 455) eloquently wrote,

> With Michal Kalecki's death, the world lost a unique individual of extremely high principles, powerful energy, and brilliant mind, and economics lost a model and inspiration. His legacy, however, cannot be erased.

Kalecki was largely a self-taught economists, after having studied mathematics and engineering in Poland—studies that were interrupted due to family reasons. His interest in economics, however, was the result of his interest in political questions, which brought him to read Marx. In 1933, he published his first book, in Polish, *An Essay on the Theory of the Business Cycle*, where he laid out his ideas regarding the importance of effective demand.

Indeed, Kalecki's long-lasting contributions to heterodox economics is now well cemented; today, Kalecki is recognized not only as a contributor to heterodox economics, but as a founder as well. In his wonderful book on *The History of Post Keynesian Economics since 1936*, King (2002, p. 36) refers to Kalecki as "a major figure in the history of Post Keynesian economics", and Arestis and Skouras (1985) dedicate their book on post-Keynesian economics "to the memory of the first post-Keynesians", specifically mentioning Michał Kalecki among them.[1] Harcourt (1977, p. 93) refers to him as a "most important patron saint of the post-Keynesians."

Without doubt, Kalecki had a profound impact on the development of heterodox and post-Keynesian economics, through his own writings but also through his influence on John Robinson, and in most recent years, perhaps more so than Keynes himself. Arestis (1996, p. 11) argues "there is very little doubt that Kalecki's role in post-Keynesian economics is both extensive and paramount," and Sawyer (1985, p. 147) goes further, claiming that "the work of many post-Keynesians owes more to Kalecki than to Keynes." Some thirty-five years later, this claim is perhaps even more valid.

The claim is certainly due to the fact that over these years, there has been a proliferation of works done on Kalecki (see for instance, Feiwel 1975; Sawyer 1985; Sebastiani 1986; King 1996a,b; Toporowski 2013, 2018; Assous and Lopez Gallardo 2010); as well as Kalecki's collected works edited by Osiatynski (1990, 1991), which certainly

---

[1] In addition, they mention Joan Robinson, Piero Sraffa and Sidney Weintraub.

contributed to a resurgence of interest), and on Kaleckian economics (far too many to list). His work is also now being extended to new areas, including gender (see Hein 2020, see this issue of the journal; see also Seguino 2006), ecological economics (see Fontana and Sawyer 2016; Monserand 2019; Sawyer 2020), and financialization (see Hein 2012, 2015). Sawyer (2020a) has recently discussed the fields to which Kaleckian economics has now been applied.[2] This is all evidence of what Sebastiani (1986, xi) calls "the widespread rediscovery of Kalecki."

As a result, when picking up any of the many heterodox journals, we are perhaps more likely to come across a paper on Kalecki or in the Kaleckian tradition than on Keynes. Moreover, much of what passes for 'post-Keynesian' economics today is more rooted in the Kaleckian tradition, with many authors labeling their work as 'post-Keynesian' simply out of habit. In this sense, a dilemma arises: is it time to abandon the term 'post-Keynesian' altogether, or are there strategic reasons to keep the expression 'post-Keynesian', as it is now well entrenched.[3]

Regardless of what we call ourselves, the above discussion shows how far the Kaleckian tradition has come since Harcourt (1975; cited in Sawyer 1985, p. 1) described Kalecki as "the most neglected of all great modern economists', and King (1996, p.1) referred to him as 'underrated". Writing some 25 years ago, Dymski (1996, p. 115) had also claimed that Kalecki had exerted "less influence than Keynes, even among heterodox economists." Today, no one can claim Kalecki's work is neglected, underrated or less influential.

Much has also been written about Kalecki's independent discovery of the principle of effective demand and other key features of Keynes's work prompting many to ask if Kalecki was 'Keynesian before Keynes'? Robinson (1952, p. 159) defended "Mr. Kalecki's discovery of the General Theory independently of Keynes", as did King (2013, p. 487) who claims Kalecki "discovered the principle of effective demand more or less simultaneously with Keynes." Lawrence Klein (1951, p. 447), rightly concludes Kalecki "created a system that contains everything of importance in the Keynesian system, in addition to other contributions" (see also Asimakopulos 1989). Robinson also claims that "Kalecki was able to weave the analysis of imperfect competition and of effective demand together and it was this that opened up the way for what goes under the name of post-Keynesian economic theory" (Robinson 1977 [1979], pp. 193–4).

In turn, this has led some to ask whether Kalecki's work should be considered more foundational to post-Keynesian/heterodox economics than Keynes's, in particular the *General Theory* (Sawyer 1985). This assessment is based on the idea that Kalecki's work was rooted in a more Marxian approach, and as such was free(r) of the neoclassical shackles, which for Keynes, ramified 'into every corner of his mind', and leading as a result to a "growing dissatisfaction with Keynes's theory" (Sebastiani 1986, p. xi).

Indeed, by focusing on the importance of social classes and power, of class struggle, and linking his theory of price to income distribution, Marx's influence is at the core of Kalecki's approach: "Kalecki however gave to this principle [of effective demand] a distinctive flavour, much closer to the Marxian than to the Marshallian tradition.

---

[2]Perhaps another reason why Kaleckian economics is growing is tied to the rise of empirical research and use of modeling within post-Keynesian economics. In this sense, Kalecki's work perhaps lends itself more to modeling than Keynes's.
[3]One cannot help but wonder how different the *après* Keynes period would have looked like had Kalecki's work been taken seriously earlier on. King (1996b) hints at this in his wonderful chapter on 'Kalecki and the Americans.'

Embedding it in the framework of business-cycle analysis" (Assous and Lopez 2010 p. vi; for a discussion on whether Kalecki was a Marxist, see Kriesler and Halevi 2020, this issue).

Kalecki's work, therefore, is said to be more realistic and superior, and "surpassed" that of Keynes (King 1996, p. 1) as it is based on oligopolistic markets, mark-up pricing, income distribution, social classes and conflict, as well as a more dynamic investment function that does not rest on the interest rates channel.

Because of the different backgrounds, followers of Keynes and Kalecki have often clashed over ideas and policies. But does this mean that Kalecki's economics is incompatible with Keynes's work? King (2013, p. 486, emphasis added) refers to "three *distinct* schools" within post-Keynesian economics. It is for this reason, for instance, that Sawyer (1985, p. 178) has claimed that "the differences between Kalecki and Keynes are substantial, such that their approaches should be separately developed and not conflated together, although there may be some places where there could be a useful cross-fertilisation of ideas." Sawyer (1985, p. 180) then unapologetically claims that Kalecki developed "a superior macroeconomics."[4]

We think this may be too harsh a position to take, and that these differences between the two approaches can only be minimized compared to their similarities (Lavoie 2015). After all, it has been three decades since the participants of the famous Trieste Summer Schools fought over who was a more faithful disciple to their respective master. Heterodox economics today seem to be less about adhering to a specific critical approach, and younger scholars have less interest in who said what first or dissecting the differences between different approaches. As Lavoie (2014, p. 44) argues, we should perhaps spend less time "following the idiosyncrasies" of one economist or the other.

Moreover, it is undeniable that, despite the "superiority" of Kalecki's work, Keynes still brings much to the heterodox table, such as an important emphasis on uncertainty and a monetary theory of production—ideas that can perfectly fit within an overall Kaleckian vision of capitalism.

The way forward, especially for many of the younger scholars in particular, is to have a less sectarian approach and a more eclectic one, borrowing the more relevant parts from various sources, or as Lavoie (2014, p. 42) says, "taking the best elements from each": a bit of Keynes, a bit of Kalecki and a bit of Sraffa—combined to make a coherent whole, while excluding many of the more extreme ideas in their writings.

The virtual conference

The papers published in this symposium were presented at a (virtual) conference we organized on 24–26 September 2020 to honour the work of Kalecki on the 50th anniversary of his death. The interest in this symposium was evident from the beginning: well over 400 participants registered for the two-day conference. One of the objectives of this symposium is to alert younger readers of the importance of Kalecki's work, and his central and dominant role within the heterodox landscape.

---

[4]For those wishing to look at the differences between Keynes and Kalecki, see Sawyer (1985), especially chapter 9. See also Lopez (2002).

The conference was sponsored by not only this journal, but also by the *Association for Social Economics*, and the *Lipinski Foundation*. Created in 2019, the foundation is a Polish-based organization that shares the idea that the dominant neoclassical school of economics is not sufficiently relevant to enable us and our economies to meet pressing challenges of our time. For this reason, the Foundation's mission is to promote pluralism in economics, as the only credible way of moving forward.

Edward Lipiński (1888–1986) was a professor of Economics at both the Warsaw School of Economics and at the University of Warsaw; he was a humanist economist and a social thinker, but also an organizer and a mover who laid the foundation for many important economic institutions in twentieth-century Poland. Crucially, in 1928, he established the *Institute for Research on Business Cycles and Prices* in Warsaw, where he discovered the economic talent in a young and unknown economist, Michał Kalecki.

By co-sponsoring the conference, the Lipinsky Foundation aims at actively rebuilding the "very lively and original Kaleckian school of thought that had been created" in Poland (Assous and Lopez 2010, p. 21).

Acknowledgement

We thank Marc Lavoie and Mario Seccareccia for comments. All errors remain ours.

References

Arestis, P. 1996. 'Kalecki's Role in Post Keynesian Economics: An Overview.' In *An Alternative Macroeconomic Theory: The Kaleckian Model and Post-Keynesian Economics*, edited by J. King. Dordrecht: Springer.

Arestis, P., and T. Skouras. 1985. *Post-Keynesian Economic Theory: A Challenge to Neo Classical Economics*. Armonk: M.E. Sharpe.

Asimakopulos, A. 1989. 'Kalecki and Robinson.' In *Kalecki's Relevance Today*, edited by M. Sebastiani, 10–24. London: Macmillan.

Assous, M., and J. Lopez. 2010. *Michał Kalecki*. London: Palgrave Macmillan.

Dymski, G. 1996. 'Kalecki's Monetary Economics.' In *An Alternative Macroeconomic Theory: The Kaleckian Model and Post-Keynesian Economics*, edited by J. King. Dordrecht: Springer.

Feiwel, G. R. 1975. *The Intellectual Capital of Michal Kalecki: A Study in Economic Theory and Policy*. Knoxville: The University of Tennessee Press.

Fontana, G., and M. Sawyer. 2016. 'Towards post-Keynesian ecological macroeconomics.' *Ecological Economics* 121: 186–195.

Harcourt, G. C. 1975. "Capital Theory: Much Ado about Something." *Thames Papers in Political Economy, Autumn 1975*.

Harcourt, G. C. 1977. 'Review of The Intellectual Capital of Michal Kalecki.' *Economica* 44 (173): 92–94.

Hein, E. 2012. *The Macroeconomics of Finance-Dominated Capitalism – And Its Crisis*. Cheltenham: Edward Elgar.

Hein, E. 2015. 'Finance-Dominated Capitalism and Redistribution of Income: A Kaleckian Perspective.' *Cambridge Journal of Economics* 39 (3): 907–934.

Hein, A. 2020. 'Gender Issues in Kaleckian Distribution and Growth Models: On the Macroeconomics of the Gender Wage Gap.' *Review of Political Economy* 32 (4).

King, J., ed. 1996a. *An Alternative Macroeconomic Theory: The Kaleckian Model and Post-Keynesian Economics*. Dordrecht: Springer.

King, J. 1996b. 'Kalecki and the Americans.' In *An Alternative Macroeconomic Theory: The Kaleckian Model and Post-Keynesian Economics*, edited by J. King. Dordrecht: Springer.

King, J. E. 2002. *A History of Post Keynesian Economics Since 1936*. Cheltenham: Edward Elgar.

King, J. 2013. 'An Introduction to Post Keynesian Macroeconomics.' *Jahrgang* 39: 485–507.

Klein, L. 1951. 'Review of R. Harrod, The Life of John Maynard Keynes.' *Journal of Political Economy* 59 (5): 443–451.

Kriesler, P., and J. Halevi. 2020. 'Was Kalecki a Marxist?' *Review of Political Economy* 32: 4.

Lavoie, M. 2014. *Post-Keynesian Economics: New Foundations*. Cheltenham: Edward Elgar.

Lavoie, M. 2015. 'Kalecki and Post-Keynesian Economics.' In *Michał Kalecki in the 21st Century*, edited by J. Toporowski, and Ł Mamica. London: Palgrave Macmillan.

Lopez, J. 2002. 'Two Versions of the Principle of Effective Demand: Kalecki and Keynes.' *Journal of Post Keynesian Economics* 24 (4): 609–621.

Monserand, A. 2019. 'Degrowth in a Neo-Kaleckian Model of Growth and Distribution: A Theoretical Compatibility and Stability Analysis.' CEPN Working Papers 2019-01, Centre d'Economie de l'Université de Paris Nord.

Osiatynski, J., ed. 1990. *Collected Works of Michal Kalecki. Volume 1: Capitalism: Business Cycles and Full Employment*. Oxford: Oxford University Press.

Osiatynski, J., ed. 1991. *Collected Works of Michal Kalecki Volume II: Capitalism: Economic Dynamics*. Oxford: Oxford University Press.

Robinson, J. 1952. *The Rate of Interest and Other Essays*. London: MacMillan.

Robinson, J. 1977[1979]. *'Michal Kalecki', Collected Economic Paper Volume 5*. Oxford: Basil Blackwell.

Sawyer, M. 1985. *The Economics of Michał Kalecki*. New York: Springer.

Sawyer, M. 2020. 'Financialisation, Industrial Strategy and the Challenges of Climate Change and Environmental Degradation.' *International Review of Applied Economics*, forthcoming.

Sawyer, M. 2020a. 'The Past, Present and Future of Evolutionary Macroeconomics.' *Review of Evolutionary Political Economy*, forthcoming.

Sebastiani, M., ed. 1986. *Kalecki's Relevance Today*. London: Macmillan.

Seguino, S. 2006. 'Feminist-Kaleckian Macroeconomic Policy for Developing Countries.' *Levy Economics Institute of Bard College*, Working Paper 446.

Toporowski, J. 2013. *Michał Kalecki: An Intellectual Biography: Volume I: Rendezvous in Cambridge 1899-1939*. London: Palgrave MacMillan.

Toporowski, J. 2018. *Michał Kalecki: An Intellectual Biography: Volume II: By Intellect Alone 1939–1970*. London: Palgrave MacMillan.

Remembering Kalecki: 22/05/1899–18/04/1970

Jerzy Osiatyński ⓘ

ABSTRACT

In this memoir article, I reminisce on the life of Michał Kalecki, a distinguished scholar, self-taught economist, strong intellectual, loving husband and a rigorous teacher. Kalecki is often portraited as being rather timid and modest in personal relations. Nonetheless, he was a bright and self-confident speaker when presenting his own ideas and challenging those of others. I first met Kalecki in 1963 when I was a graduate student of economics at the Main School of Planning and Statistics (today known as the Warsaw School of Economics). At that time, Kalecki was an undisputable intellectual leader and the economic guru for many young economists, myself included. However, in 1968, due to political pressures and the rising antisemitism in Poland, Kalecki resigned from his professorship at the Main School. A few months after his death, in 1970, with no prospects of doing economic research in Poland, I decided to move to England. Joan Robinson helped me get a guest-fellowship in Clare Hall, Cambridge, where I spent the next two years. Eventually, with the help and invaluable support from Ada Kalecka, Tadeusz Kowalik and Włodzimierz Brus, I became the editor of Kalecki's Collected Works.

1. Introduction

Remembering anyone is a difficult exercise. First, good memories are what we should — and wish — to treasure. Therefore our memory becomes selective. However, as many other scholars, I have only good memories of Michał Kalecki. Second, I knew him personally for a few years only, between 1963 and 1970, at which time I also met his wife, Mrs. Adela (Ada) Kalecka with whom, after Kalecki passed away, my wife and I became close friends. We also met her brother, Ari Szternfeld, his wife and their two daughters, as well as other relatives of Ada, all of which also visited us in our home. I have spent many hours in Kalecki's apartment every week, both as a result of more than twenty years of friendship with Ada (until her death in 1994), and also as my role as the editor of Kalecki's *Collected Works*. As such, I have spent many more hours studying his papers and consulting with her about many details of his professional life, but also learning about their personal relationship, their travels, their families, relatives and friends.

Even when Kalecki was still among us, I made friends with many of his friends and close collaborators, for instance, professors Kazimierz Łaski, Ignacy Sachs, Tadeusz Kowalik, Władysław Sadowski, and Wiktor Herer. In all discussions I had with them, Kalecki, his theories, his policy advise, as well as his principles and integrity of character have been the key points of reference and a guide of conduct. When I am now remembering him, looking at his books that Ada gave me and which I store with care in my personal library, at the small heirlooms from her that we treasure in our home, I wonder whose memories these are — mine, Ada's, or our friends'. These memories are all of that.

2. Meeting Kalecki

I met Kalecki in 1963, as a fourth-year student at the Department of Foreign Trade of the Main School of Planning and Statistics (presently — the Warsaw School of Economics). Kalecki had been teaching at the School since 1962. Łaski was the deputy Rector of the School and thanks to his perseverance he persuaded Kalecki to start teaching there. Kalecki has never been an academic lecturer and he taught only his own theory, thinking its presentation would not need as much as 30 hours a term. When later in his life he was offered a teaching position that involved 60 hours of teaching a term, he rejected it on the grounds that he would first have to work for several years on developing his theory to subsequently teach it to his students.

Yielding to Łaski's pressure who in turn wanted to bring to the School only the best quality teachers, Kalecki agreed to give a regular course on his theory of economic dynamics and business fluctuations, and another one for foreign postgraduate students and government officials, on planning economic development in third world countries. He was also involved in other post-graduate teaching and research projects. In order to exempt him from administrative burdens, formally he was merely a tenured professor at the Chair of Political Economy at the Department of Foreign Trade — a Chair that was held by Łaski. However, in all teaching and research projects in which Kalecki was involved, he was an undisputable intellectual leader and guru.

With the beginning of the 1962–63 academic year, Łaski invited me to attend his MA seminar and write my thesis under his supervision. This was a rare distinction and I happily accepted his generous invitation. In early 1963, Kalecki's *Introduction to the Theory of Growth in a Socialist Economy* was published (Kalecki [1963] 1993), and Łaski asked me to attend Kalecki's new course, which started in the second term. In the following academic year, I also attended Kalecki's lectures in his theory of economic dynamics and business cycles.

Each of Kalecki's lectures were composed of two parts. In the first 45 minutes he lectured to his audience. He explained the dynamics and modus operandi of the economy in question, in line with his own theory. As I used to joke at the time, Kalecki taught 'a capella', never using any lecture notes, hardly ever referring to any textbooks, including his own publications. However, each lecture was very clear-cut, carefully worded, as if he were dictating it to a stenographer. This way of lecturing was very unusual at the School and Łaski once asked Kalecki how he managed to be that precise and concise without using any notes. Kalecki replied 'I walk in the green and thoroughly prepare myself for presenting all that I want to say. I know all that I have to explain' (Kowalik 2011, p. 44).

The second part of his lecture was a Q & A session. His lectures were attended by many Polish top academic economists, some high-ranking economic policy makers, as well as PhD students, some junior staff of the faculty and a few undergraduates. Some were even traveling from academic centers some distance from Warsaw. Although his listeners might have had different opinions on issues Kalecki explained, or simply might not fully understand his line of thought, which were often not easy to follow, questions were seldom asked. If there were no questions from the audience Kalecki asked them himself, addressing the points he thought especially important or complex. However, if a question did arrive, Kalecki would repeat more or less exactly what he had already said before, but in a bit lauder voice, and if his answer was not understood, or the question repeated, he would again repeat his answer but still lauder. No doubt, he was not a charismatic teacher and found it difficult to accept that some people in his audience might not follow his fast and incredibly condensed argument.

In 1964, I graduated with a Master's degree, and Łaski arranged for an assistantship under his Chair. In October that year, he asked me to become research secretary to Kalecki's and Łaski's newly organized workshop on problems of growth in a centrally planned economy. In addition to that workshop, Kalecki also ran two other study groups. The better-known was the workshop organized under the joint auspices of the Main School and the University of Warsaw, and led by Kalecki in tandem with professors Czesław Bobrowski and Ignacy Sachs. It focused on issues of economic development and planning of 'Third World' countries. The other workshop focused on problems of economic dynamics and business fluctuations in developed capitalist countries. Similarly as in the case of Kalecki's lectures, all these workshops were attended by prominent Polish academic economists, PhD students, and high-ranking economic policy-makers. When in November 1964 Joan Robinson came to Warsaw to attend the joint celebrations of Kalecki's 65' and Lange's 60' birthdays, impressed by Kalecki's and his collaborators' achievements in all those areas of macroeconomic research, she said in amazement that what Kalecki established in Warsaw was a true 'Socialist Cambridge'. All this lasted until 1968 when his school of thought was chased away as a result of political purges.

In my capacity as the workshops' managing secretary, I had rather regular contact with Kalecki and Łaski, discussing the agenda of successive meetings, the recommended reference literature and the would-be referees for individual presentations. With time, I started asking Kalecki questions about the substance of his theory, and beginning with the 1965–66 academic year, I began teaching it to our undergraduate students. In 1964, possibly because of my involvement in the workshop and of my interest in his theory, Kalecki introduced me to Joan Robinson when she came to Warsaw. Subsequently, she helped me in 1970 get a scholarship at the Faculty of Economics, and a guest-fellowship in Clare Hall, Cambridge, where I spent the next two years.

While not being an outstanding lecturer, Kalecki was also not much demanding from his students. He gave a course on his theory of growth in a socialist economy for the fourth-grade students while I and another assistant taught the second-graders. At one point, we asked Kalecki if we could listen to him examining his students so that we could do the same when examining ours. He agreed, as did the students, and to our surprise he was passing some of his fourth-graders for answers that we would judge inadequate from our second-graders. Not that we would formally fail them, but we would make another appointment, and perhaps still another one, until we knew the student in question comprehended the essence of Kalecki's theory. Once he finished examining the students, we asked him for the causes for his leniency with his students. I still remember his reply. 'If you had heard the nonsense which I had so often been told by senior officials of the Planning Commission you would be as lenient as I am with those kids.'

Kalecki would come to his office at about 9 am and stay until 1 pm, coming again in the afternoon to attend seminars or meetings of many research committees or supervisory boards, which he either headed or of which he was a member. For lunch he walked home since the Kaleckis lived only about a mile away from the School. They had a maid, Pani Zosia, who was a good cook herself but who gladly and accurately followed Mrs. Kalecka's cooking instructions, and Pani Ada really knew the Polish and the Jewish cuisine. The cooking at their home was superb, and the boletus mushroom soup had no equals. The boletus mushrooms, as well as occasionally some caviar, would come all the way from Moscow, along the route that will become clear later on.

When in the office, Kalecki would come to the common room for morning tea. Sometimes he was accompanied by Łaski or Sachs, very rarely by one of his PhD students; often, however, he sat alone. Of course, everybody in the room knew who and what he was. This, I think, might have discouraged people from disturbing him. They might have thought — there sits a world-famous economist and though he is not in a company, he may be thinking over yet another extension of his theory, or pondering over economic policy measures, and must not be interrupted. Would he mind if he were? Those who dared to join him for his tea could immediately find out what a gentle and friendly person he was, curious to know the news, the gossip, ready to help with our personal problems, and at the same time very witty, with a sardonic sense of humor.

Kalecki's sense of humor is well reflected in short limericks, and proverbial aphorisms and maxima that he wrote in the 1960s. The limericks were patterned a little on Krylov whose writings Kalecki knew well, and were closely related to his critical and mocking observations of current economic and political developments as well as on some political and economic celebrities of his day. Some of these limericks and aphorisms had to wait for 50 years before their publication (see Łaski and Osiatyński 2015), lest personal rights of some of their 'heroes' were harmed. His sense of humor is also rather well reflected in an anecdotal evidence given by Mrs. Ada Kalecka and related to the Kaleckis' visiting the Keynes'.

It goes like this: after arriving in London, in April 1936, the Kaleckis rented a room in the Bloomsbury area, unaware that at the time Keynes used to live just around the corner (see Toporowski 2013, p. 80). Joan Robinson, who met Kalecki soon after he arrived to London and was very fond of him, was keen to introduce Kalecki to Keynes, and she eventually persuaded Keynes that he and his wife — the famous prima ballerina of the Moscow Ballet, Lidia Lopokova — to invite the Kaleckis to tea. Interested to know how the meeting went, the following morning Joan telephoned Kalecki and asked how was the tea? Kalecki replied: 'The tea was good. Mrs. Keynes behaved like a don, and Mr. Keynes like a prima ballerina'.

Kalecki might have given an impression of being rather timid and modest in personal relationships, but that did not apply to him when presenting his own ideas, and challenging those of others. A very accurate evidence of the latter is given by Kaldor in his colorful summary of Kalecki's participation, in 1936, in the Lionel Robbins' regular seminar at the

London School of Economics. The seminar was of an 'open' nature and was attended by professors and lecturers as well as the graduate and post-graduate students of the LSE:

> Kalecki was an active member of the seminar from the very beginning. At the outset he gave the impression of a little man with a loud and creaking voice, who spoke English completely unintelligibly. He spoke with a very strong and peculiar accent, and nobody could follow what he meant. But he persisted in making frequent interventions, and gradually the situation changed. At first, he was a source of annoyance to most people, but then we gradually learnt to respect him, including Robbins, because it gradually emerged more clearly what he said, and his contributions were always relevant and appropriate for the occasion. And so he emerged, I would say, almost as an important figure. (Quoted in Toporowski 2013, p. 81.)

While kind and friendly in personal relations, at the same time Kalecki was a highly principled man, of great integrity, often ready to submit his resignations from his positions, in defense of freedom of speech and criticism, or of the fundamental moral and value standards. Mrs. Kalecka used to say her husband's life could be presented as a series of resignations, starting with his 1936 resignation from the Institute for the Study of Business Cycles and Prices, in protest against the firing of his two close collaborators, who wrote a critical notes on Government policy measures, through his leaving the Oxford Institute of Statistics in 1945, resigning his senior position in the United Nations Secretariat in 1954, then his position in the Planning Commission in Poland in 1964, and finally — one year ahead of his retirement — his professorship at the Main School of Planning and Statistics, in 1968.

Since I was a witness of the circumstances surrounding Kalecki's last resignation, let me share with you my recollections of what happened. Given that the course and the repressions that followed the March 1968 student and intellectuals revolt in Poland have been already much discussed in the literature, there is no need to give them special attention here (for their comprehensive summary see e.g., the entry: '1968 Polish Political Crisis', *Wikipedia*; see also Davis 1982, pp. 589–591). Let me therefore address only the process of destruction of Kalecki's School in Warsaw. There were two different causes of attacks on Kalecki and his collaborators.

First, the top leaders of the communist party could not forgive Kalecki's criticism of successive five-year plans, as well as pointing out their internal inconsistencies and lack of realism, especially in promising improvements in living standards, which at the time were simply not achievable. What made the outrage even stronger, was that in the course of the implantation of these plans, Kalecki was proven right. Władysław Gomułka, then Secretary General of the Polish communist party, infuriated by yet another of Kalecki's criticism of the 1966–70 Economic Plan (see Kalecki 1992, pp. 243–254), contemptuously dismissed it by saying: 'Professors with titles, grown-up people, instead of conducting research, or helping, write nonsensical theses' (Kalecki 1992, p. 422). Following this public attack by Gomułka, Kalecki resigned his position in the Planning Commission.

The second factor was triggered by Gomułka's speech given at the national conference of the Polish communist trade unions, shortly after the 5–10 June 1967 Israeli — Arab war. In his speech Gomułka talked about the alleged Jewish 'fifth column' among the Polish intellectual elites, in government structures and in the army. This was consistent with demands by the nationalist faction within the leadership of the Polish communist party, which for several years demanded 'cleansing' of the party apparatus from 'alien elements'. Following Gomulka's aforementioned speech, this led to an aggressive 'anti-

Zionist' campaign. Although neither Kalecki, nor any of his associates at the Main School were involved in those factional feuds and power-struggle, they became the prime object of attacks and subsequent purges, especially if they were Polish Jews.

The campaign aimed at breaking up Kalecki's School was initiated by a conference on 'The Situation in the Political Economy of Socialism' organized in early May 1968 by the Central Party School (affiliated with the Central Committee of the Polish communist party). It was shortly followed by a conference of the Polish Economic Society, and another one at the Main School of Planning and Statistics. Organized on 17–18 June by the Rector of the School and the School's communist party Executive Committee, the conference discussed 'The Main Problems of the Political Economy and Teaching It' (for an account of those conferences, see Editor's Notes to Kalecki 1993, pp. 255–258). Because of his health problems (at the time of the conference he was in an early phase of recovering from diabetes), Kalecki did not attend the first day of the debate and spoke only the next day. In the morning of the first day of the conference, shortly after he came to his office, I popped in to ask how he was and to share some conference-related gossip. When I opened the door, he set at his desk with a pencil in his hand (he often drafted his texts in pencil to facilitate rubbing out a word or two when he wanted to replace them with more appropriate ones; some of Kalecki's original manuscripts that survived are written in pencil), so I apologized for disturbing him. He said I hadn't, and invited me to come in. He said he was not writing anything new but was merely bolding his handwriting of the speech he was to give the next morning, to make it easier to read. Then he read his short speech to me and asked if I liked it.

I was rather shocked. True, in the past I would occasionally make a comment on a way of formulating one sentence or another in his theory, usually by asking questions rather than making positive suggestions, but in this specific case, Kalecki asked me for my opinion on his speech. Incredible I thought, and possibly only because of the political context of the conference, or to check if what he intended to say would not be over-complicated to the young members of the faculty. Anyway, as a critic I proved useless: I said I liked the text, especially his outright defense of professors Kazimierz Łaski, Włodzimierz Brus and Jerzy Tepicht who were all under heavy and ad personam attacks in the conference papers (for his speech at that conference, see Kalecki 1992, pp. 259–264). I know that once I left, he saw Łaski and also consulted his speech with Sachs since their many joint research projects were in jeopardy (see Kalecki 1993, pp. 210–211; Osiatyński 2015, pp. 45–49).

The organizational consequences of those orchestrated actions appeared very quickly and ended up breaking up Kalecki's School. Łaski, Sachs and others were dismissed from the Main School of Planning and Statistics, several were forced to emigrate. In October 1968, Kalecki resigned his professorship at the Main School. A few months after he passed away, in 1970, I decided to leave for England since I could not get any research job in my country. In lieu of her late husband, Pani Ada wrote me a letter of recommendation. She was also instrumental, next to Kowalik and Brus, in my getting the job of the editor of Kalecki's Collected Works, when I returned from Cambridge at the end of 1972.

For all those reasons, you would not be surprised that at the end of those recollections I shall also remember Mrs. Kalecka, a true and lifelong companion to Michał. She was born in 1903 in Sieradz, a small town near Łódź, in a merchant Jewish family. Later the family moved to Łódź where she finished her primary and secondary education, and in 1921–26 she studied biology at the Jagiellonian University in Kraków. Having graduated in 1926, she returned to Łódź where she met Kalecki who had given tuition to her older sister, Franciszka. In June 1930 Adela and Michał married, and according to Toporowski (2013, pp. 28–29),

> Adela Kalecki was to be her husband's lifelong companion and confidante. Although she was not an economist, he told her of his plans and the fears and insecurities that arose from their professional insecurity that plagued him virtually throughout his working life. Her accounts and notes are a record of his thoughts on his situation. She was also close to him politically. … Adela, like Kalecki, avoided party politics.

However, next to being Kalecki's wife, Ada was also the sister of Ary Szternfeld, the world famous co-founder of modern aerospace science. His advances on aerospace could not be understood either in his native Poland, nor in France where he sought better comprehension of his research. In 1923 he ultimately ended up in Moscow, where he collaborated with Konstantin Tsiolkovsky. Szternfeld had calculated with great precision the trajectories of the aerospace rockets, including the one along which the first Soviet Sputnik traveled, in 1957. In France, he lived in poverty, and then again in Russia, following the late 1930s Stalinist terror and the closing of the Institute where Szternfeld worked. The Szternfelds spent several years in the city of Serov, in the Urals. He returned to Moscow in 1944 and lived there until his death in 1980.

Szternfeld, known also as the 'Lord Paradox' for his disclosing numerous paradoxes related to the future interplanetary flights, has a star in the space named after him, and a honorary citizenship of the Sieradz town, where he was born. Yet, the Kaleckis for many years had to help him and his family to make a modest living. The aforementioned boletus mushrooms and occasionally a can of caviar were tokens of gratitude passed to the Kaleckis through family members or close friends traveling between Moscow and Warsaw.

When I and my wife, Elżbieta, some years after Kalecki's death met Ary Szternfeld, invited by Pani Ada for dinner, he impressed us with his modesty and openness. Human greatness, we thought, does not go well, nor does it need, any wedges. Kalecki and Szternfeld were both exceedingly good examples of that.

Pani Ada, as she herself often admitted, in all her life in a way stood between those two intellectual giants, one of who was opening new ways in economic theorizing and the other in the aerospace travel. She shared the joy of their respective discoveries and the honors bestowed upon each of them, but was constantly concerned about their personal downturns and troubles. Once they both passed away, until the end of her life she spared no effort to propagate and consolidate the opus magnum of them both. For all that we must be grateful to her.

Disclosure Statement

No potential conflict of interest was reported by the author(s).

ORCID

Jerzy Osiatyński ⓘ http://orcid.org/0000-0001-5539-2556

References

Davis, N. 1982. *God's Playground: A History of Poland.* 2nd ed. Oxford: Clarendon Press.

Kalecki, M. 1992. *Collected Works of Michał Kalecki.* Vol. III, *Socialism: Functioning and Long-Term Planning.* Edited by J. Osiatyński. Oxford: Clarendon Press.

Kalecki, M. (1963) 1993. *Introduction to the Theory of Growth in a Socialist Economy.* In *Collected Works of Michał Kalecki.* Vol. IV, *Socialism: Economic Growth and Efficiency of Investment.* Edited by J. Osiatyński. Oxford: Clarendon Press.

Kalecki, M. 1993. *Collected Works of Michał Kalecki.* Vol. V, *Developing Economies.* Edited by J. Osiatyński. Oxford: Clarendon Press.

Kowalik, T. 2011. 'Unpublished Autobiographical Interview with Łaski.' Osiatyński's Papers.

Łaski, K., and J. Osiatyński, eds. 2015. *Michał Kalecki: Kapitalizm: dynamika gospodarcza i pełne zatrudnienie.* Warsaw: iTON Society.

Osiatyński, J. 2015. 'Introduction.' In *Michał Kalecki: Kapitalizm: dynamika gospodarcza i pełne zatrudnienie,* edited by K. Łaski and J. Osiatyński. Warsaw: iTON Society.

Toporowski, J. 2013. *Michał Kalecki: An Intellectual Biography. Volume I: Rendezvous in Cambridge 1899–1939.* Houndmills: Palgrave.

Kalecki and Cambridge

Maria Cristina Marcuzzo

ABSTRACT

This paper discusses Michał Kalecki's impact on Cambridge's major protagonists and, in turn, the impact they had on him during the time he spent in Cambridge. It concentrates on the criticisms he was met with on the part of Keynes, Kahn and Robinson, especially on his notion of the 'degree of monopoly'. This was the reason for his departure from Cambridge, although he continued to receive support from his Cambridge friends. The rift between him and Cambridge can be explained by the fact that, Sraffa excepted, Keynes, Kahn and Robinson were (at the time) thinking within the Marshallian framework of price determination and— quite rightly—found Kalecki's approach to be incompatible with it. Robinson later became converted to an approach to prices and distribution which has Kalecki, alongside Sraffa, as one of the contributors and now it is part of what she herself had christened post-Keynesian economics.

Do you think Kalecki will induce Piero [Sraffa] to take the General Theory seriously?
JVR to RFK, 20 March 1937 in RFK/13/90/2/166

Kalecki writes he has accepted Piero's offer, so all well so far. You must judge the best moment for telling Maynard—Mind you put it on Piero.
JVR to RFK, 25 July 1937, RFK/13/90/2/178

I am delighted Maynard is pleased with Kalecki's book. Did the delicate question of priority come up at all?
JVR to RFK, 11 January 1939, RFK/13/90/3/243

1. Introduction

There is ample literature on Michał Kalecki, his life and work, and indeed his importance for the development of post-Keynesian economics, but there are still issues which attract scholarly attention and lively theoretical debates on how to draw on his legacy.

This paper has a narrower scope: it takes a close look at Kalecki's impact on Cambridge's major protagonists and, in turn, the impact they had on him during the time he spent in Cambridge. The reason for doing so is to explore further the connection between two approaches that, although distant in inspiration, form part of the theoretical constellation that we recognize as an alternative to neoclassical economics. Historical reconstructions of the events, as they unfolded at the time, are only one side of the story because there is another approach to exploring the connections, i.e. *post factum* to analyze similarities or complementarities in the two approaches, taking into account also their later developments. In fact, Kalecki's theory evolved over time until his death in 1970, and during this time many theoretical developments also occurred within the close circle of his Cambridge supporters. Therefore, by concentrating on Kalecki's Cambridge period, this paper limits the focus on the matter. It is hoped, however, that by taking a closer view, with the benefit of some unpublished correspondence, what is lost in depth and breadth of picture is gained in terms of detail.

The paper is organized as follows: Section Two is a brief summary of the well-known story of Kalecki's encounter with the leading Cambridge protagonists and his visits there between 1936 and 1939; Section Three discusses the criticisms he received mainly from Keynes and Kahn, in particular of the notion of the 'degree of monopoly' and its role in explaining wage behaviour in the cycle; Sections Four and Five focus on Robinson's role in recruiting Kalecki to the post-Keynesian cause; Section Six addresses some general questions regarding the compatibility of the various different approaches within the post-Keynesian constellation; and Section Seven offers some concluding remarks.

2. The timeline

Kalecki arrived in England in 1936, on a Rockefeller Foundation grant, and spent the academic year 1936–1937 mostly at the London School of Economics, with occasional visits to Cambridge; Kaldor (1989) describes his impact in the Robbins Seminar at the LSE in which he eventually emerged 'almost as an important figure' (p. 3). Sometime in Summer 1936 Kalecki met Joan Robinson and made a lasting impression on her, as she mentioned several times and as testified by the support she gave him on several occasions and the influence that he had on her work.

In November 1936, in protest at the dismissal of two of his closest friends and collaborators from the Polish ISBCP (Institute for the Study of Business Cycles and Prices), Kalecki resigned from his post at the Institute. Luckily, his Rockefeller fellowship was extended for another 12 months and at the end of 1937 he moved to Cambridge, where he remained until the end of 1939. He received a research grant, from 1 January until June 1938, from the University of Cambridge. When the grant ended, Kalecki found himself without a permanent job and moved to London. In November he was able to return to Cambridge, where he was offered a research job in the newly created 'Cambridge Research Scheme of the National Institute of Economic and Social Research into Prime Costs, Proceeds and Output', established at the end of 1938. The members of the Board were Austin Robinson, Kahn, Kalecki, Champernowne and Sraffa, while Keynes was Chairman.

While in Cambridge, Kalecki was very active at Sraffa's seminars. We have plenty of evidence of this. See, for instance, the letter from Piero Sraffa to Joan Robinson dated 28 December 1938: '[Rothbarth and Kalecki] both come to my seminars and add considerably to the interest of the discussions, although they don't allow much to say to the research students, not even to the Americans [John Dunlop and Lorie Tarshis]' (quoted in Osiatynski 1990, p. 523).

After one year's work with the Cambridge Research Scheme, Kalecki presented the main results of his research, which met with extremely critical comments from Keynes and Kahn, and, to a lesser extent, Robinson. As a result, Kalecki resigned and left Cambridge for Oxford, where he joined the Oxford University Institute of Statistics, his salary still being paid by the same National Institute of Economic and Social Research. Apparently, Kalecki did not express any bad feelings about this situation, if we are to believe the following account: 'Kalecki has swallowed the Oxford job without a murmur' (Joan Robinson to Richard Kahn, 14 January 1940, in Kahn papers, RFK/13/90/4/12).[1] In fact, Kalecki's disappointment regarding the comments he received, which forced him to leave Cambridge and take up the Oxford job, must have troubled him deeply, as the following letter to Kahn, 9 June 1939, amply demonstrates:

> After a careful consideration of what you told me yesterday, I came to the definite conclusion that I would not stay for the next year in Cambridge. Do not consider it please a hysterical gesture. I formed the best possible expectations of my work in the next year and arrived at the result that I cannot venture the enterprise. The success of the inquiry I proposed for next year is much less certain than what could have been expected from my work next year. I thought that the latter was considered more or less satisfactory I could risk a possibly negative result in the next year. But I cannot take the risk that two years will be considered wasted. I would probably object that this year is not considered wasted … fully. But it is hard for me to find consolation in the wastage coefficient's being slightly less than 100 per cent. I simply think that if in a case like that the results of research are not considered satisfactory one must draw the consequences. The more that I cannot promise anything better for the next year.
>
> The rest of the time of this year I should like to devote to bringing in order the work done and writing a theoretical interpretation of the results. (Kahn papers, RFK/5/1/146-7, quoted in Toporowski 2013, p. 133)

The story has been amply documented in the literature (Harcourt and Kriesler 2011; Toporowski 2013), together with the reasons why Cambridge was not and could not become the intellectual home for Kalecki: there was a lack of a meeting of minds, leading to mutual disagreements and, finally, to distancing. There is no lack of evidence that the leading Cambridge economists were disappointed by his approach to cost analysis and price formation within the Research Scheme and that Kalecki was not always convinced of the correctness or relevance of their criticisms.

In particular, Toporowski (2013) has given us a balanced and full account both of the efforts made especially by Kahn—in the name also of Keynes, Sraffa and Robinson—to get Kalecki a job, evidencing the intellectual respect they had for him, and their reservations about his approach. In fact, they were never fully persuaded by Kalecki's unorthodox approach, which implied rejection of several Marshallian postulates, including, for instance, the assumption of rising marginal costs, which in the Marshallian framework is a necessary condition for the determination of equilibrium under perfect competition.

Kalecki collected data on industrial production by industry and the share of prime costs (labour and raw materials) in the total output of the coal, cotton, steel, tobacco, shipbuilding and electricity supply industries and used them 'to show that the standard

---

[1]However, six months later she noted: 'I get a short and bitter letter from Kalecki from time to time. Anyway he seems well dug in at Oxford' (Joan Robinson to Richard Kahn, 27 July 1940, in Kahn papers, RFK/13/90/4/231; quoted in Marcuzzo and Rosselli 2015, p. 187).

Marshallian upward sloping average or marginal cost curves were not characteristic of production. Instead there was a stable "prime cost" (the cost of wages and raw materials) that was the basis of industrial price formation.' In fact, Kalecki explicitly stated that his purpose had been to verify 'where diminishing returns were at operation' (quoted in Osiatynski 1990, p. 523).

As Toporowski (2013, p. 149) neatly put it, 'Kalecki's refusal to fit price theory into Marshallian methodology condemned his Cambridge research.'

3. Criticisms of Kalecki's approach by Keynes, Kahn and Robinson

The relationship between Keynes and Kalecki has understandably attracted most attention in the literature, as evidenced by examination of the correspondence between them and comparison of their different methodologies and the contents of their theories. Once again, let me stress that I will concentrate here on one aspect only of the multifarious issues involved, namely, Kalecki's approach to price theory and the doubts he encountered regarding the soundness of his assumptions.

When Kalecki came up with an explanation for the constancy of the wage rate in the cycle—which had puzzled Keynes, who had written to Sraffa to ask his research students to 'rack their brains' to find an explanation—both Kahn and Keynes were already showing a certain lack of conviction. In a previous article in this journal (Marcuzzo 1996), I discussed this issue at length; it suffices here to summarize the main points.

Kalecki had classified firms according to the shape of their average cost curves (increasing, constant and decreasing) and showed that the stability of the wage share in national income can be accounted for by the offsetting effects of the behaviour of the degree of monopoly (the ratio of the difference between price and marginal cost to price) and of the ratio of turnover to income (salaries, wages, profits and depreciation) (Kalecki 1938). Kalecki' s results found support in the empirical work carried out by two Cambridge research students, John Dunlop and Lorie Tarshis, who analyzed the behaviour of real wages in Great Britain and the United States with a view to testing the proposition set out by Keynes in the *General Theory*. According to Keynes, real wages were expected to vary in the opposite direction to money wages, but they showed that real and money wages vary in the same direction. These findings led Keynes to admit the possibility that constant marginal costs may be an important factor in accounting for the positive correlation between real and money wages. Nevertheless, he remained sceptical of the procedure Kalecki adopted to explain the constancy of the wage share.

Nor was Kahn persuaded. Many years later, in an interview with me, he said:

> If Kalecki's conclusion [that if real wages were not lower at the height of the boom than in a slump, there need not be an inverse relationship between real wages and unemployment] was valid, Keynes attributed this validity to a curious coincidence: that (for some reason not clearly explained by Michał Kalecki) with a rising level of output the degree of imperfection of competition increases to an extent that offsets the fall of productivity of labour working on the least efficient plants. (Marcuzzo 2020, p. 46)

Keynes, Kahn and Robinson all joined in, criticizing Kalecki's findings in the Research Scheme project. Their main criticism was levelled at the notion of 'degree of monopoly', which was questioned, for instance, as not being a 'thing in itself' (Kahn papers, RFK/5/1/138) in a three-page comment that was unsigned, but most certainly written by Robinson. Since the degree of monopoly depends on several factors (various kinds of market imperfection, wage changes and the state of demand), 'to say that there has been "a change in the degree of monopoly" is never a final account of what has happened, and it is often unreasonable to expect a constant degree of monopoly in [the] face of other changes, e.g., a change in demand' (Ibid.).

But more fundamentally, the criticism was, according to one of Kahn's comments on Kalecki's reports:

> [That o]ne of the questions, perhaps the main question to be answered, is whether the price always moves in exact proportion to the cost of raw materials and labour. Mrs Robinson demonstrates in her memorandum that the ratio of proceeds to prime costs provides only a partial answer to this question. I agree with her that one ought to try to adjust the price for changes in the price of raw material and labour. (Kahn papers, RFK/5/159)

Kahn was never in favour of abandoning the hypothesis of profit maximization, albeit interpreted as a 'trial and error' method rather than a manifestation of an optimizing rationality, not to speak of a resort to marginal calculation on the part of entrepreneurs. He never accepted explanations of the price formation mechanism of the descriptive type or based on a hypothesis of non-rational behaviour. Kahn's keenly critical position with regard to price formation theories based on 'what the entrepreneurs say they do', harking back to Hall and Hitch's (1939) article, matched his rejection of Kalecki's mark-up pricing formation (see Marcuzzo and Sanfilippo 2007).

For her part, the apparatus Robinson chose to object to Kalecki's methodology in his inquiry into proceeds and costs came straight from her *Economics of Imperfect Competition*, an approach that she abandoned later, possibly under the influence of Kalecki himself and certainly of Sraffa. In the Preface to the second edition of her book, she conceded that, 'Prices are formed by setting a gross margin, in terms of a percentage on prime costs, to cover overheads, amortization and net profit' (Robinson 1969, p. vii). However, she still believed that Kalecki's degree of monopoly could not fully explain how prices are determined, because some long period elements had to be allowed for. This is where Sraffa's price of production could be made use of. She wrote that, '[t]he post Keynesians must make use of Sraffa to build up a type of long-period analysis which will prevent neoclassical equilibrium from oozing back into the General Theory' (Robinson 1978[1980], p. 82).

However, this endeavour proved more of a project than something already accomplished:

> Post-Keynesian theory has plenty of problems to work on. We now have a general framework of long- and short-period analysis which will enable us to bring the insights of Marx, Keynes and Kalecki into a coherent form and apply them to the contemporary scene, but there is still a long way to go. (1978[1980], p. 85)

4. Robinson's change of mind

There are several inaccuracies in Robinson's later account of Kalecki's initial reaction to the *General Theory*, which were pointed out to me in a private letter written by Osiatynski in October 1985.[2] However, the contemporary impression of her first encounter with Kalecki, as she told Kahn in a letter dated 16 September 1936, corresponds with her later reminiscences:

> My Pole is a really intelligent man (tho' lacking in charm). His claim to have anticipated a lot of the General Theory is substantiated by an article in Econometrica written in 1933, and he is really possible to talk to. What a change. He is interested in the James-Roy business about investment inducing investment. If you have got James' paper with you would you bring it along and I will bring the Pole's product. I want to see how they fit together. (quoted in Marcuzzo and Rosselli 2005, p. 273)

As we saw, at the beginning she was not convinced by Kalecki's approach to cost and prices:

> Keynes's system as you say, is unrealistic, but yours is troublesome because marginal prime cost as you define it is not equal to marginal revenue, or is only equal to it if entrepreneurs are very foolish. It falls short of m[arginal] revenue by some vague margin corresponding to Keynes's marginal' user cost. (Joan Robinson to Michal Kalecki, 16 September 1936; quoted in Osiatynski 1990, p. 502)

Kalecki (1936) had constructed a marginal labour cost curve (MLC) and a marginal value-added curve (MVA), both derived by subtracting, respectively, from the prime costs curve and the marginal revenue curve (supposed to be decreasing) the cost of raw materials. The curves are first derived for the individual firm and then aggregated for the system as a whole, in the determination of the short-period equilibrium level of output.

The position of the marginal labour cost curve is fixed by assumption in the short period, since capital equipment is fixed. But the position of the marginal value-added curve depends on the level of the capitalists' expenditure, on the basis of the well-known Kaleckian assumption that only capitalists save and can change their level of expenditure. Thus, the marginal value-added curve moves until the short-period equilibrium is reached.

It is not clear whether Robinson is objecting to an equilibrium defined at the point of intersection between the MVA curve and the MLC curve or to the lack of a specific assumption regarding the entrepreneur's behaviour when choosing the level of the firm's output, but it is clear that she was not ready to follow Kalecki in his abandonment of the profit maximization rule.

Nevertheless, shortly after their first encounter, Robinson started supporting Kalecki; she was impressed by his qualities and, as she stated, 'made it [her] business to blow his trumpet for him' (Robinson 1977[1979], p. 186). In turn, Kalecki had a substantial influence on the development of her thought, and in particular her appreciation of Marx. Since 1940 she had been studying Marx (Robinson 1973, p. x); Maurice Dobb

---

[2]Let me record that Mrs Kalecki strongly denies that Kalecki might have said what Joan Robinson attributed to you in the two sentences of your quotation after her: 'I confess I was ill. Three days I lay in bed.' Not only Mrs Kalecki does not recall any such 'illness' (and she was together with her husband in 1936), moreover, she is almost certain it could not have happened; this, she says, would be totally contradictory to her husband's character and nature to become 'ill and stay in bed for three days for such a reason'. I am afraid, we have no means to support either of the two claims/ Feiwell, who also mentioned Kalecki's illness, took the information from Joan/. However, from my own memory of Kalecki as a man, and what I am told by others who knew him, I tend to think that Mrs Kalecki's memory is closer to the facts, the scene painted by Joan Robinson allegedly after Kalecki seems to me very Un-Kalecki in spirit.

was one of her 'tutors',[3] but Kalecki was the main influence. She wrote that Piero Sraffa used to tease her by saying that she 'treated Marx as a little-known forerunner of Kalecki' (Robinson 1942[1966], p. vi). In December 1941 she published the article 'Marx on Unemployment', in which she explicitly recognized that 'Mr. Kalecki's epigram "The tragedy of investment is that it causes crisis because it is useful" has a close affinity with Marx: "The real barrier of capitalist production is capital itself"' (Robinson 1948 [1951], p. 134). In fact, when her booklet *Essay on Marxian Economics* came out in 1942, Kalecki's response was highly appreciative. He wrote to her: 'I think that your analysis of Marx is very valuable: it has shown that one conception in his writing is a quite consistent theory; while Marxists who wanted to show that everything is right and consistent failed to show even that' (Michal Kalecki to Joan Robinson, 30 July 1942, J. Robinson papers, JVR: vii).

Although she initially had some reservations about the methodology employed by Kalecki in his work within the Research Scheme, she was satisfied with Kalecki's revisions, as evidenced in the following letter to Kahn, dated 15 December 1939: 'I have decided to OK the Kalecki document. He has set it out very clearly and makes a lot of remarks to point out that his estimates are not exact etc, so I think our former harsh remarks have done good' (Kahn papers, RFK/13/90/3/328-31).

5. The way to post-Keynesian economics

Robinson famously offered a staunch defence of Kalecki's approach in face of Keynes's criticism. Kalecki's influence on her is well documented in a paper by Harcourt and Kriesler (2011), which builds on work completed over the years, and also by others (possibly the earliest being Asimakopulos 1989).

The nature of the methodological differences between Keynes and Kalecki is also well documented (Sawyer 1985; Kriesler 1987; Osiatynski 1990; Toporowski 2013) and there is no need to go back over it here. I would rather take on a related point, carefully addressed by Carabelli and Cedrini (2017), who focus on the different strands of post-Keynesian economics which have emerged, and examine the implications of following either the Kaleckian or the Keynesian route. There can be no disputing the fact that the superiority of Kalecki's version of the theory of effective demand for further developments was originally argued by Robinson.

The constructive element of post-Keynesian economics, she claimed, comes from 'Kalecki's version of the *General Theory*, rather than Keynes" (Robinson 1975[1980], p. 122); she later added: 'Kalecki was able to weave the analysis of imperfect competition and of effective demand together and it was this that opened up the way for what goes under the name of post-Keynesian economic theory' (Robinson 1977[1979], pp. 193–194). She gave two reasons: (i) Kalecki's background as a Marxist allows for a better integration of Marx's major insights (such as the reproduction schemes, the reserve army of labour); and (ii) Kalecki's dual approach to price determination—supply and demand and competition for primary commodities, and mark-up and monopolistic competition for industrial goods—are closer to the realities of the contemporary world (Robinson 1978, p. xx).

---

[3]See the exchange of letters between January and May 1941 in Joan Robinson papers, JVR: vii.

Thus, according to Robinson's views in the 1970s, Kalecki's version was 'in some ways more truly a *general* theory than Keynes's', because he brought 'imperfect competition into the analysis and emphasized the influence of investment on the share of profits' (Robinson 1972[1978], p. 5). Nevertheless, she maintained, there was something missing (the role of money, uncertainty and the multiplier) in Kalecki, but it could and should be supplemented by Keynes.

In conclusion, she came to believe that it was Kalecki's rather than Keynes's version of effective demand that should be incorporated in what she saw as a true alternative to neo-classical economics, which she labelled post-Keynesian: 'The classical tradition, revived by Sraffa, which flows from Ricardo through Marx, diluted by Marshall and enriched by the analysis of effective demand of Keynes and Kalecki' (Robinson 1973, p. xii). She was, however, aware of the difficulty of achieving such an integration because, she wrote:

> The post-Keynesian theory reaches back to clasp the hands of Ricardo and Marx, skipping over the sixty years of dominance of neoclassical doctrines from 1870 to the great slump. This accounts for the paradox that post-Keynesian analysis derives equally from two such apparently incompatible sources as Piero Sraffa's interpretation of Ricardo and Michal Kalecki's interpretation of the theory of employment. (Robinson 1974[1978], p. 126)

The words 'apparently incompatible' lie behind many disagreements among the post-Keynesians (see Marcuzzo 2018), but at the same time no one would question the importance and significance of Kalecki's approach in any attempt to overcome neoclassical economics. Since, as Robinson remarked: 'Kalecki was free from the remnants of old-fashioned theory which Keynes had failed to throw off ... Kalecki gets Keynes back onto the rails where his "classical" education had led him astray' (1975[1980], pp. 192–193). Thanks to Sraffa and Kalecki, the initial incompatibility between the Continental (Marxist) tradition and the Cambridge approach is overcome in post-Keynesian economics and there is no doubt that Robinson was instrumental in bringing it about.

6. What are the questions?

There is a point in the fine, well-documented biography of Kalecki with which I disagree. Toporowski writes:

> Any notion that the originality of Keynes and Kalecki was due to their shared emphasis on the importance of aggregate demand as a determinant of output and employment may also be dismissed. By the 1930s such ideas were hardly original; they could be found, for example, in Ralph Hawtrey's well-known *Good and Bad Trade*, which had been published in 1913. (2013, p. 140)

Also Malthus, for that matter, can be credited with having grasped the role of aggregate demand in determining output and, stretching the point, we can go back even further, to Cantillon's insights. Marx came closer to appreciating the possibility that Say's law may not hold but by taking a different route. In fact, none of the predecessors of Keynes and Kalecki (Hawtrey included) came to a real understanding of the mechanism by which investment generates an equal amount of saving through variations in the level of income. This is the element of originality that Kalecki and Keynes shared.

Moreover, Kalecki's superiority does not lie in the assumption of imperfect competition, as Robinson had it, but rather in having given us a theory of effective demand without the Marshallian postulates. One postulate in particular has a damaging effect on the Keynesian message, namely, the idea that to reduce unemployment wages need to be cut. -Even if Keynes's argument is that when employment rises wages fall, and not that the cause of rising employment lies in falling wages, as indeed it can be read and was in fact rapidly incorporated in the neoclassical synthesis, the inverse relationship between wages and employment is troublesome in Keynes's theory, as he himself later admitted. He explained the reasons for his acceptance of the classical postulate as follows:

> The supposed empirical fact, that in the short period real wages tend to move in the opposite direction of the level of output, appeared that is to say, to be in conformity with the more fundamental generalizations that industry is subject to increasing marginal cost in the short period, that for a closed system [The qualifications required, if the system is not closed, are dealt with below (JMK's fn.)] a whole marginal cost in the short period is substantially the same thing as marginal wage cost, and that in competitive conditions prices are governed by marginal cost; all this being subject, of course, to various qualifications in particular cases, but remaining a reliable generalization by and large. (Keynes 1973, Appendix, pp. 399–400)

Then, in a letter to L. Tarshis, dated 10 December 1938, he admitted: 'It is clear that I have made a mistake in saying that real wages usually fall when money wages are rising. There are two or three explanations of how I came to make the mistake, and which of them is correct is not very clear to me' (quoted in Marcuzzo 1993).

Thanks to Kalecki's version of the theory of effective demand, we can get rid of the inverse relationship because there is no assumption of decreasing marginal productivity of labour in his system. With a similar argument we can use the principle of effective demand without endorsing the mark-up price determination and endorse Sraffa's production prices. A similar point, namely, whether Sraffa is compatible with Keynes, has been endlessly debated in the literature. Disputing the idea in Pasinetti's (2007) book that there was a common denominator in the work of Keynes, Kahn, Kaldor, Robinson and Sraffa, I maintained that:

> Historians of the Cambridge group should have no qualms about bringing out the differences, and must continue to cast light on all the evidence that helps us to understand the authors in their historical context. In this theoretical work there is, in a certain sense, more 'freedom' to interpret, integrate and combine concepts and propositions that were quite distinct when formulated. This does not mean making free and easy with the work of the historian, but having a clearer sense of the fact that a different aim is being pursued. (Marcuzzo 2014, p. 23)

The point is that historical investigations and theoretical constructions are quite different exercises. So while it is closer to the truth to say that Cambridge economics and Kalecki's economics had different visions and analytical tools, it is legitimate to pursue the goal not so much of 'integrating' them as, rather, making use of both of them, as the problems in hand may require. By abandoning pursuit of a unified theory, we can accommodate Kalecki, Keynes and Sraffa in our box of tools serving to understand the actual working of an economy without being committed to one all-purpose model.

Pasinetti labelled what was happening in Cambridge in the 1930s a 'revolution in economics to be accomplished'; even though Kalecki neither belongs to that tradition nor shares the same 'style', he is substantively part of that approach as an alternative to neoclassical economics.

7. Concluding remarks

Kalecki refined his theory over the years (see Kriesler 2011) and even the concept of degree of monopoly was better specified in his subsequent work (see Osiatynski 1991; Reynolds 1983); however, when he used it to present his results in Cambridge he encountered great opposition on the part of Keynes, Kahn and Robinson. They were not the only critics he faced, as well documented by Osiatynski's editorial note to his *Collected Works* and subsequent literature, but their criticisms were the reason for his departure from Cambridge, despite the support he continued to receive from his Cambridge friends.

It can be admitted that Kalecki's findings in his preliminary Interim Report were not altogether satisfactory and some of the criticisms he received were therefore justified, but, as agreed by the best commentators on Kalecki's work, the rift between him and Cambridge had a deeper explanation. Sraffa excepted, Keynes, Kahn and Robinson were (at the time) thinking within the Marshallian framework of price determination and—quite rightly—found Kalecki's approach to be incompatible with it.

Moreover, Keynes was opposed to Kalecki's unstated assumption and his sweeping generalizations from a limited set of data. The odd case is Kahn. In his Fellowship dissertation he had made use of an inverted L-shape cost curve, which he abandoned in his 1931 Multiplier article,[4] and subsequently remained a keen supporter of standard profit maximization assumptions with rising marginal costs, albeit interpreted as a trial-and-error method rather than intended to be a calculation-based marginal magnitude. Eventually, in 1960, Sraffa produced his masterpiece, demonstrating to the world that prices could be determined without reliance on marginal analysis. As a result of the arguments of both Kalecki and Sraffa, Robinson changed her tune and by early 1950 had been converted to an approach to prices and distribution that freed her from the Marshallian cocoon.

In conclusion, Joan Robinson was the midwife of what she herself christened post-Keynesian economics, while Kalecki, alongside Marx, Keynes and Sraffa, constitutes one of the pillars upon which it stands.

Disclosure Statement

No potential conflict of interest was reported by the author.

References

Asimakopulos, A. 1989. 'Kalecki and Robinson.' In *Kalecki's Relevance Today*, edited by M. Sebastiani. Basingstoke: Macmillan.

Carabelli, A., and M. Cedrini. 2017. 'Keynes Against Kalecki on Economic Method.' *Journal of Post Keynesian Economics* 40 (3): 349–375.

Hall, R. L., and C. J. Hitch. 1939. 'Price Theory and Business Behaviour.' *Oxford Economic Papers* os-2: 12–45.

---

[4]According to Keynes, this led him to accept the standard assumptions. He wrote: 'my own readiness to accept the prevailing generalisation, at the time when I was writing my General Theory was much influenced by an *a priori* argument which had recently won wide acceptance, to be found in Mr. R.F. Kahn s article on The Relation of Home Investment to Employment, published in the Economic Journal for June 1931' (Keynes 1973, p. 400).

Harcourt, G. C., and P. Kriesler. 2011. 'The Influence of Michał Kalecki on Joan Robinson's Approach to Economics.' In *Microeconomics, Macroeconomics and Economic Policy. Essays in Honor of Malcom Sayers*, edited by P. Aresti. Basingstoke: Palgrave Macmillan.

Kalecki, M. 1936. 'A Theory of the Business Cycle.' *The Review of Economic Studies* 4: 77–97.

Kalecki, M. 1938. 'The Determinants of Distribution of the National Income.' *Econometrica* 6 (2): 97–112.

Keynes, J. M. 1973. 'The General Theory of Employment, Interest, and Money.' In *The Collected Writings of John Maynard Keynes, Vol. VII*, edited by D. A. Moggridge. London: Macmillan.

Kriesler, P. 1987. *Kalecki's Microanalysis*. Cambridge: Cambridge University Press.

Kriesler, P. 2011. 'Kalecki's Pricing Theory Revisited.' In *Post-Keynesian Essays from Down Under Volume I: Essays on Keynes, Harrod and Kalecki. Theory and Policy in an Historical Context*, edited by J. Halevi, G. C. Harcourt, P. Kriesler, and J. W. Nevile. Basingstoke: Palgrave Macmillan.

Marcuzzo, M. C. 1993. 'La Relazione Salari-Occupazione Tra Rigidità Reali e Rigidità Nominali.' *Economia Politica* 10 (3): 439–463.

Marcuzzo, M. C. 1996. 'Alternative Microeconomic Foundations for Macroeconomics: The Controversy Over the L-Shaped Cost Curve Revisited.' *Review of Political Economy* 8 (1): 7–22.

Marcuzzo, M. C. 2014. 'Luigi Pasinetti and the Cambridge Economists.' *History of Economics Review* 60 (Summer): 15–29.

Marcuzzo, M. C. 2018. 'Joan Robinson's Challenges on How to Construct a Post-Keynesian Economic Theory.' *Annals of the Fondazione Luigi Einaudi* LIII (Winter): 121–135.

Marcuzzo, M. C. 2020. 'Richard F. Kahn: A Disciple of Keynes.' *History of Economics Review* 76: 2–57.

Marcuzzo, M. C., and A. Rosselli. 2005. *Economists in Cambridge: A Study Through Their Correspondence, 1907–1946*. London: Routledge.

Marcuzzo, M. C., and E. Sanfilippo. 2007. 'Profit Maximization in the Cambridge Tradition of Economics.' In *Post-Keynesian Macroeconomics Economics: Essays in Honour of Ingrid Rima*, edited by M. Forstater, G. Mongiovi, and S. Pressman. London: Routledge.

Osiatynski, J., ed. 1990. *Collected Works of Michal Kalecki, Volume I. Capitalism: Business Cycles and Full Employment*. Oxford: Clarendon Press.

Osiatynski, J., ed. 1991. *Collected Works of Michal Kalecki, Volume II. Capitalism: Economic Dynamics*. Oxford: Clarendon Press.

Pasinetti, L. 2007. *Keynes and the Cambridge Keynesians*. Cambridge: Cambridge University Press.

Reynolds, P. J. 1983. 'Kalecki's Degree of Monopoly.' *Journal of Post Keynesian Economics* 5 (3): 493–503.

Robinson, J. V. 1942 [1966]. *An Essay on Marxian Economics*. London: Macmillan.

Robinson, J. V. 1948 [1951]. 'Marx and Keynes.' In *Collected Economic Papers, Vol. I*. Oxford: Blackwell.

Robinson, J. V. 1969. *The Economics of Imperfect Competition*. 2nd ed. London: Macmillan.

Robinson, J. V. 1972 [1978]. 'The Second Crisis of Economic Theory.' In *Contributions to Modern Economics*. Oxford: Blackwell.

Robinson, J. V. 1973. 'Preface.' In *The Reconstruction of Political Economy: an Introduction to Post-Keynesian Economics*, edited by J. A. Kregel. London: Macmillan.

Robinson, J. V. 1974 [1978]. 'History Versus Equilibrium.' In *Contributions to Modern Economics*. Oxford: Blackwell.

Robinson, J. V. 1975 [1980]. 'Survey: 1960s.' In *Further Contributions to Modern Economics*. Oxford: Blackwell.

Robinson, J. V. 1977 [1979]. 'Michal Kalecki.' In *Collected Economic Papers, Vol. V*. Oxford: Blackwell.

Robinson, J. V. 1978. 'Reminiscences.' In *Contributions to Modern Economics*. Oxford: Blackwell.

Robinson, J. V. 1978 [1980]. 'Keynes and Ricardo.' In *Further Contributions to Modern Economics [FCM]*. Oxford: Blackwell.

Sawyer, M. 1985. *The Economics of Michael Kalecki*. London: Macmillan.

Toporowski, J. 2013. *Michal Kalecki: An Intellectual Biography. Vol. 1: Rendezvous in Cambridge, 1899–1939*. Basingstoke: Palgrave Macmillan.

Overhead Labour Costs in a Neo-Kaleckian Growth Model with Autonomous Non-Capacity Creating Expenditures

Marc Lavoie [ID] and Won Jun Nah

ABSTRACT

A notable feature of income distribution is the widening wage differential among workers: there is a redistribution in favour of managers at the detriment of ordinary workers. The paper incorporates this distinction between overhead managerial labour and direct labour into a neo-Kaleckian growth model with target-return pricing, where an autonomously growing demand component ultimately determines the long-run path of an economy. Our aim is to explore the role of overhead labour costs in the coevolution of income distribution and economic growth. We find that the profit share becomes an increasing function of the rate of capacity utilization, implying that empirical research based on the post-Kaleckian specification of investment is likely to be biased in finding a profit-led regime. Our model also features convergence to a fully adjusted position. We examine the parametric conditions under which the model achieves a wage-led growth regime in the long run, in the restricted sense that both the average rates of accumulation and utilization decrease during the transitional dynamics arising from an upward adjustment of the normal profit rate. Moreover, it is shown that a more equitable wage distribution between managers and ordinary workers will strengthen the wage-led nature of the economy.

1. Introduction

The popular success of the book of Thomas Piketty (2014) has rekindled interest in the study of income inequality (and possibly wealth inequality) among all strands of economic thought. One of the key features of post-Keynesian economics is its concern with the effects of changes in functional income distribution on economic activity as well as the impact of the evolution of economic activity on income distribution. Over the last twenty years, an enormous literature has been developed by post-Keynesian authors on the relationship between the profit share, or the wage share, and economic activity or economic growth, both from a theoretical angle and through empirical studies (Lavoie and Stockhammer 2013). What the work of Piketty and his colleagues throughout the world has however also underlined is the importance of income inequality arising from an

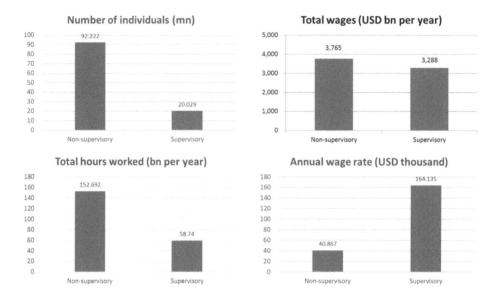

Figure 1. Labour indices of non-supervisory and supervisory workers. Source: Mohun (2014), Computations based on data provided by Simon Mohun.

unequal income distribution within wage-earners — a feature that had been left relatively unexplored by post-Keynesian authors.

Thus one of most notable feature of income distribution over the last 40 years is the widening wage differential among workers: there is a redistribution in favour of top management at the detriment of ordinary workers. How can this be taken into account within a macroeconomic model of growth and income distribution which, by tradition, only distinguished between wages and profits, or at best between wages, net profits and rentier income? In this paper we propose to subdivide wage-earners into two categories, overhead labour and direct labour. Overhead labour, or white-collar workers, will be associated with persons holding managerial positions or what the Bureau of Labor Statistics (BLS) in the United States calls supervisory workers. By contrast, direct labour, or blue-collar workers, will be associated with persons designated as non-supervisory workers.

Simon Mohun is one of the few scholars who has taken interest in this distinction at the empirical level. Figure 1 below shows numbers for the year 2010 and is taken from data that he collected from the BLS and that he to one of the current authors, and which is at the origin of the study found in Mohun (2014). Figure 1 shows that the distinction between non-supervisory and supervisory workers is not innocuous and has a substantial sociological and economic meaning. While supervisory workers represent less than 20 per cent of all workers (more exactly, 18 per cent), their average annual salary is over four times that of non-supervisory workers, so that they gather nearly half of all the wages and salaries that were paid out in 2010.[1] As one would expect from the work of Piketty, there has been a huge evolution through the years. Back in 1964, while supervisory

---

[1]A large part of this discrepancy in annual salary income can be attributed to the big difference in the number of hours worked per year. On the basis of a 50-week year, non-supervisory workers work 33.1 hours per week, while supervisory workers appear to compile no less than 58.6 hours per week. The discrepancy in worked hours is similar throughout the 1964–2010 period.

workers also represented slightly less than 18 per cent of the workforce, their annual wage income was only 2.3 times that of non-supervisory workers, so that their share of total wages and salaries was less than one third. This is a further justification for devising macroeconomic models that can take some account of this evolution in the widening annual wage differential between workers.

Our intent in this paper is to introduce the distinction between non-supervisory (direct labour) and supervisory workers (overhead labour) into a neo-Kaleckian model of growth and distribution. While there are dozens of such models, only very few of them incorporate this distinction. The first authors to do so, but in static models, were Asimakopulos (1970) and Harris (1974). In growth models, the distinction was introduced by Rowthorn (1981), Kurz (1990), Nichols and Norton (1991), Lavoie (1992, 1995, 1996, 2009, 2014), Dutt (1992, 2012) and Nikiforos (2017). In all these works, overhead labour is indeed a fixed cost and 'assumed to move in proportion to production capacity' (Steindl 1979, 3).[2] A second set of authors — Tavani and Vasaudevan (2014), Ederer and Rehm (2020) as well as Palley (2005, 2015, 2017) — also consider two classes of wage earners (workers and managers), but the relative wage revenue of the two classes remains constant whatever the level of economic activity, thus implicitly assuming that employment in both classes move in proportion to output. We believe this is a shortcoming, as it cannot capture the short-run fluctuation of the profit share. We shall follow instead the lead of the first set of authors, where the salaries of managers are truly considered as a fixed cost.

Relative to these previous works, the peculiarity of our paper is that this distinction between overhead and direct labour is set within a neo-Kaleckian growth model with autonomously growing expenditures that do not by themselves create production capacity. There is now a general recognition that this may be an appropriate way to model basic stylized facts of modern economies with access to credit, as argued in particular by Fiebiger (2018), who claims that what he calls semi-autonomous expenditures — household investment made possible by mortgages and debt-financed personal consumption expenditures — are the main drivers of the US economy (cf. Leamer 2015). Published papers developing this new approach, which is related to the so-called Sraffian supermultiplier of Freitas and Serrano (2015) and Serrano and Freitas (2017), can first be found in Allain (2015) and Lavoie (2016). A number of other papers have extended this line of research in various directions and with different autonomous expenditures, as in Allain (2019), Dutt (2019), Hein (2018), Fazzari, Ferri, and Variato (2020), Lavoie (2017a), Pariboni (2016), and Nah and Lavoie (2017, 2019a, 2019b). All these papers provide a new closure consistent with fundamental Keynesian features, where saving adjusts to investment through an endogenous average propensity to save despite constant marginal propensities to save, while requiring neither an endogenous rate of capacity utilization nor an endogenous pricing mark-up.

The next section presents the key equations of our model, notably how the amount of direct and overhead labour are determined, and it calculates the algebraic values of the various shares of income that go to profits, the salaries of managers and the wages of direct labour when firms set prices on the basis of a target-return pricing formula. We

---

[2]As far as we know, Rolim (2019) is the only empirical work on wage-led and profit-led demand regimes that splits the wage share into the shares going to supervisory and non-supervisory personnel. More about this will be said in the conclusion.

shall see that the profit share and the share of wage income going to managers depend on the realized rate of capacity utilization. As Steindl (1979, p. 3) puts it, 'we need to distinguish between those shifts to or from profits which are due to effective demand, and those that result from changed price-cost relations independent of demand'. This means that in a neo-Kaleckian model with overhead costs the profit share can no longer be considered as an exogenous parameter, being instead an endogenous variable. This means that a slightly different definition of wage-led demand is needed, one that in our model will depend on the target rate of return of firms. In the third section we analyse the determinants of the short-run equilibrium, having previously discussed the shape of the saving and investment functions. In particular we discuss the conditions under which an increase in the target rate of return or in the wage rate of managers relative to that of direct workers has a negative impact on the rate of capacity utilization. We also study the impact of such changes on the profit share, taking note that an increase in the target rate of return does not necessarily lead to an increase in the profit share. In the fourth section, we shall study the long-run equilibrium of the model. At this stage we introduce a path-dependent adjustment, such that the growth rate of sales expected by firms react to realized values. We examine what happens in the long run when a less equitable wage distribution between supervisory and non-supervisory workers is being imposed to our model economy. We also examine the conditions under which the model achieves a wage-led demand regime, in the restricted sense that both the average rates of accumulation and of utilization decrease during the transitional dynamics arising from an upward adjustment of the target rate of return in the pricing equation. The last section will recap the main features of the model and its main results, relating some of these to two very recent empirical studies.

2. The Model Economy

The model economy is a closed economy with no government, where households and monopolistically competitive firms interact. We borrow the basic assumptions from Lavoie (2009) for our artificial economy. Firms are owned and managed by a subset of households, who are the shareholders of firms while at the same time providing managerial, or supervisory, i.e., overhead labour services for the firms. On the other hand, the rest of households, do not save and provide ordinary, i.e., direct labour services for the firms. The (nominal) wage rate is given by w for direct labour and σw for overhead labour, where σ is the wage premium of overhead labour over that of direct labour, with $\sigma > 1$.[3]

The number of direct workers, L_d, varies proportionally to the level of production, q, while that of overhead workers, L_f, for fixed labour, hinges on productive capacity, q_{fc} i.e., full-capacity output. For some constants y_d and y_f, we have $q = y_d L_d$ and $L_f = q_{fc}/y_f$. This implies that direct labour costs are variable and overhead labour costs are fixed with respect to q, once the stock of capital, K, is given. With $f \equiv y_d/y_f$, we can measure the size of L_f relative to L_d when the economy is operating at full capacity (when $q = q_{fc}$). The productivity of direct labour is given by y_d. As to the overall labour

---

[3]Other formulations of the wage remuneration of overhead labour are possible. Lavoie (2009, p. 390) suggests that the real wage of overhead workers be a given, thus avoiding that autonomous increases in the mark-up of firms reduce their real remuneration.

productivity y, taking both direct and overhead labour into account, it is a pro-cyclical variable as it depends positively on the rate of capacity utilization, $u = q/q_{fc}$, as shown below:[4]

$$y = \frac{q}{L_d + L_f} = \frac{y_d}{1 + f/u} \tag{1}$$

National income is divided into profits and wages, and the latter is again divided into wages to overhead labour and wages to direct labour. Let π denote the *net* share of profits out of national income, while m, where m stands for '*managers*', denotes the share of national income that goes to overhead labour. Hence, $(\pi + m)$ amounts to what we can call the gross share of profits, as it is determined by the percentage gross costing margin of firms over direct unit costs (Lee et al. 1986). From now on we will refer to π as simply the share of profits.

Let us assume that workers involved with direct labour, save nothing and consume all their wages.[5] In our model economy, total saving is then made up of three components: saving from the retained earnings of firms; saving out of the salaries of the managers and out of received dividends; and a negative component, which is dissaving due to autonomous consumption.[6] Let us further assume that firms retain a proportion s_f of their net profits, and that households who receive overhead salaries and dividends save a constant proportion s_h of both components of these revenues.[7] These dividends are thus a proportion $(1 - s_f)$ of net profits. We assume that $0 < s_f < 1$ and $0 < s_h < 1$.

With Z the real autonomous consumption expenditure, total saving can then be expressed as:

$$s_f \pi q + s_h[mq + (1 - s_f)\pi q] - Z \tag{2}$$

Dividing equation 2 by K, the capital stock, we have a saving function expressed in *growth* terms, g_s, such that:

$$g_s = s_f \frac{\pi u}{v} + s_h\left[\frac{mu}{v} + (1 - s_f)\frac{\pi u}{v}\right] - z \tag{3}$$

---

[4]As Kaldor (1964, p. xvi) puts it, 'short-period labour costs per unit of output are not constant, but falling (mainly on account of the influence of "overhead labour")'.

[5]Of course, some of the non-supervisory workers may dissave, but we shall assume that as a group they neither save nor dissave. Similarly, a fraction of supervisory workers may be dissaving by getting access to credit. Explicit dissaving by direct workers would require an analysis of household debt and wealth dynamics, which would greatly complicate the model, as others who have dealt with poor and rich households have found out in previous articles, and it would lead us away from our main task.

[6]These two components of saving and dissaving by managers are among the peculiarities of our model compared to Lavoie (1995, 2014) for instance.

[7]This comes down, as mentioned earlier, to assume that shareholders are at the same time managers. Making a distinction between managers (who earn salaries, save and hence receive profits on their accumulated financial wealth) and pure capitalists (who only receive capital income) would imply the consideration of three classes and the addition of the dynamics of the shares of capital accumulated by managers on one hand and pure capitalists on the other, and thus make our model even more complex. Ederer and Rehm (2020) have something of the sort, with either workers who save and capitalists who don't work in their basic model, or with both workers and managers who work and save in their extended model, thus considering in both models the determinants of their respective shares of financial capital with differential rates of return. Dutt (1990), assuming the presence of pure capitalists and workers who save, as did Pasinetti (1962), was the first author to examine the endogenous determination of the shares of wealth in a neo-Kaleckian model. Palley (2017) has a structure similar to Ederer and Rehm's extended model, but his shares of wealth are exogenous.

where $v = K/q_{fc}$ is the capital-to-capacity output ratio which is assumed to be constant, and where $z = Z/K$ is the relative magnitude of non-capacity creating autonomous expenditures compared to the volume of capital.

There is quite a bit of empirical evidence that firms use target-return pricing (Lee 1998). Under this pricing procedure, the price is set in such a way that a normal rate of profit r_n will be achieved when the economy is running at the normal rate of utilization of capacity, i.e., when $u = u_n$.[8] Lavoie (2014, p. 333) shows that under these conditions the price is given by:

$$p = \left[1 + \frac{r_n v}{u_n - r_n v}\right]\left[\left(1 + \frac{\sigma f}{u_n}\right)\left(\frac{w}{y_d}\right)\right] = \left[1 + \frac{r_n v + \sigma f}{u_n - r_n v}\right]\frac{w}{y_d} = \left[\frac{u_n + \sigma f}{u_n - r_n v}\right]\frac{w}{y_d} \quad (4)$$

The first expression reflects the necessary percentage net costing margin on the normal unit cost which is the sum of the unit direct labour cost and of the unit normal overhead labour cost. The next two expressions reflect the percentage gross costing margin on the unit direct labour cost (w/y_d). Obviously, any increase in the target rate of return r_n or in the relative overhead cost σf requires a higher mark-up. For equation 4 to be positive, it must be that:

$$u_n > r_n v \quad (5)$$

Notice that the inverse of the last term inside the squared bracket, given by $(u_n + \sigma f)/(u_n - r_n v) > 1$, happens to be the income share of direct labour, d, where d is for 'direct labour', since the numerator of equation 6 is the revenue (in real terms) of direct labour while the denominator is total output:

$$d = \frac{(w/p)L_d}{q} = \frac{(w/p)}{y_d} = \frac{u_n - r_n v}{u_n + \sigma f} \quad (6)$$

From equation 6, we can see that an increase in the target rate of return — the normal rate of profit r_n — will lead to a fall in the share of income going to direct labour. Similarly, when there is an increase in the proportion of supervisory workers (measured by f at full capacity) or in the wage premium going to managers (measured by σ), the share of income going to direct labour gets reduced. This is because the percentage mark-up on unit direct costs, as can be ascertained from equation 4, is raised.

In a similar way, the income share that goes to overhead salaries, m, becomes:

$$m = \frac{(\sigma w/p)L_f}{q} = \frac{\sigma f}{u}\left[\frac{u_n - r_n v}{u_n + \sigma f}\right] \quad (7)$$

It follows that the share of profits is equal to:

$$\pi = 1 - d - m = 1 - \left[1 + \frac{\sigma f}{u}\right]\left[\frac{u_n - r_n v}{u_n + \sigma f}\right] \quad (8)$$

We may thus gather from the above that the overall share of income that goes into the hands of the managers/shareholders is equal to $M = m + (1 - s_f)\pi$. But we will not

---

[8]Target-return pricing is a specific version of normal-cost pricing, where the estimated unit cost is calculated at the standard rate of capacity utilization, which corresponds to normal output, also called nowadays *budgeted output* (Lee 2013).

deal with this measure anymore, except to say that it can be shown that this share becomes smaller with a higher rate of capacity utilization, all else equal.

From equations 7 and 8, it is clear that the share of profits, π, is an increasing function of the rate of utilization of capacity, u, while the share of overhead salaries, m, decreases in u. With overhead labour present, an increase in the rate of utilization due to an increase in effective demand brings about changes in the composition of labour, increasing the relative proportion of direct labour and decreasing that of overhead labour. Thus, as Steindl (1952, p. 46) made clear,

> the net profit margin can, in fact, change for two quite different reasons: either because of a change in utilisation of capacity, with an otherwise unchanged structure of costs and prices; or the net profit margin can change at a *given level of utilisation of capacity*. The latter type of change will take place, for example, if the gross profit margins change.[9]

This will happen in particular if the target rate of return r_n changes or if there is a change in the relative overhead labour cost, represented by the combined parameters σf.

That the profit share has a contemporaneous positive response to an increase in the actual rate of capacity utilization implies that the share of profits itself can be a poor indicator either of the expected profitability or of the relative bargaining position of capital in the class conflict. The point was made early on by Rowthorn (1981, p. 21) when he noted that there was no necessary positive relationship between the mark-up and the profit share, and it was reasserted by Lavoie (1995, 2014, p. 422, 2017b). And as Palley (2017, p. 50) puts it: 'If the profit share is a positive function of capacity utilization, shifts of the IS schedule can make it look empirically as if the economy is profit-led when it is in fact wage-led'. It was in this vein that Weisskopf (1979) suggested the concept of the 'corrected share of profits', which here we denote by π_c, and which we define as follows:

$$\pi_c = 1 - d - m\frac{u}{u_n} \tag{9}$$

Evidently, π_c corrects the actual share of overhead salaries by making it proportional to the actual utilization rate relative to its normal rate.[10] Hence, the uncorrected share of profits seen from the cost (or supply) side, which we shall call π^s, and the corrected one π_c can be contrasted by comparing equations 10 and 11 below, obtained after some manipulations of equations 8 and 9, respectively:

$$\pi^s = \frac{(\sigma f + r_n v)u - (u_n - r_n v)\sigma f}{u(u_n + \sigma f)} \tag{10}$$

$$\pi_c = \frac{r_n v}{u_n} \tag{11}$$

Notably, out of (d, m, π^s, π_c), only d and π_c are independent of the rate of utilization while the others are not. In this respect, we argue that, when we consider the post-Kaleckian investment function of the Bhaduri-Marglin (1990) type, the true indicator of the expected profitability or of the relative power of capital in the class struggle should be

---

[9]Original emphasis.
[10]Weisskopf (1979) defined the corrected profit share by multiplying the income share of overhead labour by the ratio of output relative to full-capacity output, but consistency with the target-return formula requires that it be multiplied by the ratio of output relative to normal output.

π_c (or inversely d), or rather r_n itself, instead of the traditional measure π. This is because, in the presence of overhead labour, the traditional share of profits π will not succeed in isolating the pure effects of profitability on accumulation, as has been repeatedly argued by Weisskopf (1979), Sherman and Evans (1984), and most recently by Lavoie (2017b), to name a few.

It is interesting to note that the corrected share of profits π_c is impervious to any change in the wage differential between supervisory and non-supervisory workers. By contrast, the share of profits π will move up or down as a consequence of an increase in the wage premium going to managers, measured by σ,[11] depending on whether the actual rate of capacity utilization is higher or lower than the normal rate of utilization, as the following equation shows:

$$\frac{\partial \pi^s}{\partial \sigma} = \frac{f(u - u_n)(u_n - r_n v)}{u(u_n + \sigma f)^2} \tag{12}$$

Note that this partial derivative is valid for a given rate of utilization. This means that the profit-share curve seen from the supply side (equation 10), drawn in (u, π) space, shifts down if $u < u_n$ and shifts up if $u > u_n$ as σ increases. This is illustrated in Figure 2.

We may now deal with the last elements of the model. The saving function can be reformulated with an explicit consideration of our target-return pricing formula as can be found in Appendix 1. In this paper, we assume that the investment function takes the standard form of those neo-Kaleckian models that are concerned with a possible convergence towards the normal rate of capacity utilization:[12]

$$g_i = \gamma + \gamma_u(u - u_n) \tag{13}$$

g_i is the rate of accumulation of capital, i.e., investment divided by K. The first term on the right-hand side, γ, represents the secular expected growth rate of sales. The coefficient γ_u captures the sensitivity of induced investment to changes in effective demand, i.e., to changes in the rate of capacity utilization.

3. Equilibrium in the Short Run

For analytical tractability, we introduce a distinction between the short and the long run into our model economy. We define the short run as the time period during which the capital stock, K, does not change, thus implying that there is no expansion of production capacity as of yet. It is also assumed that over the short run there is no change in the expectation of the firms about future sales growth, γ, and in the autonomous consumption of managers, Z. All these variables will be allowed to adjust in the long run.

---

[11]This is also true of a change in the proportion of supervisory workers, measured by f at full capacity. However, we focus on σ because, as recalled in the introduction, the variable f seems to have hardly changed through time.

[12]Some readers may wonder why we don't use the investment function advocated by Bhaduri and Marglin (1990), with the share of profits as an additional component to the function used here. Besides the reason given in the main text, with overhead costs the share of profits becomes an endogenous variable that does not measure profitability at normal capacity utilization. Furthermore, Pariboni (2016, p. 426) has shown that in a model with autonomous non-capacity creating expenditures and the Bhaduri-Marglin investment function, the profit-led regime 'is no longer a feasible option: an increase in the profit share leads to a reduction in the equilibrium degree of capacity utilization, regardless of the relative magnitude of the parameters involved'. There is thus no advantage in making use of this more complicated investment function.

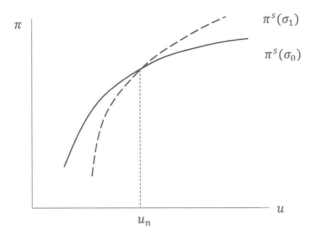

Figure 2. Profit curves seen from the supply side for a larger overhead wage premium, $\sigma_0 < \sigma_1$.

The short-run equilibrium is achieved by adjustments in the rate of utilization of capacity so as to equate g_s to g_i (so that saving equals investment, or alternatively, so that aggregate supply equates aggregate demand). The equilibrium rate of utilization of capacity will be denoted by u^*, as determined in Appendix 1. For the short-run equilibrium to be stable, the following Keynesian stability condition must be met, derived from the fact that the slope of the saving curve (equation A2) must be steeper than that of the investment curve (equation 13), which also implies that the denominator of u^* as determined in Appendix 1 must be positive:

$$[s_f(1 - s_h) + s_h](\sigma f + r_n v) - \gamma_u v(u_n + \sigma f) \equiv A > 0 \tag{14}$$

We can also obtain the short-run equilibrium values of the share of profits, π^*, the rate of profit, r^*, and the rate of accumulation, g^*, as found in Appendix 1.

A simple comparative statics exercise shows that both the short-run equilibrium values of the rate of capacity utilization and of the rate of accumulation are lower when there is a higher normal rate of profit r_n. This reveals, as expected from the chosen investment function, the wage-led nature of demand and accumulation of the present model in the short run:

$$\frac{\partial u^*}{\partial r_n} = \frac{-\sigma f v \{s_f(1 - s_h) + u^*[s_f(1 - s_h) + s_h]\}}{A} < 0 \tag{15}$$

$$\frac{\partial g^*}{\partial r_n} = \gamma_u \frac{\partial u^*}{\partial r_n} < 0 \tag{16}$$

Furthermore, we can evaluate the short-run effects of widening the gap σ between the wage rate obtained by overhead labour and the wage rate of direct labour. We have:

$$\frac{\partial u^*}{\partial \sigma} = \frac{f(u_n - r_n v)\{u_n s_f(1 - s_h) - u^*[s_f(1 - s_h) + s_h]\}}{A(u_n + \sigma f)} \tag{17}$$

Three cases need to be considered:

(a) $\partial u^*/\partial\sigma > 0$ and $\partial g^*/\partial\sigma > 0$, if

$$u^* < \left[\frac{s_f(1-s_h)}{s_f(1-s_h)+s_h}\right] u_n \tag{18}$$

(b) $\partial u^*/\partial\sigma < 0$ and $\partial g^*/\partial\sigma < 0$, if

$$u^* > \left[\frac{s_f(1-s_h)}{s_f(1-s_h)+s_h}\right] u_n \tag{19}$$

And finally, (c) $\partial u^*/\partial\sigma = 0$ and $\partial g^*/\partial\sigma = 0$, if

$$u^* = \left[\frac{s_f(1-s_h)}{s_f(1-s_h)+s_h}\right] u_n \tag{20}$$

A permanent increase in σ has a twofold effect. Obviously, it directly increases overhead expenses incurred by firms. This reallocates income from the firms to their managers. With income going to firms, only the ratio $(1-s_f)(1-s_h)$ gets to be spent on consumption by managers; with income going directly to managers, the ratio $(1-s_h)$ gets spent. The former is strictly less than the latter. Moreover, when the value of s_f is higher, the difference between the former and the latter gets bigger. Thus, an increase in σ may lead to an increase in consumption and in the rate of utilization as in the (a) case, and this positive redistribution effect is amplified with a bigger s_f. We can see that, the higher is s_f, the more likely is the (a) case, since the term inside the squared bracket on the far right of (18) increases in s_f. The (a) case is more likely once the term inside the bracket is big enough, and vice versa:

$$\frac{\partial}{\partial s_f}\left[\frac{s_f(1-s_h)}{s_f(1-s_h)+s_h}\right] > 0 \tag{21}$$

However, this is not the whole story. As is evident from equation 6, an increase in σ lowers the income share that goes to direct labour, whose propensity to consume is assumed to be unitary. This is because of the target-return pricing strategy: as equation 4 shows, an increase in overhead costs will lead to an increase in the percentage mark-up over unit direct labour costs and hence to a fall in the real wage of direct labour. A widening gap in wage rates shifts income away from the poor to the rich. Due to the difference in their respective propensities to save, this change yields a shrinking effect on the economy as in the (b) case. This is to be expected because if managers receive higher wages but save most of it, the potential positive effect of this change will be that much smaller. Also, it is apparent that, as s_h gets smaller, the difference in the propensities to consume of direct labour and overhead labour diminishes, and hence the negative effect caused by the redistribution towards the overhead labour is dampened. This makes the (b) case less likely. It is consistent with the fact that the term in the squared bracket on the far right of (19) decreases in s_h:

$$\frac{\partial}{\partial s_h}\left[\frac{s_f(1-s_h)}{s_f(1-s_h)+s_h}\right] < 0 \tag{22}$$

These two effects are in conflict with each other. The former positive effect is due to the redistribution towards the managers away from the retained earnings of the firms, and the latter negative effect is due to the redistribution towards managers away from direct labour. Unless the former dominates the latter, the less equitable structure of wages resulting from an increase in σ turns out to reduce effective demand in the short run, as in the (b) case. From the discussions above, we can conclude that the (b) case is more likely to occur than the (a) case when the marginal propensity to save of managers, which is s_h, is high and when the retention ratio of firms, which is s_f, is low. We can also conclude from the fact that the term inside the bracket of the right hand side of either equation 18 or 19 is smaller than unity that in the neighbourhood of the normal rate of capacity utilization u_n, the effect on economic activity of an increase in wage dispersion will be negative.[13]

Coming now to the effects on the profit share as a consequence of an increase in the wage premium obtained by overhead labour, i.e., of an increase in wage dispersion, we plug (equation 7) into the saving function (equation 3), thus obtaining a saving function with only the profit share and the rate of utilization as endogenous variables, and then equate this saving function to the investment function (equation 13) to get the profit share as a function of the rate of utilization:

$$\pi^d = \frac{1}{s_f + s_h(1 - s_f)}\left[v\gamma_u - s_h\sigma f\left(\frac{u_n - r_n v}{u_n + \sigma f}\right)\right] + \frac{v(\gamma - \gamma_u u_n + z)}{u[s_f + s_h(1 - s_f)]} \tag{23}$$

Equation 23 is the profit share seen from the demand side and can be contrasted with equation 10, which is seen from the opposite cost side. Evaluating the partial derivative with respect to σ, while holding the rate of utilization constant in equation 23, we have:

$$\frac{\partial \pi^d}{\partial \sigma} = -\frac{f s_h u_n(u_n - r_n v)}{[s_f + s_h(1 - s_f)](u_n + \sigma f)^2} < 0 \tag{24}$$

This implies that the profit-share curve seen from the demand side (equation 23), drawn in (u, π) space, shifts down in a parallel fashion when the wage premium of managers, σ, increases. This is illustrated in either Figure 3(A or B), depending on whether the term $(\gamma - \gamma_u u_n + z)$ in equation 23 is positive or negative.[14]

Table 1 summarizes the effects of an increase in σ (the wage premium of overhead labour) on the rate of utilization and on the share of profits when the combined effects on the demand and supply sides are taken into consideration. With regards to the impact of an increase in the wage differential on the short-run equilibrium share of profit, an analytical discussion is provided in Appendix 2. As to the impact of this increase on the rate of capacity utilization, the possible cases were explained above with the help of equation 17. The detailed graphical illustrations corresponding to the various cases of Table 1 can be found in Figure 4(A and B).

---

[13]As an illustration if the retention ratio of firms is 0.6 while the propensity to save of managers is 0.1, and with a normal rate of utilization equal to 0.8, an increase in σ will have a negative impact on the rate of utilization as long as $u^* > 0.675$. So this should be the more frequent case.

[14]Obviously, in the case where managers do not save ($s_h = 0$), there will be no shift of the demand-side profit-share curve, as occurred in Lavoie (1995). Note that we consider only the case where the profit-share curve (equation 10) is steeper than (equation 23) as in Figure 4(B) because the rate of utilization must decrease when there is an increase in the target rate of return, as shown by the sign of the derivative given by equation 15, and this can only happen if the slope of equation 10 is steeper than that of equation 23.

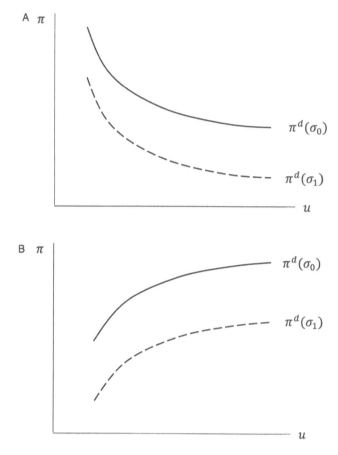

Figure 3. (A) Profit curves seen from the demand side for a larger overhead wage premium, with $\gamma - \gamma_u u_n + z > 0$ and $\sigma_0 < \sigma_1$. (B) Profit curves seen from the demand side for a larger overhead wage premium, with $\gamma - \gamma_u u_n + z < 0$ and $\sigma_0 < \sigma_1$.

We may also briefly examine what happens to the rate of capacity utilization and to the share of profit in the short-run equilibrium when there is an increase in the target rate of return. We already know from equation 15 that the rate of capacity utilization will be lower. What happens to the share of profits can be ascertained by checking Figure 5

Table 1. The short-run effects of an increase in σ, the wage premium of overhead labour.

	Utilization rate	du	$d\pi$	Figure
$\gamma - \gamma_u u_n + z > 0$	$u > u_n$	(−)	?	4(A1)
	$\left[\dfrac{s_f(1 - s_h)}{s_f(1 - s_h) + s_h}\right]u_n < u \leq u_n$	(−)	(−)	4(A2)
	$u < \left[\dfrac{s_f(1 - s_h)}{s_f(1 - s_h) + s_h}\right]u_n$	(+)	(−)	4(A3)
$\gamma - \gamma_u u_n + z < 0$	$u > u_n$	(−)	(−)	4(B1)
	$\left[\dfrac{s_f(1 - s_h)}{s_f(1 - s_h) + s_h}\right]u_n < u \leq u_n$	(−)	(−)	4(B2)
	$u < \left[\dfrac{s_f(1 - s_h)}{s_f(1 - s_h) + s_h}\right]u_n$	(+)	?	4(B3)

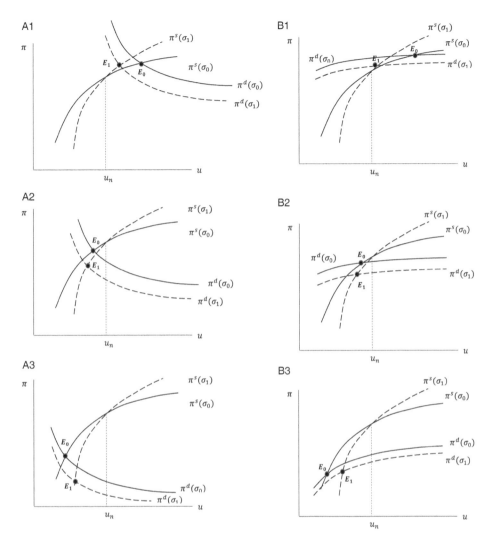

Figure 4. (A1) The effects of an increase in the overhead wage premium σ for the case of $\gamma - \gamma_u u_n + z > 0$ and $u > u_n$. Note: Due to an increase in σ, the π^s curve tilts counterclockwise and the π^d curve shifts down. The economy moves to point E_1 once it starts from point E_0. The same explanation applies to Figure 4(A2, A3, B1, B2 and B3). (A2) The effects of an increase in the overhead wage premium σ for the case of $\gamma - \gamma_u u_n + z > 0$ and $\left[\frac{s_f(1-s_h)}{s_f(1-s_h)+s_h}\right]u_n < u < u_n$. (A3) The effects of an increase in the overhead wage premium σ for the case of $\gamma - \gamma_u u_n + z > 0$ and $u < \left[\frac{s_f(1-s_h)}{s_f(1-s_h)+s_h}\right]u_n$. (B1) The effects of an increase in the overhead wage premium σ for the case of $\gamma - \gamma_u u_n + z < 0$ and $u > u_n$. (B2) The effects of an increase in the overhead wage premium σ for the case of $\gamma - \gamma_u u_n + z < 0$ and $\left[\frac{s_f(1-s_h)}{s_f(1-s_h)+s_h}\right]u_n < u < u_n$. (B3) The effects of an increase in the overhead wage premium σ for the case of $\gamma - \gamma_u u_n + z < 0$ and $u < \left[\frac{s_f(1-s_h)}{s_f(1-s_h)+s_h}\right]u_n$.

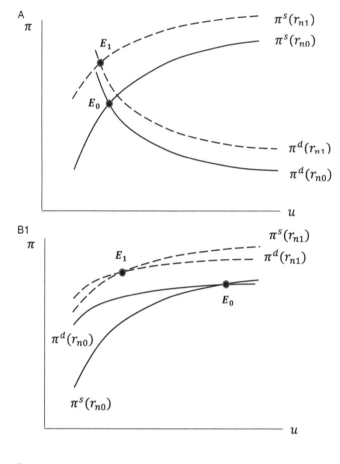

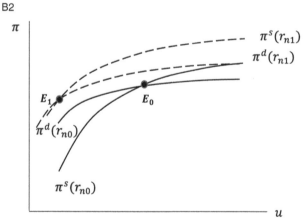

Figure 5. (A) The effects of an increase in the target rate of return r_n for the case of $\gamma - \gamma_u u_n + z > 0$. Note: Due to an increase in r_n, both the π^s curve and the π^d curve shift up. The economy moves to point E_1 once it starts from point E_0. The same explanation applies to Figure 5(B1 and B2). (B1) The effects of an increase in the target rate of return r_n for the case of $\gamma - \gamma_u u_n + z < 0$: $\Delta \pi^* > 0$. (B2) The effects of an increase in the target rate of return r_n for the case of $\gamma - \gamma_u u_n + z < 0$: $\Delta \pi^* < 0$.

(A and B). From equation 10, it is obvious that a rise in the normal rate of profit r_n shifts up the curve representing the profit share π^s seen from the cost side:

$$\frac{\partial \pi^s}{\partial r_n} = \frac{(\sigma f + u)v}{u(u_n + \sigma f)} > 0 \qquad (25)$$

From equation 23, we can ascertain that a rise in the normal rate of profit also shifts up the curve representing the profit share π^d seen from the demand side:

$$\frac{\partial \pi^d}{\partial r_n} = \frac{s_h \sigma f v}{[s_f + s_h(1 - s_f)](u_n + \sigma f)} > 0 \qquad (26)$$

However, it can be worthwhile to emphasize that, for any value of u, the π^s curve seen from the cost side shifts upward vertically more than does the π^d curve seen from the demand side, when responding to an increase in r_n. This can be verified by comparing the relative magnitude of the two partial derivatives as follows:

$$\frac{\partial \pi^s}{\partial r_n} - \frac{\partial \pi^d}{\partial r_n} = \frac{v}{u_n + \sigma f} \left[\left(1 + \frac{\sigma f}{u} \right) - \frac{s_h}{s_h + s_f(1 - s_h)} \sigma f \right] > 0 \qquad (27)$$

The very last fraction in the squared brackets is smaller than unity and it is multiplied by σf which we can also safely assume to be smaller than unity, on the basis of the data provided in Figure 1[15] in the introduction of this paper.[16] Furthermore, it is also evident that the degree with which the π^s curve moves up when responding to an increase in r_n decreases in u while the π^d curve shifts upward in a parallel fashion, since

$$\frac{\partial}{\partial u} \frac{\partial \pi^s}{\partial r_n} < 0 \qquad (28)$$

$$\frac{\partial}{\partial u} \frac{\partial \pi^d}{\partial r_n} = 0 \qquad (29)$$

Figure 5(A) corresponds to the case where the term $(\gamma - \gamma_u u_n + z)$ in equation 23 is positive. A rise in the target rate of return is necessarily associated with a higher equilibrium profit share π^*. Hence in that case the evolution of the profit share will adequately represent the evolution of the stronger bargaining position of firms and this will allow researchers to appropriately assess that the economy is in a wage-led demand regime since the rate of utilization is necessarily lower.

By contrast, in the case where the term $(\gamma - \gamma_u u_n + z)$ in equation 23 is negative, a rise in the target rate of return could associate a lower rate of capacity utilization with a lower equilibrium profit share π^*, as illustrated with Figure 5(B2). This is apparent due to the

---

[15]Considering the data presented in Figure 1, we can assume that the employment share of overhead labour at full capacity is 0.2. This implies we can pinpoint the value of f being close to 0.2. Also, considering that the overhead salary rate is close to the quadruple of the wage rate obtained by direct workers, we can pinpoint the value of σ being close to 4. Hence, we may safely assume that $\sigma f < 1$, in accordance with the empirical facts.

[16]If the π^s curve shifts upward less than the π^d curve does, i.e., $\partial \pi^s / \partial r_n < \partial \pi^d / \partial r_n$, then the rate of utilization *increases* after an increase in r_n. If the degree to which the two curves shift is the same, i.e., $\partial \pi^s / \partial r_n = \partial \pi^d / \partial r_n$, then the rate of utilization stands still, since the increase in the utilization rate due to the upward shift of the π^d curve exactly offsets the decrease in it due to the same amount of vertical shift of the π^s curve. However, these two cases are ruled out because equation 15 must hold.

fact that the π^s curve shifts up more than the π^d curve does after an increase in r_n. This is more likely to happen when the propensity to save of managers is close to zero.[17] Empirical researchers would then mistakenly assess that the economy is in a profit-led demand regime.

This can be analysed algebraically. The effect of an increase in the target rate of return r_n upon the equilibrium profit share π^* in Appendix 1, is not uniquely determined. It can be shown that it depends on the magnitude of the effect of r_n on u^*, and hence on the value of u^*, since from:

$$\frac{\partial \pi^*}{\partial r_n} = \frac{(\sigma f / u^*)(u_n - r_n v)\dfrac{\partial u^*}{\partial r_n} + v(u^* + \sigma f)}{u^*(u_n + \sigma f)} \tag{30}$$

it follows that

$$\frac{\partial \pi^*}{\partial r_n} > 0 \quad \Leftrightarrow \quad \frac{u^* v(u^* + \sigma f)}{\sigma f(u_n - r_n v)} > \left| \frac{\partial u^*}{\partial r_n} \right| \tag{31}$$

and

$$\frac{\partial \pi^*}{\partial r_n} \leq 0 \quad \Leftrightarrow \quad \frac{u^* v(u^* + \sigma f)}{\sigma f(u_n - r_n v)} < \left| \frac{\partial u^*}{\partial r_n} \right| \tag{32}$$

4. Equilibrium in the Long Run

We now move on to a longer time horizon, and let autonomous consumption, Z, increase at the exogenously given rate of $\bar{g}_z$. In this paper, we define the 'long run' as the time period during which our artificial economy ultimately reaches a fully adjusted position, in the sense that the growth rate of sales expected by firms, γ, is allowed to adjust, while the flow of autonomous consumption relative to the stock of capital, given by z, is allowed to move through time. These two variables change through time according to the laws of motion given by equations 33 and 34, where '$\wedge$' represents the rate of change,

$$\hat{z} = \bar{g}_z - g^* \tag{33}$$

$$\hat{\gamma} = \phi_\gamma (g^* - \gamma) \tag{34}$$

Equation 33 arises straightforwardly from the definition of $z = Z/K$. The assumed given rate of growth of autonomous consumption expenditures is represented by $\bar{g}_z$. Equation 34, where we assume that $\phi_\gamma > 0$, implies that the sales expectations of firms in growth terms react positively to the realized rate of growth. For instance, when the actual growth rate of the economy turns out to be surprisingly high, the expected growth rate of sales will be modified upwards accordingly. This reaction function is often referred to as the Harrodian instability mechanism.

---

[17]When $s_h = 0$, the π^d curve given by equation 23 does not shift at all when there is a change in r_n and hence an increase in r_n necessarily leads to a fall in the profit share.

From equations 33 and 34, the long-run equilibrium solutions are given by:

$$g^{**} = \bar{g}_z \tag{35}$$

$$\gamma^{**} = \bar{g}_z \tag{36}$$

$$u^{**} = u_n \tag{37}$$

The long-run values of other variables can be determined. Straightforwardly from equation 10, the long-run share of profits, π^{**}, is equal to:

$$\pi^{**} = \frac{r_n v}{u_n} \tag{38}$$

As to the long-run income shares of direct wages, d^{**}, and overhead salaries, m^{**}, they are:

$$d^{**} = \frac{u_n - r_n v}{u_n + \sigma f} \tag{39}$$

$$m^{**} = \frac{\sigma f}{u_n}\left[\frac{u_n - r_n v}{u_n + \sigma f}\right] \tag{40}$$

Then from equation 3, we have:

$$z^{**} = [s_f(1 - s_h) + s_h]\, r_n + s_h \frac{\sigma f}{v}\left[\frac{u_n - r_n v}{u_n + \sigma f}\right] - \bar{g}_z \tag{41}$$

It is shown in Appendix 3 that, essentially, in this model of autonomously growing non-capacity creating expenditures with overhead labour costs, just as in the standard model without such costs, the presence of the short-run Keynesian stability condition, which is $A > 0$, given by equation 14, also guarantees dynamic stability towards a long-run fully adjusted position, provided there exists a Harrodian adjustment mechanism tied to the investment function and provided this Harrodian instability mechanism is sufficiently weak so that it gets tamed by the growth of autonomous expenditures.

Finally, we evaluate some of the important partial derivatives of z^{**}:

$$\frac{\partial z^{**}}{\partial r_n} = s_f(1 - s_h) + \frac{s_h u_n}{u_n + \sigma f} > 0 \tag{42}$$

$$\frac{\partial z^{**}}{\partial \sigma} = \frac{s_h f u_n d^{**}}{v(u_n + \sigma f)} > 0 \tag{43}$$

Recall that the numerator of z grows at a constant rate. Hence, equation 42 implies that when there is an upward adjustment to the target rate of return set by firms, on average the stock of capital grows more slowly than do autonomous expenditures (which grow at the rate $\bar{g}_z$) during the whole traverse between the old and the new long-run equilibrium. Considering the transition dynamics after the change, we can say that the average rate of accumulation has gone down. This is indicative of the wage-led nature of growth in the long run, in the restricted sense that the rate of capital accumulation *on average* gets reduced during the traverse, until it reaches a new long-run position after an increase in the normal rate of profit. This means that the *level* of output will be lower than otherwise it would have been if firms had not decided to raise the target rate of return. What we have is a level effect.

Likewise, for the same reasons, equation 43 implies that a widening gap in the wage obtained by overhead workers relative to that attained by direct workers slows down the accumulation of capital during the traverse to the new long-run solution. During the transition period from the initial to the final state, the average rate of accumulation goes down after an increase in the wage differential between supervisory and non-supervisory workers. This can be interpreted as supporting the prospect for the 'income (or wage) equality-led growth'.[18]

Last but not least, the wage-led nature of growth in the present model economy, which is evident from equation 42, can be shown to be more prominent when wage distribution is more equitable, and hence when the relative wage gap is smaller. This can be demonstrated by the inequality below:

$$\frac{\partial}{\partial \sigma}\left[\frac{\partial z^{**}}{\partial r_n}\right] = -\frac{s_h u_n}{(u_n + \sigma f)^2} < 0 \tag{44}$$

In words, an economy where wage distribution is highly unequal, all else equal, will turn out to be less strongly wage-led in the long run. The positive association that our paper reveals between the wage-led feature of growth and a more equal wage distribution is in line with the recent claims of Carvalho and Rezai (2016) and Palley (2017).

5. Conclusion

We have devised a neo-Kaleckian model of growth and distribution where capital accumulation depends on the expected growth rate of sales and on the discrepancy between the actual and the normal rate of capacity utilization, but where the economy is driven by the growth rate of autonomous non-capacity creating expenditures, more specifically by the growth rate of autonomous consumption expenditures, those that Fiebiger (2018) and Fiebiger and Lavoie (2019) call semi-autonomous household expenditures.

The novelty in this neo-Kaleckian model with autonomous expenditures arises from combining three features. First, we distinguish between managerial labour — overhead labour or supervisory workers — on the one hand, and direct labour — or non-supervisory workers — on the other hand. Non-supervisory workers do not save, whereas managers have a given marginal propensity to save out of their salaries and out of the capital income they receive from firms. Managers are the social class that has autonomous consumption expenditures. The saving function is thus more complex than usual in this kind of model.

The employment of direct labour moves proportionately with the level of actual output whereas the employment of managers is tied to the level of full-capacity output. In accordance with the stylized facts noted in the introduction, there is a substantial differential between the wage rate received by overhead labour compared to that obtained by direct labour. It follows that the profit share becomes an endogenous variable, which is a positive function of the level of capacity utilization in the short run, as is often observed in the early

---

[18]This point has been recognized from the recent experiences in South Korea, where the policies for 'income-led growth' have been implemented, but where it has been observed that the fragmentation of the labour market is a major structural obstacle to the success of the policies. For more on this, see Nah (2018) and Joo et al. (2020).

phase of the business cycle. In addition, because of the presence of overhead labour, the overall labour productivity is a pro-cyclical variable. A possible implication of this feature for future empirical research on wage-led and profit-led demand regimes is that econometricians should be using the corrected profit share π_c of equation 9 instead of the actual profit share when doing their estimations.

The second key feature of our model is that we suppose that firms set prices on the basis of a target-return pricing formula. As a consequence, an increase in the wage rate of overhead labour relative to that of direct labour will lead to an increase in the percentage mark-up set by firms, thus modifying in general the income distribution between profits and wages, as well as the distribution between wages going to managers and wages going to direct workers.

The third key feature of the present model with autonomous non-capacity creating expenditures is that in the long run we introduce a slow Harrodian instability mechanism, whereby firms increase the expected growth rate of sales when the actual growth rate is above the one expected by firms.

Several interesting results directly arise from the target-return pricing formula combined to the distinction between overhead and direct labour. First an increase in the target rate of return or in the relative real wage of overhead labour, at a given rate of capacity utilization, leads to a fall in the income share of direct labour. Second, at a given rate of capacity utilization, this increase in the relative real wage of overhead labour will lead to an increase (decrease) in the profit share if this given actual rate of capacity utilization is bigger (smaller) than the normal rate.

Third, in an economy with overhead labour, all else equal, that is, with no change whatsoever in the percentage mark-up over unit direct labour costs, an increase in the rate of utilization leads to a fall in the income share of overhead labour and an increase in the share of profits. Thus, unless the measures of the profit share are corrected for this effect, statistical enquiries will be biased towards finding that the aggregate demand regime is profit-led. We have computed an amended version of the corrected profit share suggested by Weisskopf (1979), where the income share of overhead labour is corrected by the actual rate of utilization relative to the normal rate, and have shown that this measure is both impervious to a change in the actual rate of capacity utilization and in the wage differential between supervisory and non-supervisory workers, as it ought to be when firms use a target-return pricing formula.

Combining now the above supply-side with the demand-side effects, we have shown that in the short run an increase in the bargaining power of firms as reflected by their target rate of return always leads to a fall in the equilibrium rate of capacity utilization and in the rate of accumulation. The model is thus wage-led in the short run, in the sense that an autonomous increase in the costing margin of firms calculated at the normal rate of capacity utilization, i.e., an autonomous increase in the mark-up, leads to a fall in the rate of utilization. In general, this will be accompanied by a rise in the profit share, as one would expect from a wage-led model; but the higher target rate of return may also be associated with a fall in both the rate of utilization and the profit share, thus yielding a false profit-led result.

We have also identified the conditions under which an increase in the wage differential favouring overhead labour (necessarily accompanied by an increase in the mark-up and a fall in the income share of direct labour) will lead in the short run to a fall in the rate of capacity utilization and in the rate of accumulation. This will necessarily occur when the actual rate of utilization is higher than the normal rate of utilization, but it may also happen if the actual rate of utilization is smaller than the normal rate of utilization, provided the actual rate is greater than a certain fraction of the normal rate. This fraction depends on the retention ratio of firms and on the marginal propensity to save of managers. The higher is their marginal propensity to save, the smaller will that fraction be, and hence the more likely it is that more inequality in the distribution of wages will generate lower rates of utilization and of accumulation. This result is intuitive because the redistribution of income from direct labour, who do not save, towards overhead labour, who do save, will reduce aggregate demand, so this negative effect will be particularly strong if the marginal propensity to save of overhead labour is high.

As to the effect of a redistribution of income towards overhead labour on the short-run equilibrium profit share, we have shown that its effect is particularly uncertain. The only thing that can be said with certainty is that if the actual rate of utilization is in-between the same fraction of the normal rate of utilization evoked above and the normal rate of utilization, then more wage inequality will generate a fall in the short-run equilibrium value of the profit share. Otherwise the effect of this redistribution on the profit share can go one way or another. However, it can be asserted that the consequence of an increase in the relative wage of overhead labour is more likely to have a negative than a positive impact on the profit share. Changes in the way wages are split between managers and direct labour thus has effects on the rate of utilization and the profit share, and this ought not to be omitted when doing empirical work on demand regimes.

Finally, we consider the results obtained for the long-run equilibrium of the model. The adjustment mechanism involving the expected growth rate of sales (the Harrodian instability mechanism), combined with the dynamic behaviour of the relative weight of the autonomous consumption expenditures, drives the economy towards a fully adjusted state, at a normal rate of capacity utilization, provided the Keynesian short-run stability condition holds and provided Harrodian instability is not overly strong.

We have shown that an increase in the target rate of return set by firms leads to a fall in the average growth rate during the traverse to the new long-run equilibrium — a result which is consistent with what we had observed in the short run. The economy is thus clearly wage-led, a result which is not really surprising given the formulation of the investment function, given by equation 13, which does not include a term ascertaining expected profitability (at the normal rate of capacity utilization), in contrast to the post-Kaleckian model of Bhaduri and Marglin (1990).

What is more surprising and particularly interesting in the study of the long-run effects of our model is that, despite the ambiguous short-run effect on the rate of capacity utilization and the rate of accumulation of an increase in the wage differential favouring supervisory workers, there is no ambiguity with respect to the long-run effect. We have demonstrated that increased inequality in wage distribution necessarily leads to a fall in the average rate of growth of the economy during the traverse from the old to the new long-run equilibrium, thus implying a lower level of economic activity and lower potential output in the long run compared to a situation with no change in wage dispersion.

The main implication of these results, if the model is sufficiently faithful to reality, is that governments should pursue policies that tend to reduce wage dispersion between managerial jobs and non-supervisory jobs, as Palley (2017) also advocates. This calls for a return to egalitarian wage policies or solidarity wage policies. In other words, besides the possibility of a wage-led growth regime, our long-run results provide support for a growth strategy based on wage equality and the imposition of constraints on the perks and salaries obtained by executive managers, such as the imposition of a maximum ratio between executive income and the average or median wage of the other employees of a firm. Efforts to shrink the dispersion of wages by raising the remuneration of those workers at the bottom of the scale also ought to be pursued.

Some final remarks ought to be made regarding the main assumption of our model, which is that by construction the model has a wage-led demand regime. Neo-Kaleckian models of growth and distribution, as well as their empirical versions based on structural equations, have been criticized, among other features, for omitting the possible distributive impact of changes in the rate of utilization on the wage share. Empirical studies conducted with the so-called aggregative VAR approach, which entertain the simultaneous impact of rates of capacity utilization on the wage share and of wage shares on the rate of utilization, used to find systematic evidence of profit-led demand regimes and of profit-squeeze effects (meaning that positive shocks to the rate of utilization lead to a fall in the profit share) — neo-Goodwinian results as alluded to above. But these aggregative results have recently been questioned by new research, which provides support for the Kaleckian model with overhead labour costs that has been presented here, or at least its short-run results.

Michael Cauvel (2019) has pointed out that these aggregative studies use a restrictive specification, such that 'the utilization rate does not have a contemporaneous effect on the wage share'. When that restriction is removed, 'an increase in the wage share is generally found to have a positive effect on the utilization rate … The response of the wage rate to a utilization rate shock is generally small and insignificant' (2019, p. 30). Recall that it is a key feature of the Kaleckian model with overhead labour costs that the rate of utilization has a contemporaneous effect on the wage and profit shares. Furthermore, when dealing with an adjusted wage share and adding the cyclical component of labour productivity, Cauvel (2019, pp. 37–38) finds that 'demand appears to be wage-led and the effects of demand on distribution are found to be mixed or insignificant. Therefore, the results of this disaggregated analysis suggest that the relationship between these variables would be better characterized by wage-led demand and cyclical effects of demand on productivity, rather than a Goodwin cycle pattern'.[19]

Lilian Rolim (2019) has provided further evidence that the Goodwinian profit-led demand regimes and profit-squeeze distributive effects may be spurious. Using the wage and profit shares based on the same data provided by Mohun (2014) as done here, Rolim has verified that using the standard aggregative approach yields the usual Goodwinian results. The results are misleading because they fail to take into account the impact and role of overhead costs. When the wage share is split into the income shares of non-supervisory and supervisory workers, this alternative specification yields results which are quite consistent with the model that has been presented here:

> A positive shock of the workers' share will lead to a decrease in the supervisors' share and to an increase in capacity utilization. A positive shock on the supervisors' share will lead to a

---

[19]In the working paper version of this article (Nah and Lavoie 2018), we have provided figures illustrating numerical simulations which show that changes in the target rate of return or in the wage premium of overhead labour can produce transitional dynamics that generate a clockwise loop in the (u, π) space, and thus loops similar to those defending the neo-Goodwinian profit-led/profit-squeeze story, thus generating a pseudo-Goodwin loop.

decrease in both the workers' share and in capacity utilization. Finally, a positive shock in capacity utilization will lead to an increase in both the workers and the supervisors' share, but in the first period, there is a small decrease in the latter ... There is evidence that both the workers' and supervisors' shares Granger-cause capacity utilization and that capacity utilization Granger-causes the supervisors' share. (Rolim 2019, pp. 765–766)

Thus, both Caudel and Rolim provide empirical evidence that supports the neo-Kaleckian wage-led model of growth and distribution with overhead labour costs the details of which have been presented here.

Taking into account the strength of the accumulated response functions found by Rolim, there does seem to exist a profit-squeeze mechanism, but the squeeze is done through the supervisors' remuneration, and not through the wages obtained by the non-supervisory workers. The increase in capacity utilization leads to a (non-significant) small increase in the income share of non-supervisory workers and a Granger-caused substantial increase over time in the income share of managers, and thus to a fall in the share of profits. It is the increase in the wage-income share of managers, presumably obtained through various bonuses and salary increases when the economy is doing well, that leads to an eventual fall in the rate of capacity utilization. Thus the political implications that we have already mentioned in our conclusion can be reasserted: to raise aggregate demand, governments should pursue wage-led policies and policies that tend to reduce wage dispersion between managerial jobs and non-supervisory jobs. This conclusion is of course reinforced when considering that a more equal wage distribution could be said to be desirable, on its own, based on ethical grounds.

Acknowledgments

We thank the two anonymous referees of the journal for their detailed comments which certainly helped to clarify some of the statements of our paper. This research has benefitted in the past from a grant for the study of income distribution issues provided by the Institute for New Economic Thinking (INET). The paper was presented at the 22nd Conference of the Forum for Macroeconomics and Macroeconomic Policies (FMM) in October 2018.

Disclosure Statement

No potential conflict of interest was reported by the author(s).

ORCID

Marc Lavoie (iD) http://orcid.org/0000-0002-9942-1803

References

Allain, O. 2015. 'Tackling the Instability of Growth: A Kaleckian-Harrodian Model with an Autonomous Expenditure Component.' *Cambridge Journal of Economics* 39 (5): 1351–1371.
Allain, O. 2019. 'Demographic Growth, Harrodian (In)Stability and the Supermultiplier.' *Cambridge Journal of Economics* 43 (1): 85–106.
Asimakopulos, A. 1970. 'A Robinsonian Growth Model in One-Sector Notation – an Amendment.' *Australian Economic Papers*, December: 171–176.

Bhaduri, A., and S. Marglin. 1990. 'Unemployment and the Real Wage: the Economic Basis for Contesting Political Ideologies.' *Cambridge Journal of Economics* 14 (4): 375–393.

Carvalho, L., and A. Rezai. 2016. 'Personal Income Inequality and Aggregate Demand.' *Cambridge Journal of Economics* 40 (2): 491–505.

Cauvel, M. 2019. 'The neo-Goodwinian Model, Reconsidered.' FMM Working paper, No 47, https://www.econstor.eu/bitstream/10419/213403/1/1670248771.pdf.

Dutt, A. K. 1990. 'Growth, Distribution and Capital Ownership: Kalecki and Pasinetti Revisited.' In *Economic Theory and Policy*, edited by B. Datta, S. Gangopadhyay, D. Mookherjee, and D. Roy. Bombay: Oxford University Press.

Dutt, A. K. 1992. 'Stagnation, Growth and Unproductive Activity.' In *The Economic Surplus in Advanced Economies*, edited by J. B. Davis. Aldershot: Edward Elgar.

Dutt, A. K. 2012. 'Growth, Distribution and Crises.' In *From Crisis to Growth? The Challenge of Debt and Imbalances*, edited by H. Herr, T. Niechoj, C. Thomasberger, A. Truger, and T. van Treeck. Marburg: Metropolis.

Dutt, A. K. 2019. 'Some Observations on Models of Growth and Distribution with Autonomous Demand Growth.' *Metroeconomica* 70 (2): 288–301.

Ederer, S., and M. Rehm. 2020. 'Making Sense of Piketty's "Fundamental Laws" in a Post-Keynesian Framework: The Transitional Dynamics of Wealth.' *Review of Keynesian Economics* 8 (2): 195–219.

Fazzari, S., P. Ferri, and A. M. Variato. 2020. 'Demand-led Growth with Accommodating Supply.' *Cambridge Journal of Economics* 44 (3): 583–605.

Fiebiger, B. 2018. 'Semi-Autonomous Household Expenditures as the Causa Causans of Postwar US Business Cycles: The Stability and Instability of Luxemburg-Type External Markets.' *Cambridge Journal of Economics* 42 (1): 155–175.

Fiebiger, B., and M. Lavoie. 2019. 'Trend and Business Cycles with External Markets: Non-Capacity Generating Semi-Autonomous Expenditures and Effective Demand.' *Metroeconomica* 70 (1): 247–262.

Freitas, F., and F. Serrano. 2015. 'Growth Rate and Level Effects: The Stability of the Adjustment of Capacity to Demand and the Sraffian Supermultiplier.' *Review of Political Economy* 27 (3): 258–281.

Harris, D. J. 1974. 'The Price Policy of Firms, the Level of Employment and Distribution of Income in the Short Run.' *Australian Economic Papers* 13 (22): 144–151.

Hein, E. 2018. 'Autonomous Government Expenditure Growth, Deficits, Debt and Distribution in a Neo-Kaleckian Growth Model.' *Journal of Post Keynesian Economics* 41 (2): 316–338.

Joo, S. Y., K. K. Lee, W. J. Nah, and S. M. Jeon. 2020. *The Income-led Growth in Korea: Status, Prospects and Lessons*. Korea Institute for International Economic Policy. (Forthcoming).

Kaldor, N. 1964. 'Introduction.' In *Essays on Economic Policy, Volume 1*, edited by N. Kaldor. London: Duckworth.

Kurz, H. D. 1990. 'Technical Change, Growth and Distribution: A Steady State Approach to Unsteady Growth.' In *Capital, Distribution and Effective Demand: Studies in the Classical Approach to Economic Theory*, edited by H. D. Kurz. Cambridge: Polity Press.

Lavoie, M. 1992. *Foundations of Post-Keynesian Economic Analysis*. Aldershot: Edward Elgar.

Lavoie, M. 1995. 'The Kaleckian Model of Growth and Distribution and its Neo-Ricardian and Neo-Marxian Critiques.' *Cambridge Journal of Economics* 19 (6): 789–818.

Lavoie, M. 1996. 'Unproductive Outlays and Capital Accumulation with Target-Return Pricing.' *Review of Social Economy* 54 (3): 303–321.

Lavoie, M. 2009. 'Cadrisme Within a Kaleckian Model of Growth and Distribution.' *Review of Political Economy* 21 (3): 371–393.

Lavoie, M. 2014. *Post-Keynesian Economics: New Foundations*. Cheltenham: Edward Elgar.

Lavoie, M. 2016. 'Convergence Towards the Normal Rate of Capacity Utilization in Neo-Kaleckian Models: The Role of Non-Capacity Creating Autonomous Expenditures.' *Metroeconomica* 67 (1): 172–201.

Lavoie, M. 2017a. 'Prototypes, Reality and the Growth Rate of Autonomous Consumption Expenditures: A Rejoinder.' *Metroeconomica* 68 (1): 194–199.

Lavoie, M. 2017b. 'The Origins and Evolution of the Debate on Wage-led and Profit-led Regimes.' *European Journal of Economics and Economic Policies: Intervention* 14 (2): 200–221.

Lavoie, M., and E. Stockhammer. 2013. *Wage-led Growth: An Equitable Strategy for Economic Recovery*. Basingstoke: Palgrave Macmillan.

Leamer, E. E. 2015. 'Housing Really is the Business Cycle: What Survives the Lessons of 2008–09?' *Journal of Money, Credit and Banking* 47 (1) supplement: 43–50.

Lee, F. S. 1998. *Post Keynesian Price Theory*. Cambridge: Cambridge University Press.

Lee, F. S. 2013. 'Post-Keynesian Price Theory.' In *The Oxford Handbook of Post-Keynesian Economics: Volume I: Theory and Origins*, edited by G. C. Harcourt and P. Kriesler. Oxford: Oxford University Press.

Lee, F. S., J. Irving-Lessman, P. Earl, and J. E. Davies. 1986. 'P.W.S. Andrews's Theory of Competitive Oligopoly: A New Interpretation.' *British Review of Economic Issues* 8 (19): 13–39.

Mohun, S. 2014. 'Unproductive Labor in the U.S. Economy: 1964–2010.' *Review of Radical Political Economics* 46 (3): 355–379.

Nah, W. J. 2018. 'The First Year of Income-led Growth Policies in Korea: a Post-Keynesian View.' *Journal of Korean Economic Development* 24 (3): 35–64.

Nah, W. J., and M. Lavoie. 2017. 'Long-Run Convergence in a neo-Kaleckian Open-Economy Model with Autonomous Export Growth.' *Journal of Post Keynesian Economics* 40 (2): 223–238.

Nah, W. J., and M. Lavoie. 2018. 'Overhead Labour Costs in a Neo-Kaleckian Growth Model with Autonomous Expenditures.' Working Paper, No. 111/2018, Hochschule für Wirtschaft und Recht Berlin, Institute for International Political Economy (IPE), Berlin. https://www.econstor.eu/bitstream/10419/188924/1/1041257600.pdf.

Nah, W. J., and M. Lavoie. 2019a. 'Convergence in a Neo-Kaleckian Model with Endogenous Technical Progress and Autonomous Demand Growth.' *Review of Keynesian Economics* 7 (3): 275–291.

Nah, W. J., and M. Lavoie. 2019b. 'The Role of Autonomous Demand Growth in a Neo-Kaleckian Conflicting-Claims Framework.' *Structural Change and Economic Dynamics* 51 (December): 427–444.

Nichols, L. M., and N. Norton. 1991. 'Overhead Workers and Political Economy Macro Models.' *Review of Radical Political Economy* 23 (1-2): 47–54.

Nikiforos, M. 2017. 'Uncertainty and Contradiction: An Essay on the Business Cycle.' *Review of Radical Political Economics* 49 (2): 247–264.

Palley, T. 2005. 'Class Conflict and the Cambridge Theory of Distribution.' In *Joan Robinson's Economics: A Centenial Celebration*, edited by B. Gibson. Cheltenham: Edward Elgar.

Palley, T. I. 2015. 'The Middle Class in Macroeconomics and Growth Theory: A Three-Class neo-Kaleckian-Goodwin Model.' *Cambridge Journal of Economics* 39 (1): 221–243.

Palley, T. I. 2017. 'Wage- vs Profit-led Growth: the Role of the Distribution of Wages in Determining Regime Character.' *Cambridge Journal of Economics* 41 (1): 49–61.

Pariboni, R. 2016. 'Autonomous Demand and the Marglin-Bhaduri Model: A Critical Note.' *Review of Keynesian Economics* 4 (4): 409–428.

Pasinetti, L. L. 1962. 'Rate of Profit and Income Distribution in Relation to the Rate of Economic Growth.' *Review of Economic Studies* 29 (4): 267–279.

Piketty, T. 2014. *Capital in the Twenty-First Century*. Cambridge, MA: Harvard University Press.

Rolim, L. N. 2019. 'Overhead Labour and Feedback Effects Between Capacity Utilization and Income Distributions: Estimations for the USA Economy.' *International Review of Applied Economics* 33 (6): 756–773.

Rowthorn, B. 1981. 'Demand, Real Wages and Economic Growth.' *Thames Papers in Political Economy*, Autumn: 1–39.

Serrano, F., and F. Freitas. 2017. 'The Sraffian Supermultiplier as an Alternative Closure for Heterodox Growth Theory.' *European Journal of Economics and Economic Policy: Intervention* 14 (1): 71–90.

Sherman, H. J., and G. R. Evans. 1984. *Macro-Economics: Keynesian, Monetarist and Marxist Views*. New York: Harper & Row.

Steindl, J. 1952. *Maturity and Stagnation in American Capitalism*. Oxford: Blackwell.

Steindl, J. 1979. 'Stagnation Theory and Stagnation Policy.' *Cambridge Journal of Economics* 3 (1): 1–14.

Tavani, D., and R. Vasaudevan. 2014. 'Capitalists, Workers, and Managers: Wage Inequality and Effective Demand.' *Structural Change and Economic Dynamics* 30 (December): 120–131.

Weisskopf, T. E. 1979. 'Marxian Crisis Theory and the Rate of Profit in the Postwar U.S. Economy.' *Cambridge Journal of Economics* 3 (4): 341–378.

Appendices

Appendix 1. Characterization of the short-run equilibrium

Taking an explicit account of our target-return pricing formula, we can rewrite our saving function as equation A1, by making use of equations 7 and 8 into equation 3 and rearranging.

$$g_s = \frac{[s_f(1-s_h)+s_h](\sigma f + r_n v)u - s_f(1-s_h)\sigma f(u_n - r_n v)}{v(u_n + \sigma f)} - z \tag{A1}$$

The equilibrium rate of utilization, u^*, is then solved for from equations A1 and 13, for given values of z and γ.

$$u^* = \frac{\gamma - \gamma_u u_n + z + \dfrac{s_f(1-s_h)\sigma f(u_n - r_n v)}{v(u_n + \sigma f)}}{\dfrac{[s_f(1-s_h)+s_h](\sigma f + r_n v)}{v(u_n + \sigma f)} - \gamma_u} \tag{A2}$$

Applying u^*, we can solve for the short-run equilibrium values of the share of profits, π^*, the rate of profit, r^*, and the rate of accumulation, g^* as follows.

$$\pi^* = \frac{(\sigma f + r_n v)u^* - (u_n - r_n v)\sigma f}{u^*(u_n + \sigma f)} \tag{A3}$$

$$r^* = \frac{(\sigma f + r_n v)u^* - (u_n - r_n v)\sigma f}{v(u_n + \sigma f)} \tag{A4}$$

$$g^* = \gamma + \gamma_u(u^* - u_n) \tag{A5}$$

Note that for π^* and r^* to take on positive values, for otherwise unit direct and overhead costs will not be covered by the value of sales, u^* must be such that:

$$u^* > \left[\frac{u_n - r_n v}{\sigma f + r_n v}\right]\sigma f . \tag{A6}$$

Appendix 2. The effect of an increase in the wage premium going to overhead labour on the short-run equilibrium profit share

Starting from equation 8, we can write

$$\frac{\partial \pi^*}{\partial \sigma} = \frac{u_n - r_n v}{u^{*2}(u_n + \sigma f)^2}\left[\sigma f \frac{\partial u^*}{\partial \sigma} + u^*(u^* - u_n)\right]. \tag{A7}$$

This indicates that, if there is an increase in σ, the short-run equilibrium share of profits may either increase or get reduced, depending on the sign of the sum of the terms found inside the squared brackets on the far right. It can easily be shown that $\partial\pi^*/\partial\sigma < 0$ if

$$\left[\frac{s_f(1-s_h)}{s_f(1-s_h)+s_h}\right] u_n \leq u^* \leq u_n . \tag{A8}$$

This makes sense because we have already seen that, for a given rate of utilization which is lower than its normal level, an increase in the wage differential will generate a decrease in the profit share, while we have just found that if the left-hand side inequality in the relation shown above is verified, then the actual rate of utilization will fall, which means a further fall in the profit share. Otherwise, the sign of $\partial\pi^*/\partial\sigma$ is indeterminate. The first term in the bracket is positive, while the second term is negative, if

$$u^* < \left[\frac{s_f(1-s_h)}{s_f(1-s_h)+s_h}\right] u_n \tag{A9}$$

Contrarily, the first term is negative, while the second is positive, if this time

$$u^* > u_n . \tag{A10}$$

This relates to the determination (or indetermination) of the signs of $d\pi$ in Table 1.

Appendix 3. Long-run stability

Equation 41 in the text implies another inequality constraint for autonomous expenditures Z to be positive in the long run. Its growth rate $\bar{g}_z$ cannot be too high:

$$\bar{g}_z < [s_f(1-s_h)+s_h] r_n + s_h \frac{\sigma f}{v}\left[\frac{u_n - r_n v}{u_n + \sigma f}\right] \tag{A11}$$

We can also see that the long-run share of saving from firms out of total saving is given by the following relation:

$$\Omega^{**} = \frac{s_f \pi u_n/v}{(\pi+s_h m)u_n/v - z} \tag{A12}$$

This is because both the firms and managers/shareholder should save equal proportions of their own capital stocks in the steady state, so that Ω converges to a certain constant, Ω^{**}.

$$\frac{s_f \pi q}{\Omega K} = \frac{s_h[mq+(1-s_f)\pi q] - Z}{(1-\Omega)K} \tag{A13}$$

To evaluate the long-run stability of the model, let us form a Jacobian J to be:

$$J = \begin{bmatrix} \frac{\partial\hat{z}}{\partial z} & \frac{\partial\hat{z}}{\partial\gamma} \\ \frac{\partial\hat{\gamma}}{\partial z} & \frac{\partial\hat{\gamma}}{\partial\gamma} \end{bmatrix} \tag{A14}$$

Now, we can evaluate each element of J using equations 33 and 34.

$$J = \begin{bmatrix} -\frac{\gamma_u}{B} & -1-\frac{\gamma_u}{B} \\ \frac{\phi_\gamma\gamma_u}{B} & \frac{\phi_\gamma\gamma_u}{B} \end{bmatrix}, \tag{A15}$$

where

$$B \equiv \frac{v(u_n + \sigma f)}{A} \tag{A16}$$

with A being the denominator of the short-run rate of utilization as computed in Appendix 1, which must be positive as implied by the short-run stability condition (equation 14) of the main text. From this it follows that

$$Det(J) = \phi_\gamma \gamma_u \nu(u_n + \sigma f) A > 0 \qquad (A17)$$

$$Tr(J) = \frac{(\phi_\gamma - 1) \gamma_u}{B} . \qquad (A18)$$

The determinant of J is necessarily positive as long as the usual short-run Keynesian stability condition is fulfilled. It is easy to see that the trace of J can be negative, so that our system turns out to be dynamically stable in its long run, under the condition that

$$\phi_\gamma < 1. \qquad (A19)$$

This proves that the long-run stability of the current system of two differential equations is guaranteed by the usual short-run Keynesian stability condition (which implies in particular that the growth rate of capital accumulation of firms does not react too strongly to the discrepancy between the realized and the standard rate of capacity utilization), as long as Harrodian instability is not too severe, i.e., as long as the secular growth rate of sales does not react too strongly to the discrepancy between the actual and the expected growth rate of the economy.

Reforming Capitalist Democracies: Which Way?

Amit Bhaduri

ABSTRACT

The debate about how to reconcile political with economic democracy is translated within the framework of wage and profit-led growth in this article. The inherent tension between providing sufficient profit incentive to motivate investment by the capitalist class and maintaining electoral accountability to the economically less privileged majority is examined through an analysis of the effectiveness of policies to raise the social wage. This article shows how wider circumstances characterizing regimes as wage- or profit-led matter for reconciling a higher profit share with a higher social wage.

1. Introduction

The higher real wage plays a two-sided role in a capitalist economy closed to international trade. While it increases consumption demand (C) through distribution of income in favor of the working class with a higher propensity to consume, it depresses private investment expenditure (I) due to its unfavorable effect on the profitability of investment. Assuming constant marginal and average labor productivity that ensures that the higher real wage means both lower profit share (h) and margin, a skeleton Kalecki-type model was presented in Bhaduri and Marglin (1990) and in Marglin and Bhaduri (1990). The model has predecessors in the under-consumptionist tradition (Steindl 1952; Rowthorn 1981). However, they failed to capture this more general two-sided effect of the real wage due to the specific form of the investment function used. It should be made clear that the model of Bhaduri and Marglin (1990) is not about justifying a particular version of the investment function; rather, it is meant to capture the more general issue.

2. Mechanics of the Model with Modifications

The essential mechanics of the Bhaduri and Marglin (1990) model can be derived by writing the expenditure–income or investment–saving equality in the form:

$$I = I(z, h) = S = shz, \quad 1 > s, z, h > 0 \tag{1}$$

where s = propensity to save out of profit with no saving out of wage; $z = (Y/Y\text{max}) =$ degree of capacity utilization and $h = (P/Y) =$ share of profit. From (1) the direction of change of capacity utilization driven by change in aggregate demand due to the share of profit can be derived as the slope of the locus of investment saving (IS) equilibrium as,

$$(dz/dh) = (I_h - sz)/(sh - I_z) \qquad (2)$$

where subscripts denote partial derivatives of the relevant variables.

Assuming that the demand driven income generation process is stable, i.e. $(sh - I_z) > 0$ (Bhaduri 2008), the condition for profit-led expansion is $(dz/dh) > 0$. From (2) this requires a stronger positive impact of profit share on investment than on saving, i.e. $I_h > sz$. The opposite case of wage-led expansion with a higher profit share reducing capacity utilization, i.e. $(dz/dh) < 0$, would require $I_h < sz$. These conditions are local properties so long as the partial derivatives obey the required inequalities.

A linear investment function has global properties with the partial derivatives I_z and I_h remaining constant over the relevant domain, as postulated in several similar models (Lavoie 2016; Pariboni 2016). In this case, the investment saving equality takes the form that can conveniently be written for easy comparison with the Bhaduri–Marglin model (Rowthorn 2018) as,

$$I = I_z z + I_h h + I_0 = S = shz \qquad (3)$$

and the level of capacity utilization is given by,

$$z = \frac{I_h h + I_0}{sh - I_z} \qquad (4)$$

Assuming the Keynesian stability condition, (4) points to two different ways in which the level of capacity utilization (z) can be raised. The first is to increase profit share (h) through direct fiscal measures or less direct measures known as structural reforms aimed at restraining growth in wage in relation to labor productivity, often euphemistically called labor market flexibility through easier hire and fire policies, lowering employment benefits, casualization of labor, reform of the pension system and so on. All such reform policies are meant to work broadly through the profit incentive and would increase $I_h h$ in (4). However, since higher profit share (h) will also impact negatively on capacity utilization (z) by raising the saving ratio (sh) in the denominator of (4), such profit incentive-based policies would work only if the positive impact of higher investment on demand due to higher profit share outweighs its negative impact through higher savings.

The level of capacity utilization in the linear model (4) could be affected by a second route if the value of the intercept I_0 is treated not as a constant given by initial conditions but as a policy variable, introducing in effect an additional parameter, I_0. However, this assumption must be economically interpreted. In a laissez fare capitalist economy presumed in the Bhaduri–Marglin model, there is no room for economic activity by the government. Until we introduce the economic role of the government and public policy in influencing I_0 in Section Six, changes in I_0 must mean an autonomous change in private investment.

3. Institutional Setting of Social Wage

It would be plausible in many circumstances to think of a part of total private investment as autonomous in the sense that it is not directly guided by either profitability or the degree of capacity utilization specified in the investment function in (3). It might be investment undertaken by the local community for non-market distributive or other objectives, or by private corporations as their 'social responsibility' and public relations efforts. In so far as the government is concerned (to be discussed later, in Section Six), it would usually be the major player. Its expenditure may be funded from the current (including regular expenditure of social welfare and other subsidy items, discussed later in equation (9)) or the capital account (investment items) of the budget for expanding the capacity and delivery of welfare services. These expenditures affect the level of the 'social wage' made available in various direct and indirect ways to members of society. If it is available to all, it affects the living standards of the general public. When targeted exclusively at workers, wage net of tax minus subsidy received by the working class becomes the relevant variable. When the benefit is universal, the working class is either subsidizing or being subsidized by a wider scheme involving taxes and subsidies for the general public.

The social wage level has historically evolved in different ways in various capitalist democracies as the outcome of interactions among social actors, usually with converging as well as conflictive interests. They involve industrialists, trade unions, philanthropists, NGOs, community-based religious and non-religious organizations and so on. The evolution of this complex process is naturally both country and time specific. However, the ruling ideology has usually played a dominant role. Generally speaking, while the welfare state and the social democratic ideology played an important role in increasing the social wage level, the neo-liberal ideology tried to reverse that process by emphasizing the role of private profit motive. The intensity of the tension between the two varied historically over time, often shaped by broader geo-political considerations. The 'systems competition' between western capitalist democracies and Soviet-style socialism during the Cold War period tended to raise the social wage level in capitalist democracies markedly (Hobsbawm 1993). With the end of the Cold War and increasing globalization, the scope of market forces expanded globally in trade, investment and finance beyond the reach of the nation state, placing transnational corporations in an advantageous position. Private profit motive and rolling back government economic activities became the priority through various pro-corporate policies. This tendency is clearly witnessed in pressure on governments to provide competitive corporate tax benefits and allow liberalization, deregulation and privatization even in areas of public utilities, including water, the transport system, welfare services like health care, education, pension reform and so on.

However, the social wage mode of operation need not always be through the government. Typically, that results not in a universal but, rather, a targeted increase in the social wage for some segments of the working population. For instance, a private corporation may incur expenditure to increase the company wage with subsidized food, education, housing, health care and so on. Its main purpose is often to gain workers' dependence on and loyalty to the company. This connects with the broader view that worker discipline may be enforced using a 'carrot and stick' policy; that is, either by gaining the loyalty of workers or by creating the fear of job loss through functional unemployment in the absence of direct supervision (Shapiro and Stiglitz 1984; Akerlof and Yellen 1990). This echoes the explanation of political trade cycles suggested by Kalecki (1943), which fit well with Marx's original notion of a 'reserve army of labor', and even with the mainstream notion of a 'natural' or 'non-accelerating inflation rate of unemployment (NAIRU)'.

Most former socialist countries institutionalized such measures of augmented 'company wage'. In contrast to many social democracies, the production of most 'public goods' remained in the domain of a centralized state bureaucracy, but it became an institutional aspect of those socialist countries to provide employee access to many public goods as the social wage through employment in state enterprises. Privatization of these corporations during the period of transition to the market economy depressed violently the standard of living of the suddenly unemployed workers who lost the security of the social wage along with their private wage. This remains perhaps the clearest example of how the social wage can be reduced drastically through privatization and disinvestment.

4. Formal Representation of the Social Wage

In the formal model, the evolution of the social wage amounts to a shift of the intercept I_0 of the linear investment function (3). It results from various types of public or community investments aimed at expanding, rationalizing or modernizing social welfare benefits. In so far as the government is concerned, they would be part of the capital account of a government budget. On the other hand, expenditures related to regular maintenance and delivery of these welfare services would be classified under the current account of the budget, while the expansion of such welfare services may be either in the current or in the capital account depending on whether they are meant as temporary or permanent expansions.

Shifts in I_0 may also signify changes in the private 'investment climate' due to changes in the social wage level. At contrasting extremes, a higher social wage may be brought about by a larger positive intercept as workers are better trained as a consequence of a higher social wage, while a drastic decrease in the social wage say through large scale privatization may even turn the intercept negative. The latter typically occurred during the period of transition in former socialist countries through large disinvestment in and privatization of public enterprises and reduced aggregate demand when the proceeds of privatization were used to create artificially a budget surplus for the government. Indeed, this became the norm under neo-liberal fiscal policy (see Section Six).

Formally, a negative intercept raises problems with the existence of a meaningful economic solution in (4), i.e. for $z > 0$ it requires that,

$$(I_h h + I_0) > 0 \Rightarrow h > -\left(\frac{I_0}{I_h}\right) \tag{5}$$

So long as I_0 is positive, the inequality (5) is always true, but when it turns negative, profit share has to be higher than a positive number, which serves as a minimum value, for positive z to exist. Because $1 \geq h \geq 0$, inequality (5) allows for the existence of meaningful solution if $I_h > |I_0|$, i.e. the absolute magnitude of I_0 setting a lower bound to the level of disinvestment for a solution to exist. Setting $I_h = k|I_0|$, where $k > 1$, it can be seen from equation (4) that, under the Keynesian stability condition, $h > (1/k)$ allows for a positive degree of capacity utilization ($1 > z > 0$). This means that, for any given level of privatization ($|I_0|$), the smaller the value of k, representing a weaker profit motive I_h, the less likely is the possibility of a solution existing in the form of privatization. And yet, it is a policy mistake often made: to privatize even under recessionary conditions when the profit incentive is generally weak.

5. The Social Wage and Profit Incentive

In a capitalist democracy, increasing profit share together with income distribution neg-atively affecting the poorer working classes would raise questions about the legitimacy and acceptability of these policies to the electorate. Social democratic policies would gen-erally try to mitigate the effects of higher profit share (after tax) through a higher social wage. However, this would be resisted by those who would like to rely solely on the effec-tiveness of the profit motive to stimulate private investment. The analytics of this ideolog-ical divide can be schematized starkly by holding the level of capacity utilization constant. With capacity utilization fixed at some arbitrary level, $z = z^*$, and parameters s, I_z and I_h assumed constant, the problem boils down to examining how an increase in profit share h affects the social wage through its impact on I_0 with no variation in output allowed by assumption. Rewriting (4) as $z^*(sh - I_z) = I_h h + I_0$ and differentiating (4) with respect to h,

$$\frac{dI_0}{dh} = (sz^* - I_h) \tag{6}$$

Equation (6) is central to the argument for linking the nature of a regime with the social wage policy. It follows from the right-hand side of (6) that, in the wage-led case, as specified by the numerator of (2), the social wage denoted by I_0 would have to increase to maintain the same level of capacity utilization, z^*, at a higher profit share. On the other hand, in the profit-led case, the social wage has to decrease to accommodate the stimulus to private investment received through a higher profit share. At a higher profit share, (h), capacity utilization decreases in a wage-led regime that needs to be compen-sated by a rise in investment, I_0, in the social wage to restore effective demand and capac-ity utilization to $z = z^*$. However, in the profit-led regime, a higher h stimulates investment through higher profitability and the social wage, I_0, can be reduced keeping the level of capacity utilization constant at z^*.

A more extreme form of conservative argument often suggests that raising profit share would not be a problem; instead, it would be a part of the solution in so far as the higher profit share would strengthen further the profit incentive. This argument may be stylized by replacing I_h, which has so far been treated as a constant by the assumption that I_h is an increasing function of h while all other parameters remain constant. In this case, differen-tiating (4),

$$\frac{dI_0}{dh} = -[(I_h - sz^*) + mI_h] < 0 \tag{7}$$

where m represents the elasticity of I_h with respect to h, i.e. $m = \dfrac{dI_h/I_h}{dh/h} > 0$

For simplicity of exposition, if m is treated as a constant, the right-hand side of (7) is unambiguously negative in the profit-led case, implying that the extent of reduction in the level of I_0 with respect to h could be larger, the larger is the elasticity m at a constant level of capacity utilization z^*. However, the situation is more ambiguous in the wage-led case, as a rearrangement of (7) shows:

$$\left(\frac{dI_0}{dh}\right) > 0 \quad \text{if} \left[\frac{sz^* - I_h}{m}\right] > I_h \tag{8}$$

The square-bracketed term on the left-hand side in (8) remains positive in the wage-led case, but decreases in magnitude as m becomes larger. This ultimately violates the inequality for a sufficiently high value of m. Therefore, the wage-led regime is able to accommodate a higher social wage with a higher profit share only for relatively small values of m, indicating the relatively weak response of private investors to a higher profit share (I_h).

6. The Role of Government Fiscal and Monetary Policies

Without introducing explicitly the economic role of the government in influencing the social wage level, the story we have been trying to tell so far sounds more like that of Hamlet without the Prince of Denmark. This was necessary for expositional simplicity and may now be modified to introduce some complications due to government fiscal policies. However, for compatibility of exposition with the earlier analysis, we assume all wages as well as dividend incomes are consumed. This allows us to interpret $1 > s > 0$ as the fraction of gross profit retained by firms. Assuming government revenue is derived entirely from corporate tax on profit, (T), and spending is on subsidy and transfer to the public, (U), net government budget surplus revenue, (B), on goods and services at $z = z^*$ is,

$$B = (T - U) = t_p h z^* - U \tag{9}$$

where $1 > t_p > 0$ is corporate tax rate on gross profit. Assuming U is constant for simplicity and differentiating (9) with respect to h yields $B_h = t_p z^* > 0$. B_h is interpreted as the revenue support provided to the budget at the margin from tax on gross profit earned by raising the profit share (h) of corporations. In the opposite case, where $B_h < 0$, the budgetary support from tax on profit is negative at the margin. Equation (4) is modified to accommodate budgetary expenditure and becomes,

$$z = \frac{I_h h + I_0 - B}{sh - I_z} \tag{10}$$

With the corporate retention rate out of gross profit, s, as well as I_z and I_h held constant, at an arbitrarily given level of capacity utilization $z = z^*$, we can now see how the social wage changes with profit share by differentiating (10) with respect to h,

$$\frac{dI_0}{dh} = [(sz^* - I_h) + B_h] \tag{11}$$

Note that $B_h = t_p z^*$ in (11). In a wage-led regime, i.e. when $(sz^* - I_h) > 0$, equation (11) is positive $\left(\frac{dI_0}{dh} > 0\right)$. This points to the negative effect of budget surplus created by raising profit share at a given corporate tax rate on profit. The increase in budget surplus induced by a higher profit share would require, in a wage-led regime, higher spending on the social wage to compensate for the contraction in demand to maintain a given level of capacity utilization, $z = z^*$. In the profit-led regime with $(sz^* - I_h) < 0$, a budget surplus at a higher profit share merely strengthens further the tendency to reduce spending on the social wage. It is easy to see from (11) that these conclusions are reversed when $B_h < 0$.

The impact of running a budget surplus through privatization rather than tax proceeds is captured in equation (10). It increases B and decreases I and has a very strong negative impact on capacity utilization. This can be countered through an increase in the profit share, h, but would fail if private investors do not respond strongly enough to profit; indeed, a solution may not even exist (see end of Section Four).

Two points left out in this schematized formalism on fiscal policy need mention. First, without any change in the tax structure, the composition of budgetary expenditure can be changed to raise the social wage level, e.g. providing better schooling and health care facilities and greening of working-class areas at the expense, say, of the military budget. However, opponents of such proposals would typically argue in favor of defense expenditure for enhancing external and internal security (i.e. policing), usually claiming that a 'strong nation' and 'law and order' are most important elements of the universal social wage. What types of public good contribute to the social wage and how to prioritize them defines, at times, the ideological divide. While this issue cannot be settled logically, it is worth pointing out that a targeted social wage for workers is usually less ambiguous than a universal benefit in the name of a social wage.

Second, interest payments on accumulated public debt have increasingly become an important budget item for most countries, which have not been considered in our formulation. Financing the social wage by issuing bonds impacts adversely on income distribution in so far as the interest income mostly goes not to poorer pensioners but to a richer section of the bond-holding public. From this point of view, monetary policy affecting the bond rate raises the issue of borrowing from the bond market versus borrowing from the central bank (i.e. monetizing the budget deficit). Since making the choice between bond financing versus printing money might impact significantly on income distribution, it has implications for how a higher social wage is to be financed and also the desired degree of independence of the central bank in this respect. This is also an important example of how the conventional distinction between fiscal and monetary policy becomes blurred in some important policy issues.

7. Output Expansion and the Social Wage

The assumption of keeping capacity utilization arbitrarily constant at some level, $z = z^*$, was made for expositional simplicity. This assumption may now be relaxed. A change in capacity utilization in response to an increased share of profit is examined through logarithmic differentiation of equation (4), which, on simplification, yields

$$dz/dh = \frac{[(I_h - sz) + (dI_0/dh)]}{[sh - I_z]} \tag{12}$$

The denominator of (12), as usual, is positive for the stable Keynesian income-generation process. In view of the classification of regimes in (2), it follows that the numerator of (12) would be positive despite the decrease in aggregate demand brought about by a rise in profit share in the wage-led regime if investment for raising the social wage is increased sufficiently. This would make $dz/dh > 0$ in (12) even in a wage-led regime. In a profit-led regime, capacity utilization increases with profit share; that is, $dz/dh > 0$ in (12) so long as a higher stimulus to investment through a higher profit share compensates for a reduction in the expenditure on the social wage whereby $(dI_0/dh) < 0$. It follows that suitable variation in the level of investment in the social wage through sustained fiscal policies can bring about a regime change. Not surprisingly, budgetary measures affecting the social wage are a fiercely fought ideological territory.

8. Concluding Observations

An academic article is not meant to be a substitute for the transformative politics of either the Right or Left. However, it can help to clarify the economic logic behind ideologies. The article shows how, in keeping with the main thrust of their ideology, conservative economic reformers rely on the profit motive as the 'life blood of capitalism'. This leads them to argue for raising the profit share through various fiscal, monetary and labor market policies without concerning themselves with their negative impacts on the poor majority. They believe that a strong stimulus in terms of the profit incentive would also help to lift the poor from poverty by raising investment and growth. This is encapsulated in the idea that the benefit of higher growth will 'trickle down' to the poor, and also in the wisecrack that wealth has to be created before being distributed. And yet, even in a capitalist democracy, the holders of such views remain accountable to the electorate. If various fiscal and non-fiscal distributive measures in favor of profit leading to higher inequality do not bring about sufficient investment within a specified period of time they cannot escape reckoning with the consequences. Moderate social democrats who also believe in encouraging the profit motive are also accountable in this way. However, they would usually talk of mitigating the situation by raising the social wage, typically through extending the 'safety net' for the poor. Thus, even when the two sides of the political divide agree on the importance of stimulating private investment through the profit motive, the time period within which the impact of such a stimulus must materialize becomes decisive. In other words, the ideologies of conservatives and moderate social democrats might converge in relation to the desirability of the profit motive but diverge regarding the speed with which it is expected to work in a market economy.

Democracy imposes an institutional time horizon for political accountability, forcing at times some degree of convergence in policies among contesting ideologies because demand management by the state has an advantage in so far as its impacts on capacity utilization and employment are more immediate. In contrast, building private investors' confidence through the profit motive involves an uncertain and usually longer time horizon. The vital importance of the time horizon in defining the relationship between the profit incentive and accountability in electoral democracies deserves special emphasis in ideological debates. Instead, everybody becomes 'Keynesian' in a crisis situation! Nevertheless, precisely this short-termism might also affect the quality of public investment. A missing link for social democrats might be to prepare in advance and place in the public domain a reservoir of well-worked-out schemes for raising the social wage with or without a crisis situation.

Another theme emerges from this discussion. It shows that the same macroeconomic policy need not produce similar outcomes when wider circumstances differ. Our case in point is the broad characterization of economic regimes as wage- or profit-led. The article shows how investment regarding social wage policies would differ even if a common policy for raising profit share is accepted by both sides. A higher social wage and a higher profit share need to complement one another in a wage-led regime because a higher profit share depresses the economic activity level and the capacity utilization level can be maintained only through higher expenditure aimed at raising the social wage level. In contrast, a higher profit share is expected to stimulate investment sufficiently to maintain aggregate demand without raising or even with lowering the social wage in a profit-led regime thus making a higher social wage unwarranted in a profit-led regime.

The ideology of classical social democracy relied heavily on the concept of raising the social and not merely the private wage. It was summed up perceptively by the Swedish economist Bertil Ohlin (1938) as a shift 'from nationalization of the means of production to nationalization of consumption' (pp. 4–5). This proposition is somewhat ambiguous in so far as it leaves open the issue of private profitability in producing goods for social consumption. If a policy of providing a higher social wage in isolation tries to mitigate the effects of a higher profit share, and inequality, it would create a growing tension between the objective of socialization of consumption through sufficient availability and profitability of the compatible pattern of mass-consumption goods (like public transport, water supply, health care, a common school system and so on) and more expensive and specialized goods for the rich (e.g. specialized and expensive health services, luxurious housing, special schools and so on). This tension between raising social consumption and the profitability of private production is glaringly visible in poorer capitalist democracies where insufficient purchasing power of the masses cannot ensure sufficient profitability for private production of these basic goods. For the same reason, nationalization of basic consumption goods in keeping with a higher social wage faces opposition from large private corporations because their profit motive usually directs them in more profitable directions (e.g. highly specialized expensive health care, luxury housing, positional goods of various kind and so on). Over-bureaucratization, poor quality and delivery of public services and a greater tax burden for the general public provided further fuel to the discontent encouraged in the first instance by the corporate profit motive. As the balance of power shifted in favor of large private corporations with corporate controlled media heavily influencing public opinion, privatization became the buzz word even for producing public utilities such as public transport, water supply, health care, education, care for children and the elderly. With the shift in focus from a higher social wage to widening the scope for deregulation and privatization, social democracy had to retreat, significantly, from its original position. Undoubtedly it must reinvent itself in many ways if it wants to become relevant once more. A central issue would be how to reduce reliance on corporations to produce the pattern of goods and services needed for raising the social wage, while avoiding the past folly of centralized over-bureaucratization of the delivery of essential economic and social services by creating more community-based decentralized services. This might be the direction transformative politics would need to take to provide a perspective for fiscal, monetary and labor market policy. Capitalist democracies need to be held accountable not to the market and the profitability of corporations but to the electoral majority by bringing back into focus the importance of a rising social wage and its compatible production pattern. Many false narratives would no doubt be created to resist this transformation to hollow out further the content of an electoral democracy leaving only its populist shell. To recognize the importance of the social wage is to recognize where genuine accountability lies in a democracy.

Acknowledgment

I am grateful to Eckhard Hein, Duncan Foley, Stephen Marglin, Srinivas Raghavendra, Peter Scott, Rune Skarstein, Ajit Sinha and, especially, Francis Cripps. I also acknowledge the comments on various drafts of two anonymous referees. The usual disclaimer applies.

Disclosure Statement

No potential conflict of interest was reported by the author.

References

Akerlof, G. A., and J. L. Yellen. 1990. 'The Fair-Wage-Effort Hypothesis and Unemployment.' *The Quarterly Journal of Economics* 105 (2): 255–283.

Bhaduri, A. 2008. 'On the Dynamics of Profit-Led and Wage-Led Growth.' *Cambridge Journal of Economics* 32 (1): 147–160.

Bhaduri, A., and S. A. Marglin. 1990. 'Unemployment and the Real Wage: The Economic Basis for Contesting Political Ideologies.' *Cambridge Journal of Economics* 14 (4): 375–393.

Hobsbawm, E. 1993. *The Age of Extremes*. London: Viking.

Kalecki, M. 1943/1971. 'Political Aspects of Full Employment.' In *Selected Essays on the Dynamics of the Capitalist Economy*. Cambridge: Cambridge University Press.

Lavoie, M. 2016. 'Convergence Towards the Normal Rate of Capacity Utilization in Neo-Kaleckian Models: The Role of Non-Capacity Creating Autonomous Expenditures.' *Metroeconomica* 67 (1): 172–201.

Marglin, S. A., and A. Bhaduri. 1990. 'Profit Squeeze and Keynesian Theory.' In *The Golden Age of Capitalism: Reinterpreting the Postwar Experience*, edited by S. A. Marglin, and J. B. Schor. Oxford: Clarendon Press, 1991.

Ohlin, B. 1938. 'Economic Progress in Sweden.' *The Annals of the American Academy of Political and Social Science* 197 (1): 1–6.

Pariboni, R. 2016. 'Autonomous Demand and the Marglin-Bhaduri Model: A Critical Note.' *Review of Keynesian Economics* 4 (4): 409–428.

Rowthorn, R. E. 1981. 'Demand, Real Wages and Economic Growth.' *Thames Papers in Political Economy* (Autumn, London): 1–39.

Rowthorn, R. E. 2018. 'A Note on the Bhaduri-Marglin Model.' Cambridge, September 26 (unpublished).

Shapiro, C., and J. E. Stiglitz. 1984. 'Equilibrium Unemployment as a Worker Discipline Device.' *American Economic Review* 74 (3): 433–444.

Steindl, J. 1952. *Maturity and Stagnation of American Capitalism*. New York: NYU press.

Kalecki on Budget Deficits and the Possibilities for Full Employment

Malcolm Sawyer

ABSTRACT

This paper revisits the writings of Michal Kalecki which relate to issues of fiscal policy, budget deficits and securing full employment in capitalist economies. It seeks to relate those writings to the recent fiscal policy debates after the global financial crises. It covers the issues of the financing and funding of public expenditure and private expenditure. The relationship between the scale of budget deficit and the achievement of full employment is considered. Kalecki's approach to the 'burden' of debt is elaborated. The social and political constraints on the achievement of full employment are revisited.

1. Introduction

Kalecki wrote extensively on issues relating to fiscal policy, budget deficits and unemployment in industrialised capitalist economies, particularly in the first half of the 1930s (with papers now in Osiatynski 1990) and the first half of the 1940s (papers largely in Osiatynski 1990, 1991, 1997). These writings combined theoretical arguments alongside empirical analysis and went alongside the developments of his macroeconomic analysis. The purpose of this paper is to draw on those writings for their contemporary relevance and to illustrate how they relate to some of the recent experiences of austerity and policies of fiscal consolidation.

In section 2, I outline some features of the recent experiences with fiscal and budgetary policies as background to the subsequent discussion of Kalecki's analyses. Section 3 summarises Kalecki's approach to the financing and funding of public expenditure and budget deficits. This is followed by section 4 which deals with some issues of the financing and funding of private expenditure. Section 5 focuses on the relationship between the scale of budget and the achievement of full employment. It points to Kalecki's arguments against seeking a balanced budget at full employment, and that is extended to the case of the structural budget balance policy. In section 6, Kalecki's approach to the 'burden' of debt is elaborated. Section 7 revisits the social and political constraints on the achievement of full employment. Section 8 provides some concluding comments.

2. Remarks on Recent Fiscal Policy Debates

During the 2000s, fiscal policy and the role of budget deficits had taken something of a back seat in macroeconomic policy with the dominance of monetary policy, at least in most academic debates. The so-called great moderation (Bernanke) with the inflation targeting framework based on monetary policy and an independent central bank had appeared to have achieved steady growth with low inflation — in words of Mervyn King the NICE (non-inflationary continuous expansion) decade. The global financial crises (GFC) of 2007/09 brought that illusion to an end. In the resulting global recession, budget deficits rose as economic activity (and thereby tax receipts fell) and as governments boosted their expenditure to provide income support and business rescue packages. But this was soon followed by drives for fiscal consolidation and austerity. The fiscal policy responses varied between countries (Sawyer 2017). However, there were underlying themes which could be labelled the drive for fiscal consolidation and austerity. In the aftermath of the GFC, there was a general drive for fiscal consolidation and reductions in the budget deficits down to budget balance or even surplus. There were fears of 'excessive' debt levels, and the scares of burdening future generations with debt, and claims of inability to borrow further ('the credit card is maxed out' to use expression often used by UK Prime Minister David Cameron). The attempts to reduce budget deficits largely took the form of expenditure cuts (or at least expenditure rising less quickly) rather than tax increases: particularly in case of the UK.

The COVID-19 pandemic has led to budget deficits which were on a large scale (of the order of 15–20 per cent relative to GDP) and subject to a particularly rapid increase and rising public debt levels. Although the causes of the down-turns in economic activity are different, both the GFC and the COVID-19 pandemic raise issues for fiscal policy in terms of the role of budget deficits, responding to higher levels of public debt (relative to GDP), and responding to rising unemployment.

3. Financing and Funding of Public Expenditure

In approaching the issue of 'how can public expenditure be paid for', an important distinction which needs to be made is between initial finance and final finance (or funding), taking the terms from the monetary circuitist analysis (Graziani 1989, 2003). Initial finance is required for any expenditure to occur in that the prior possession of money is required in order for it to be spent. Final finance refers to the funding of expenditure over a particular period, that is the source of the funds (from income, from savings, from borrowing) needed to underpin the expenditure undertaken. The circuitist analysis has generally focused on the initial financing of production, where it is required to cover the costs of planned production and to enable the expenditure, and requires possession of money which may be provided through bank loans. Final finance refers to the funding in the sense of the sources and uses of funds relating (in this example) to the costs of production. Mehrling (2020, p. 2) makes the distinction between payment and funding, an 'analytical distinction … being basically the same as Graziani's (2003) distinction between initial finance and final finance.' In the discussion here I use the terminology of (initial) finance and funding. Kalecki, as many authors, often uses the term finance to mean what I term funding or final finance in the circuitist terminology.

Modern Monetary Theory (MMT) has emphasised that government expenditure can always be financed (in the sense of initial finance) through the actions of the central bank acting in its role as the bank of the government, and that a government cannot run out of money.[1]

Kalecki, writing in 1932, noted that a fiscal expansion could come from 'the government obtaining large credits from the central bank and spending them on massive public works of one sort or another. In this case the money no doubt would be spent and this would result in increased employment' (Kalecki 1932b, p. 175). In a similar vein, he spoke of 'starting up major public-investment schemes, such as construction of canals or roads, and financing them with government loans floated on the financial markets, or with special government credits drawn on their bank of issue' (Kalecki 1932a, p. 53). Similarly, 'the government raises credits in the central bank and uses them, e.g. to construct public service units' (Kalecki 1933, p. 156). In this and similar discussions, Kalecki often emphasised the effects of government spending on profits and also the constraints on the level of economic activity imposed by balance of payments considerations.

He set out another account a decade or so later when he sought to answer the question of:

> where the public will get the money to lend to the government if they do not curtail their investment and consumption. To understand this process it is best, I think, to imagine for a moment that the government pays its suppliers in government securities. The suppliers will, in general, not retain these securities but put them into circulation while buying other goods and services, and so on, until these securities will reach people or firms which retain them as interest-yielding assets. In any period of time the total increase in government securities in the possession (transitory or final) of persons and firms will be equal to the goods and services sold to the government. Thus, what the economy lends to the government are goods and services whose production is 'financed' by government securities. In reality, the government pays for the services, not in securities, but in cash, but it simultaneously issues securities and so drains the cash off, and this is equivalent to the imaginary process described above. (Kalecki 1944a, pp. 347–348)

When a budget deficit was required in order to sustain a high level of aggregate demand, Kalecki clearly set out the argument that the funding of a deficit did not constitute a problem. In a sub-section headed 'where does the money come from?', Kalecki (1944a, p. 358) wrote that 'the budget deficit always finances itself — that is to say, its rise always causes such an increase in incomes and changes in their distribution that there accrue just enough savings to finance it', nevertheless 'the matter is still frequently misunderstood' (and, of course, it is still misunderstood).

The effects of government spending and money creation were often seen in what could be described in portfolio adjustment terms. For example,

> in normal conditions [absence of hyperinflation] the accumulation of reserves does not lead to an increase in spending, but merely to so-called liquidity in the money market. Capitalists, whose reserves have increased, will invest part of them in stocks and bonds sold by other

[1] 'It is the currency issuer — the federal government itself — not the taxpayer, that finances all government expenditure.' 'We will show how MMT demonstrates that the federal government is not dependent on revenues from taxes or borrowing to finance its spending and that the most important constraint on government spending is inflation' (Kelton 2020).

capitalists. Their price will rise, that is, their rate of interest will fall. Equilibrium will be reached when bank deposits become just as attractive as securities. (Kalecki 1955, p. 358)

4. Financing and Funding of Private Expenditure

The Keynesian IS/LM framework can be used to predict the effects of changes in investment and government expenditure by shifts in the IS curve. However, within that framework, no attention was paid to how a proposed increase in expenditure would be financed — where does the money come from? Although Kalecki did not particularly emphasise this point, in his writings he did indicate how the required money would be created. He used the working assumption that 'the financing of additional investment is effected by the so-called creation of purchasing power. The demand for bank credit increases, and these are granted by the banks' (Kalecki 1935, p. 190). In Sawyer (2001, p. 487), I argued that 'Kalecki presented ideas which can be seen as now embedded in the structuralist post-Keynesian analysis of endogenous money and in the circuitist approach.' Messori (1991, p. 301), however, argued that 'Kalecki did not differentiate enough between the two different meaning of financing: the monetary flows required to finance an increase in the demand for capital goods (investment financing), and the monetary advances required to finance the purchase of working capital (production financing).' The main focus of that analysis was on investment decisions, rather than on the extension of credit, which was viewed as generally permissive.

5. Full Employment and Balanced Budgets

The adoption by 26 of the 28 member countries of the European Union of a 'fiscal compact' within the Treaty on Stability, Coordination and Governance formalised requirements for a balanced structural budget for each member country. In the UK, in the Charter for Budget Responsibility targets were updated in Autumn 2016 'to reduce cyclically-adjusted public sector net borrowing to below 2% of GDP by 2020–21' and 'for public sector net debt as a percentage of GDP to be falling in 2020–21' (HM Treasury 2017). It is puzzling as to why a target for the cyclically adjusted budget position is set for some years ahead rather than being required to be met all the time, recognising that, of course, the actual budget position will vary with the business cycle and discretionary spending. It had earlier been proposed, though not implemented, that the government to run a budget surplus. The then UK Chancellor of the Exchequer (George Osborne) announced in June 2015 his intention 'that, in normal times, governments of the left as well as the right should run a budget surplus to bear down on debt and prepare for an uncertain future', and that 'in the Budget we will bring forward this strong new fiscal framework to entrench this permanent commitment to that surplus, and the budget responsibility it represents' (Osborne 2015).[2]

From the perspective of Kalecki's work, the aim for balanced structural budget would be a recipe for austerity, and a fortiori aiming for a budget surplus. A structural budget position is calculated as that which would appertain if the economy were operating at 'potential output' and government expenditure and tax rates maintained at their

---

[2]See Sawyer (2015) for a critique.

current levels (apart from spending programmes and tax adjustments, which are explic- itly related to the state of the business cycle). 'Potential output' is the level of output at which inflation would be expected to be constant. The estimates of the 'structural balance' depend on the output gap measure, with SB = FB – eOG – OE where SB is struc- tural budget, FB is fiscal balance, e is reaction of fiscal balance to output gap, OG, and OE is discretionary (for state of business cycle) adjustments to budget deficit.

There are a range of what may be termed technical objections to the construction and use of a structural budget (further discussed in Sawyer 2012; Heimberger and Kapeller 2017). These include the issues of the estimation of 'potential output' and the degree to which estimates of 'potential output' have path dependent effects on output.

'Potential output', which may correspond with the non-accelerating inflation rate of unemployment (NAIRU), is intended to be a level of output at which rate of inflation would be constant, and corresponding for the NAIRU, a level of unemployment at which inflation would be constant. This may fall well short of full employment. The focus on 'potential output' in the context of macroeconomic policy is in effect an aban- donment of any notion of full employment. Kalecki would have viewed the achievement of full employment as requiring not only the appropriate level of aggregate demand sup- ported by fiscal policy but also the creation of sufficient productive capacity.

Kalecki (1944b) argued that there would be the need for permanent budget deficits in the face of intentions to save exceeding intentions to invest. He criticised those who accepted that budget deficits would rise during economic downswings but who did not accept the arguments for the need for permanent budget deficits. He argued that 'there will emerge out of a consistent anti-cyclical policy a certain more or less stable level of private investment which by itself, i.e. without considerable assistance by loan expenditure of the public authorities, may fall short of the level required to "fill the gap" of savings out of a full employment income.' The White Paper on Employment Policy of 1944 stated that their policy recommendation 'certainly do not contemplate any departure from the principle that the Budget must be balanced over a longer period', and there was also concern in reducing 'that part of the public debt which is a dead-weight war debt' (Ministry of Reconstruction 1944, p. 25). Kalecki argued that the White Paper on Employment Policy did not provide a programme for achieving lasting full employment which would have to be based on a long-run budget deficit policy or the redistribution of income towards wages thereby stimulating aggregate demand. He argued that even if counter-cyclical measures were successful in stabilising effective demand, it did not follow that full employment would be achieved. The simple reason was that the relatively stable level of private investment may well fall below the level required to match savings out of full employment income (Kalecki 1944b, pp. 243–244).

There has also been an important shift in macroeconomic debates from the achieve- ment of full employment especially of labour to the achievement of 'potential output'. It would have to be recognised that the meaning of 'full employment' has to evolve to accommodate changes in the labour market from one dominated by often male workers on what was regarded as full time work to one with much more variations in hours of work and other conditions. But the main point is that 'potential output' is a measure geared towards a low and constant rate of inflation without any check whether this corresponds to a socially desirable level of employment.

Nevertheless, the arguments of Kalecki that a budget deficit may well be required to underpin full employment can be applied to the case of 'potential output'. The 'impossibility' of structural budget balance comes from the following argument. Suppose that the economy was operating at 'potential output', and then:

$$G-T = S-I+M-X. \tag{1}$$

where S is private savings, T tax revenue (net of transfers), M imports, I private investment, G government expenditure on goods and services and X exports (including net income received from abroad).

The budget deficit position would then be the structural budget position (by definition): now assume that the balanced structural budget has been achieved. Then:

$$I-S+CA = 0 \tag{2}$$

However, is this equation sustainable? Have the levels of investment, savings and current account position come about as a result of voluntary decisions? Are the levels of investment, savings, and current account position those which are desired at 'potential output'? If they are not, then equation 2 would not be sustainable, and hence a balanced structural budget would not be feasible.

Keynes is frequently quoted as saying that 'look after the unemployment, and the budget will look after itself' (Keynes 1933). From the perspective of Kalecki's analysis, a revival of private demand, whether coming in some sense autonomously (e.g., upturn of the business cycle, upturn of foreign demand) or through some policy stimulus (e.g., reduction of interest rate, though Kalecki would have seen that as of limited usefulness), stimulus for investment (though if that comes through tax incentives it has fiscal implications, and Kalecki placed doubt on how far investment could be stimulated), would lower unemployment and lower the budget deficit. But the use of a fiscal stimulus to reach full employment would mean a large budget deficit — how far would depend on how far private demand especially investment revives in the face of a public stimulus. It is notable though that Kalecki viewed a long term budget deficit as the key component in securing full employment.

6. Debt Burdens

The general rise in the public debt to GDP ratios after the global financial crisis (GFC) brought arguments about the scale of the debt ratio to the fore, and these have been exacerbated by the COVID-19 pandemic with further rises in the debt ratio. The claim that budget deficits burden future generations has often been made: for example, 'public borrowing is, in essence, taxation deferred, and it would be irresponsible and unfair to accumulate substantial debts to fund spending that benefits today's generation at the expense of subsequent generations' (HM Treasury 2010, p. 11). It is strange how this argument keeps re-emerging as it is well-known to be false. Kalecki clearly stated that 'interest on an increasing national debt (as indeed on all debt) cannot be a burden to society as a whole because in essence it constitutes as internal transfer.' Pigou (1918) had earlier dismissed the 'burden on future generations' argument by noting the internal transfer nature of interest payments on debt. The present (COVID-19) situation, as with the fiscal responses to the GFC, has the common features of large deficits which will leave the government debt much higher afterwards than before, and that the budget deficit post-war/pandemic will be much smaller than during the war/pandemic. This is likely to mean that the debt ratio will begin to fall once the pandemic is over,[3] and it could then be left to decline through the effects of a lower budget deficit.

In considering issues of the size of the national debt, the following separation can be made. First, consider the case where the government runs a budget deficit which averages (relative to GDP) d. Kalecki noted that if full employment is maintained by deficit spending, then the public debt expands and the resulting interest payments on the debt also rise. But the sustainability of the debt ratio of depend on the rate of growth of the economy, and as Kalecki noted the rate of taxation 'necessary to finance the increasing amount of interest on the national debt need not rise if the rate of expansion is sufficiently high, as a result of the increase in working population and technical progress' (1944a, p. 363).

It is well-known that a continuing primary budget deficit (relative to GDP) of d leads to a debt (relative to GDP) of $b = d/(g - r)$ where g is the growth rate and r the rate of interest on government debt, and sustainability of the deficit position without the debt continuously increasing relative to GDP requires $g > r$. It had often been argued the rate of interest would be above the growth rate, thereby limiting a continuous primary deficit. However, it has recently been argued that 'safe interest rates [which] are expected to remain below growth rates for a long time, is more the historical norm than the exception' (Blanchard 2019, p. 1197).

It can be argued that the total budget deficit is the one relevant for fiscal policy and stimulus purposes. Interest payments on the public debt are income for the bond-holders. A total budget deficit (relative to GDP) of e would lead the debt ratio to converge to $b = e/g$ with the deficit (in the long term) becoming $d + r.b$ where r is the rate of interest on government debt[4] and d the primary deficit. Then $e = d + r.e/g$ and $d = e.(g - r)/r = b(g-r)$. Hence d is positive if $g > r$ (i.e., a deficit) and negative (i.e., a surplus) if $g < r$. The debt ratio converges on e/g (where g is the nominal growth rate) though the composition of the budget deficit moves towards interest payments.

The budget deficit which is relevant for the level of demand is the total deficit. Thus (as argued in Sawyer 2019) the average budget deficit required to ensure full employment would be readily funded and the resulting debt level would, in general, be sustainable.

Second, consider a situation (as at present with the pandemic, and during war-time) where the budget deficit has risen considerably to deal with an emergency, and the debt ratio has jumped substantially, though the deficit subsequently likely to fall. This was in effect the type of situation about which Kalecki was writing where the UK government had been running a budget deficit of the order of 25 per cent of GDP and the debt ratio had been rising and eventually reached over 250 per cent by the end of the war. The debt ratio will be much higher than prior to the crisis (war, pandemic), and interest payments also higher than otherwise.[5] Kalecki (1943b) discussed 'the burden of the national debt', in terms of a 'financial burden' in that interest has to be paid out. He

---

[3] $B(t) = B(t-1) + D(t)$; $b(t) = b(t-1)/(1 + g) + d$; $b(t) - b(t-1) = d.(1 + g) - g.b(t)$, and hence declines if $g.b(t) > d(1 + g)/g$, that is $d < b.g/(1 + g)$, where B is the public debt stock, D budget deficit, b,d corresponding ratios to GDP, g nominal growth rate.

[4] This is usually viewed in terms of the rate of interest on bonds; however when the deficit is partially bond funded and partially money funded it should read as the average rate of interest on borrowing, bearing in mind that current practice in many countries is that the central bank pays interest on bank reserves with the central bank.

[5] During the pandemic, as during WWII, interest rates have been rather low.

also noted that interest payments are taxable. And he did not make any reference to any 'burden on next generation'. In what sense is the interest on debt a burden?

Kalecki advocated an annual capital tax, levied on firms and individuals which would raise money to finance the interest payments on the national debt which would affect 'neither capitalists' consumption nor the profitability of investment' (Kalecki 1944a, p. 363), which may be overly optimistic as consumption may well depend on wealth. Kalecki's proposal was for the funding of the interest payments on the debt — and his quick calculations in the context of war time UK was a wealth tax levied at a rate of 1 per cent per annum. He envisaged a 'tax imposed to finance the interest on the national debt incurred after a certain fixed date' (p. 363).

With a particular level of budget deficit required to secure full employment, then a higher amount of interest payments would tend to reduce the level of government expenditure consistent with that level of budget deficit. Let B be outstanding government debt, r (net of tax) interest rate on debt. The budget deficit $D = G + rB - T$, and treat $T = t.Y$ where Y is national income and T is taxes net of transfers, G government consumption. The sectoral balance (for a closed economy) provides $S - I = s_1(1-t).Y + s_2 r.D - I$, where S is savings, and I is investment treated as exogenous, s_1 and s_2 propensities to save out of disposable income and interest payments.

To secure full employment (or supply constrained maximum output) Y^*:

$$G + rD - t.Y* = s_1(1 - t).Y* + s_2 r.D - I$$

$$G \leq s_1(1 - t).Y^* + tY^* - (1 - s_2)r.D - I$$

hence G will be constrained to be lower if tax rate is lower, interest payments on debt higher, investment higher. Other matters being equal, a higher debt (after war, pandemic) lowers constrained government expenditure unless taxes changed. Debt is a burden on government/tax payer, but not on bond holders — reflected in income received. Note, however, that the interest payments act as a stimulus, and hence in order to achieve full employment there is less need for a stimulus from other forms of public expenditure.

It has long been argued that a bond funded deficit is more expansionary in the longer term than a money funded one as the former gives rise to future interest payments which are a source of income to the bond holders, whereas the latter was viewed as not doing so. Under present circumstances in many countries, interest is paid by the central bank on the reserves held by the banks. Whether such interest payments stimulate demand is debatable: balance sheet effects need to be examined. The point to be made is that when interest payments on government debt are made, there is some addition to demand.

Some invoked the argument for a negative relationship between the size of public debt and the rate of growth (at least above some threshold level of debt). An illustration of the role which such arguments played in the fiscal responses to the GFC comes from a speech given by George Osborne in early 2010, as the then shadow chancellor of the exchequer, subsequently chancellor following a change of government. It formed a major plank in his pursuit of an austerity agenda. As Ken Rogoff himself puts it, 'there's no question that the most significant vulnerability as we emerge from recession is the soaring government debt. It's very likely that will trigger the next crisis as governments have been stretched so wide' (Osborne 2010), 'The latest research suggests that once debt reaches more than about 90% of GDP the risks of a large negative impact on long term growth become highly significant. So, while private sector debt was the cause of this crisis, public sector debt is likely to be the cause of the next one' (Osborne 2010). In the words of Reinhart and Rogoff,

> [o]ur main result is that whereas the link between growth and debt seems relatively weak at 'normal' debt levels, median growth rates for countries with public debt over roughly 90 per cent of GDP are about one per cent lower than otherwise; average (mean) growth rates are several percent lower. Surprisingly, the relationship between public debt and growth is remarkably similar across emerging markets and advanced economies. (Reinhart and Rogoff 2010, p. 573)

Further support came from a Bank of International Settlements study: 'We note the risk that persistently high levels of public debt will drive down capital accumulation, productivity growth and long-term potential growth' (Cecchetti, Mohanty, and Zampoli 2010, p. 16). The results of Reinhart and Rogoff were debunked by Herndon, Ash, and Pollin (2014). A more recent study found 'that with further hindsight, and from a time series perspective, there is little to no support for the view that higher levels of debt cause reductions in economic activity. In contrast to Reinhart and Rogoff (2010), we suggest that economic slumps tend to cause debt build-ups rather than *vice versa*' (Amann and Middleditch 2020). Ash, Basu, and Dube (2020, p. 25) re-examine the relationship between public debt and growth in advanced economies, and find 'little evidence to suggest a subtantial, causal negative relationhip. We demonstrate that there is strong indication of a reverse causal relationship from GDP growth to public debt.' In Sawyer (2017), I considered further empirical evidence and argued that the evidence for a negative relationship between debt ratio and economic growth could be severely questioned. Further, there could well be elements of a relationship running from slow growth to high debt ratios, that is slow growth may lead to high ratios.

The approach of Kalecki provides an indication of what the scale of the budget deficit should be — sufficient to underpin full employment. That scale would shift as the scale of private demand shifted — lower propensity to invest, higher propensity to save indicating the need for a larger budget deficit. A budget deficit which propelled the economy into over-full employment would probably be inflationary (in the absence of measures to constrain inflation), and would involve 'forced' savings to fund the deficit.

7. The Social and Political Constraints on Achievement of Full Employment[6]

Kalecki wrote that 'a solid of majority of economists is now [that is 1943] of the opinion that, even in a capitalist economy, full employment may be secured by a government spending programme, provided there is in existence adequate plan to employ all existing labour power, and provided adequate supplies of necessary foreign raw-materials may be obtained in exchange for exports' (see Kalecki 1943a, p. 347). This was a view which he clearly supported, and he often placed some emphasis on the possible balance of payments constraints. Kalecki argued that the right balance between capital equipment

---

[6]I have discussed 'Kalecki on the causes of unemployment and policies to achieve full employment' in Sawyer (2007).

and available labour, with sufficient capital equipment needs to employ all the available labour and to leave some capacity in reserve, would be needed to enable full employment without inflationary pressures:

> If the maximum capacity of equipment is inadequate to absorb the available labour, as will be the case in backward countries, the immediate achievement of full employment is clearly hopeless. If the reserve capacities are non-existent or insufficient, the attempt to secure full employment in the short run may easily lead to inflationary tendencies in large sections of the economy, because the structure of equipment does not necessarily match the structure of demand. (Kalecki 1943a, pp. 361–362)

It is unfortunately that case that a shortage of capital equipment can be more extensive, particularly when location taken into account than envisaged by Kalecki and that shortage of capital and equipment is a more widespread phenomenon limiting the achievement of full employment.

Kalecki (1944a) evaluated 'three ways to full employment' of which budget deficit was one, with re-distribution of income another one which Kalecki favoured, though 'back of the envelope' calculations suggest that while re-distribution could play a role it may be a relatively minor one (depending on the differences in the propensities to spend of the different income groups). The stimulation of investment would contribute to aggregate demand, but Kalecki saw there were severe limits to doing so. He argued that there would need to be continuing and cumulative stimulation of investment, and that the rate of interest, taxes on income and profits would have to continuously reduced or subsidies to investment continuously increased (cf. Kalecki 1943a, p. 377). The basis of the argument was that a high level of investment would lead to the capital: output ratio rising and the rate of profit declining, and to maintain a high level of investment would require measures to offset the effects of a declining rate of profit.

Kalecki warned that those opposed to the idea that full employment can be achieved by government spending:

> there were (and are) prominent so-called 'economic experts' closely connected with banking and industry. This suggests that there is a political background in the opposition to the full employment doctrine, even though the arguments advanced are economic. That is not to say that people who advance them do not believe in their economics, poor though it is. But obstinate ignorance is usually a manifestation of underlying political motives. (1943a, p. 349)

I cite one example amongst many of the continuing objections raised by 'economic experts'. An article in Sunday Times in March 2010 headed 'Economists warn that a failure to act could trigger a loss of confidence that could push up interest rates and threaten the recovery'. 'Leading economists say the government lacks a credible plan to cut Britain's budget deficit and that action to reduce the country's borrowing should start immediately after the election.' (https://www.thetimes.co.uk/article/tories-right-on-cuts-say-economists-n9sqxrdlt2t, 11 March 2010). George Osborne (2010) argued that 'There is a recognition that the scale of the deficit and the rapid increase in the national debt cannot safely be ignored, and that public expenditure will have to be cut.' He argued that notions that expansion fiscal policy would reduce unemployment missed the importance of expectations and confidence. Hence, he concluded that 'a credible fiscal consolidation plan will have a positive impact through greater certainty and confidence about the future'. Note the appeal to 'confidence', and the idea that consolidation and reductions in public expenditure restores confidence rather than maintaining or increasing public expenditure. Kalecki had noted that:

> under a *laissez-faire* system the level of employment depends to a great extent on the so-called state of confidence. If this deteriorates, private investment declines, which results in a fall of output and employment ... This gives the capitalists a powerful indirect control over government policy: everything which may shake the state of confidence must be carefully avoided because it would cause an economic crisis, Hence budget deficits necessary to carry out government intervention must be regarded as perilous. The social function of the doctrine of 'sound finance' is to make the level of employment dependent on the state of confidence. (Kalecki 1943a, p. 350)

Kalecki (1943a, pp. 347–356) raised a number of social and political obstacles to the achievement of prolonged full employment in a laissez faire capitalist economy. He argued that under sustained full employment 'the social position of the boss would be undermined, and the self-assurance and class consciousness of the working class would grow. Strikes for wage increases and improvements in conditions of work would create political tensions' (Kalecki 1943a, p. 351). He suggested that 'discipline in the factories' and 'political stability' would also be undermined. 'The fundamentals of capitalist ethics require that "you shall earn your bread in sweat" — unless you happen to have private means' (1943a, p. 351). Much may be read into these words, but I think it is reasonable to suggest that full employment may involve significant wage inflation and a fall in work intensity and labour productivity along with a decline of 'discipline in the factories'. The volume of profits would be higher under full employment (and hence the rate of profit, though perhaps not the share), with money wage rises leading to rising prices (to protect profits) and a squeeze on rentier income. As the threat of dismissal ceases to play its threatening role, work intensity may be lower at full employment, and labour productivity thereby lower than otherwise.

In the aftermath of the global financial crisis, although financial institutions were bailed out by large funds from government, programmes of austerity were soon pursued. Vercelli (2013) argues that while expansionary policies would have benefitted financial and non-financial businesses they gave full support to austerity policies:

> The explanations given by Kalecki in 1943 still seems to be the right one; the political interest is stronger than the economic interest. First of all the focus of mainstream indignation was redirected almost overnight from the avidity of Wall Street to the corruption of the State and profligacy of people, especially in the PIIGS [Portugal Ireland Italy Greece Spain] countries. This abrupt change of focus was implemented through a systematic campaign through friendly economists and sympathetic mass media, and crony policy officials sought to postpone and maybe to avoid or at least water down, the radical reforms of finance and corporate governance that in 2008 and 2009 had obtained great popular support. This sudden shift in public opinion after the subprime crisis and its apparent early support by many economists, policy officials, and high-level practioners terrified big businessmen, mainly in finance, and their supporters and beneficiaries, convincing them that in the absence of a prompt, vigorous and relentless counter-offensive they would lose much of their power and privilege. (Vercelli 2013, p. 85)

Kalecki saw *laissez-faire* capitalism as inconsistent with sustained full employment. Kalecki in rather typical laconic style concluded by saying that "'Full employment capitalism" will, of course, have to develop new social and political institutions which will reflect the increased power of the working class. If capitalism can adjust itself to full employment, a fundamental reform will have been incorporated in it. If not, it will show itself an outmoded system which much be scrapped' (Kalecki 1943a, p. 356). In a posthumously published paper (Kalecki and Kowalik 1971), it was argued that 'a "crucial reform" imposed on the ruling class may stabilize the system, temporarily at least ... we have to do with just such a situation in contemporary capitalism' (p. 467):

> Government intervention in the expansion of markets became an institution, making it possible to limit unemployment to a few per cent ... This state of affairs (along with a considerable expansion of social security) led to a certain transformation of the working class, which on the whole became radically reformist in its attitude towards capitalism. Preserving high employment rates in the leading capitalist countries generally gives the workers a satisfactory level of real income. With high and steady employment, real wages, at least over the long term, rise along with increases in labour productivity, unless a fall in their share in national income offsets this. (pp. 472–473)

As King (2013) argues 'by 1971 the crucial reform was already beginning to unravel' (p. 32). King lists five aspects: collapse of Bretton Woods system of fixed exchange rates, leading to increased financial instability; financialisation; unwinding of first five principles of social democracy [government commitment to full employment, unionised and tightly regulated labour market, highly progressive taxation, comprehensive welfare state, public ownership of public utilities]; tendency for the various 'varieties of capitalism' to approach the Anglo-Saxon model; and 'the so-called "Great Moderation" after 1992 appears to demonstrate the advantages of neoliberal capitalism and to confirm the case against the "crucial reform"'.

The unravelling of the 'crucial reform' and the ushering in of the eras of neo-liberalism, globalisation and financialisation have been accompanied by rising inequality and generally slower economic growth. In recent years (say the last two decades), unemployment in industrialised countries has fluctuated and has rarely come close to what may be deemed full employment. Whilst the precise definition of full employment has always presented some difficulties, in periods times when employment was predominantly on what was regarded as a full time basis then full employment could be approximated by all those relying on labour income were in employment (with some recognition that there was some labour mobility with those without work equal to job vacancies). Alternative measures of unemployment have been developed to reflect part-time working by many and the fluctuations in hours worked, e.g., by those on 'zero hours' contracts. Eurostat provides statistics on 'labour market slack' which is the sum of those who are unemployed and seeking work (the ILO definition), Underemployed part-time workers, people seeking work but not immediately available, and people available to work but not seeking. The 'labour market slack' as a percentage of what is termed extended labour force (labour force plus potential labour force), for the EU member countries averaged just under 17 per cent during the 2010s. The American U-6 measure of unemployment (total unemployed, plus all persons marginally attached to the labour force, plus total employed part time for economic reasons, as a percent of the civilian labour force plus all persons marginally attached to the labour force) averaged 14.6 per cent in the first half of the 2010s and 8.7 per cent in the second half. These figures would suggest that full employment has not been achieved.

8. Concluding Comments

Kalecki recognised that public expenditure is financed by central bank money creation and the private investment expenditure is financed by bank loans, though he did not give prominence to those features. This is particularly notable in the context of the focus placed by Modern Monetary Theory on the role played by the central bank on the creation of money (at effectively zero cost). In that way, the financing of the expansion of expenditure is in the hands of the banks, whether central bank in the case of government, commercial banks in the case of private investment. Kalecki also argued that budget deficits pursued to secure higher employment can always be funded. Kalecki doubted that a balanced budget would usually be compatible with full employment. In this paper, that line of argument has been extended to show that in general a balanced structural budget would not be attainable, and that pursuit of such a balanced budget position would, in general, be deflationary. Kalecki gave a straightforward dismissal of the argument that government debt is a burden on future generations. I have rehearsed the argument that a budget deficit designed to underpin full employment can be funded and will be sustainable. Kalecki recognised that there are fiscal costs of interest payments on an enhanced public debt (following war or a pandemic), which could be met, if required, by an annual levy on wealth.

Kalecki has become well known for his perceptions of the social and political obstacles to the achievement of full employment. His prediction that there would always be 'economic experts' ready to provide spurious arguments to undermine the pursuit of fiscal policy designed to enable full employment was clearly shown in the aftermath of the global financial crises, and are beginning to surface again following the COVID-19 pandemic. The experiences of recent decades have highlighted that there have not been the 'fundamental reforms' required to provide sustained non-inflationary full employment.

Acknowledgements

I acknowledge the generous comments from an anonymous referee. All errors remain mine.

Disclosure Statement

No potential conflict of interest was reported by the author.

References[7]

Amann, J., and P. Middleditch. 2020. 'Revisiting Reinhart and Rogoff After the Crisis: A Time Series Perspective.' *Cambridge Journal of Economics* 44 (2): 343–370.

Ash, M., D. Basu, and A. Dube. 2020. 'Public Debt and Growth: An assessment of key findings on causality and thresholds.' Political Economy Research Institute, Working Paper Series, no. 433, Re-Issued April.

Blanchard, O. 2019. 'Public Debt and Low Interest Rates.' *American Economic Review* 109 (4): 1197–1229.

---

[7]References to Kalecki's work are given under the original date of publication, with indication of where the work is reproduced in the Collected Works of Kalecki: the page references in the text refer to the Collected Works.

Cecchetti, S. G., M. S. Mohanty, and F. Zampoli. 2010. 'The Future of Public Debt: Prospects and implications.' Bank of International Settlements Working Papers No. 300.

Graziani, A. 1989. 'The Theory of the Monetary Circuit.' Thames Papers in Political Economy Spring.

Graziani, A. 2003. *The Monetary Theory of Production*. Cambridge: Cambridge University Press.

Heimberger, P., and J. Kapeller. 2017. 'The Performativity of Potential Output: Pro-Cyclicality and Path Dependency in Coordinating European Fiscal Policies.' *Review of International Political Economy* 24 (5): 904–928.

Herndon, T., M. Ash, and R. Pollin. 2014. 'Does High Public Debt Consistently Stifle Economic Growth? A Critique of Reinhart and Rogoff.' *Cambridge Journal of Economics* 38 (2): 257–279.

HM Treasury. 2010. *Budget 2010: Securing the Recovery*. London: The Stationery Office, HC 451.

HM Treasury. 2017. *Charter for Budget Responsibility: Autumn* 2016.

Kalecki, M. 1932a. 'Is a "Capitalist" Overcoming of the Crisis Possible?' *Przeglad Socjalistyczny*, English translation in Osiatyński (1990), 48–53.

Kalecki, M. 1932b. 'Inflation and War.' Reproduced in Osiatyński (1996), 175–179.

Kalecki, M. 1933. 'Stimulating the World Business Upswing.' Published in Polish in *Polska Gospodarcza*, English Translation in Osiatynski (1990), 156–164.

Kalecki, M. 1935. 'The Essence of the Business Upswing.' Reproduced in Osiatynski (1990), 188–194.

Kalecki, M. 1943a. 'Political Aspects of Full Employment.' *Political Quarterly* 14 (4): 322–331, Reprinted in Osiatyński (1990), 347–356.

Kalecki, M. 1943b. 'The Burden of the National Debt.' Reproduced in Osiatynski (1997), 163–167.

Kalecki, M. 1944a. 'Three Ways to Full Employment.' In *Oxford University Institute of Statistics, the Economics of Full Employment*, 357–376. Oxford: Blackwell, Reproduced in Osiatyński (1990).

Kalecki, M. 1944b. 'The White Paper on Employment Policy.' *Bulletin of the Oxford University Institute of Statistics* 6 (8): 137–144, Reproduced in Osiatyński (1997), 238–244.

Kalecki, M. 1955. 'The Impact of Armaments on the Business Cycle after the Second World War.' Reproduced in Osiatynski (1991), 351–373.

Kalecki, M., and T. Kowalik. 1971. 'Observations on the "Crucial Reform".' *Politica ed Economia* 2 (3): 190–196. English Version in Osiatynski (1991), 467–476.

Kelton, S. 2020. *The Deficit Myth*. London: John Murray.

Keynes, J. M. 1933. 'Radio Interview in 1933 in Collected Writings of John Maynard Keynes.' Volume XXI, Page 150.

King, J. E. 2013. 'Whatever Happened to the Crucial Reforms?' In *Economic Crisis and Political Economy, Volume 2 of Essays in Honour of Tadeusz Kowalik*, edited by R. Bellofiore, E. Karwowski, and J. Toporowski. Basingstoke: Palgrave Macmillan.

Mehrling, P. 2020. 'Payment vs. Funding: The Law of Reflux for Today.' Institute for New Economic Thinking Working Paper, No. 113.

Messori, M. 1991. 'Financing in Kalecki's Theory.' *Cambridge Journal of Economics* 15 (3): 301–313.

Ministry of Reconstruction. 1944. *Employment Policy*, Cmnd. 6527. London: HMSO.

Osborne, G. 2010. 'Mais Lecture — a New Economic Model.' February 24. https://conservative-speeches.sayit.mysociety.org/speech/601526.

Osborne, G. 2015. 'Mansion House 2015: Speech by the Chancellor of the Exchequer.' https://www.gov.uk/government/speeches/mansion-house-2015-speech-by-the-chancellor-of-the-exchequer.

Osiatynski, J., ed. 1990. *Collected Works of Michał Kalecki Volume I Capitalism: Business Cycles and Full Employment*. Oxford: The Clarendon Press.

Osiatynski, J., ed. 1991. *Collected Works of Michał Kalecki Volume II Capitalism: Economics Dynamics*. Oxford: The Clarendon Press.

Osiatynski, J., ed. 1996. *Collected Works of Michał Kalecki Volume VI Studies in Applied Economics 1927–1941*. Oxford: The Clarendon Press.

Osiatynski, J., ed. 1997. *Collected Works of Michał Kalecki Volume VII Studies in Applied Economics, 1940–1967*. Oxford: The Clarendon Press.

Pigou, A. C. 1918. 'A Special Levy to Discharge war Debt.' *Economic Journal* 28 (110): 135–156.

Reinhart, C. M., and K. S. Rogoff. 2010. 'Growth in a Time of Debt.' *American Economic Review* 100 (2): 573–578.

Sawyer, M. 2001. 'Kalecki on Money and Finance.' *European Journal of the History of Economic Thought* 8 (4): 487–508.

Sawyer, M. 2007. 'Kalecki on the Causes of Unemployment and Policies to Achieve Full Employment.' In *Unemployment: Past and Present*, edited by Philip Arestis and John McCombie. Basingstoke: Palgrave. ISBN 978-0-230-20244-3.

Sawyer, M. 2012. 'The Contradictions of Balanced Structural Government Budget.' In *From Crisis to Growth? The Challenge of Imbalances and Debt*, edited by H. Herr, T. Niechoj, C. Thomasberger, A. Truger, and T. L. van Treeck. Marburg: Metropolis Verlag.

Sawyer, M. 2015. 'The "Budget Surplus" Rule Scam.' Centre for Labour and Social Studies *Think Piece*. http://classonline.org.uk/docs/Class_thinkpiece_budgetsurplusrulescam_MalcolmSawyer. pdf.

Sawyer, M. 2017. 'Lessons on Fiscal Policy After the Global Financial Crisis.' In *Economic Policies Since the Global Financial Crisis*, edited by P. Arestis and M. Sawyer. Basingstoke: Palgrave Macmillan.

Sawyer, M. 2019. 'Approaching Budget Deficits, Debts and Money in a Socially Responsible Manner.' In *Frontiers of Heterodox Macroeconomics*, edited by P. Arestis and M. Sawyer. Basingstoke: Palgrave Macmillan. ISBN 978-3-030-23928-2.

Vercelli, A. 2013. 'Political Aspects of Persisting Unemployment.' In *Economic Crisis and Political Economy, Volume 2 of Essays in Honour of Tadeusz Kowalik*, edited by R. Bellofiore, E. Karwowski, and J. Toporowski. Basingstoke: Palgrave Macmillan.

The Eurozone in Crisis — A Kaleckian Macroeconomic Regime and Policy Perspective

Eckhard Hein and Judith Martschin

ABSTRACT
The current Covid-19 Crisis 2020 has hit the Eurozone in a highly fragile situation, with a weak and asymmetric recovery from the Great Financial Crisis, the Great Recession and the following Eurozone Crisis. These crises have revealed the weaknesses of the macroeconomic policy institutions and strategies of the Eurozone based on New Consensus Macroeconomics (NCM). Applying a Kaleckian/post-Keynesian analysis of the demand and growth regimes to the EA-12 countries, we show that the internal imbalances within the EA-12 before the Eurozone have been externalised since then. Most of the countries and the EA-12 as a whole have now turned export-led mercantilist and thus highly vulnerable to fluctuations in world demand. For an economic policy alternative we turn towards Kalecki's macroeconomic policy proposals for achieving and maintaining full employment in a capitalist economy by government deficit expenditures, in combination with re-distribution policies in favour of labour and low-income households, assisted by central banks targeting low interest rates. This approach is then applied to the Eurozone, in order to derive a policy mix which should contribute to a more rapid recovery from the Covid-19 Crisis and to a medium- to long-run non-inflationary full employment domestic demand-led regime.

1. Introduction

After the Great Financial Crisis and the Great Recession 2007–09, the European Union (EU) and the Eurozone, as well as the world economy, are currently facing the deepest recession since the crisis in the late 1920s, which has led to the Great Depression of the 1930s (IMF 2020; European Commission 2020a). The current Covid-19 Crisis has hit the Eurozone asymmetrically, while it was already in a fragile situation, since it had not fully recovered from the Great Recession and, in particular, the following Eurozone Crisis. This crisis revealed the fundamental problems of the economic policy institutions and the economic policy model of the Eurozone, which has been based on New Consensus Macroeconomics (NCM) (Arestis and Sawyer 2011, 2013; Hein 2013, 2018a).

First, in 'normal' times, i.e., in the period before the 2007–09 crisis, there were no mechanisms that prevented rising current account imbalances and divergence among member states. With the one and only Eurozone-level macroeconomic policy instrument, the nominal interest rate set by the European Central Bank (ECB) for the Eurozone as a whole, necessarily guided by Eurozone average inflation, real interest rates diverged. This contributed to even further divergence, with below average real interest rates in booming member countries with above average inflation and rising current account deficits and above average real interest rates in stagnating member states with below average inflation and rising current account surpluses. Furthermore, the introduction of structural reform policies in stagnating countries, in order to reduce the respective NAIRU in line with the NCM, further weakened domestic demand, and thus contributed to rising current account surpluses due to the dampening effect on imports in these countries.

Second, in the Eurozone crisis, it became clear that nominal interest rate policies of the ECB were insufficient to stabilise aggregate demand and economic activity. The zero lower bound for the nominal short-term ECB lending rate, the main refinancing rate, imposed a downward constraint on interest rate policies. Furthermore, lowering the short-term policy rate was not sufficient to bring down long-term interest rates when risk and liquidity premia for commercial banks and other financial intermediaries rose. To the extent that long-term interest rates were decreased, i.e., by means of direct intervention in financial markets ('quantitative easing'), this was not sufficient to stimulate investment under the conditions of depressed demand expectations.

Third, and the main reason for the Eurozone Crisis, the role of the ECB as a 'lender of last resort', not only for the banking sector, but also for member state governments, was unclear at the beginning of the crisis. Therefore, when governments went into debt in order to stabilise the financial sector, as well as the real economy when the limits of ECB monetary policies became obvious, some interest rates on member state debt started to rise and put these governments under the pressure of financial markets. As a consequence, the ECB gradually moved towards a lender of last resort and guarantor of government debt of member states. However, Draghi's (2012) statement that '(w)ithin our mandate, the ECB is ready to do whatever it takes to preserve the euro', was later qualified such that the ECB's willingness to intervene in secondary government bond markets, in the context of Outright Monetary Transactions (OMT), was made conditional on the respective countries applying to the European Stability Mechanism (ESM) and introducing macroeconomic adjustment programmes, i.e., austerity policies (ECB 2012). Linking financial rescue measures with austerity policies, however, has been detrimental to recovery (De Grauwe 2012; Hein 2013).

The initial responses towards the Covid-19 Crisis in 2020 in the EU and the Eurozone have been quite expansionary. In the area of fiscal policies, the strict budgetary rules (Stability and Growth Pact, Six-Pack, Two-Pack, Fiscal Compact) have been temporarily suspended making use of the budgetary escape clause, and discretionary fiscal expansion of more than 3.5 per cent of EU GDP has been implemented at national and EU levels, associated with liquidity guarantees of more than 25 per cent of EU GDP (European Commission 2020a). New assistant schemes, like the EU funding for short-term work scheme, have been set up and existing institutions have been targeted towards fighting the crisis, like the ESM pandemic crisis support for member states and European Investment Bank (EIB) financing for business (European Commission 2020b). Furthermore, the European Commission (2020c) has presented a recovery plan with expenditures of € 750 billion over several years, financed by debt issued by the European Commission.

In addition, the ECB (2020) has announced further expansionary measures, supporting commercial banks with longer-term refinancing operations at negative interest rates and stabilising financial markets with the continuation of its asset purchase programme (APP) and a new pandemic emergency purchase programme (PEPP). The main refinancing interest rate is kept at zero per cent, with a corridor of −0.5 to 0.25 per cent given by the deposit and the marginal lending facility rates.

Whether these expansionary measures, in particular the fiscal expansion, mark a fundamental change in the EU and Eurozone macroeconomic policy model moving away from the NCM, remains to be seen. It is too early to judge whether these measures are conceived as rather short-run rescue measures, acknowledging the severity of the crisis and the limits of central bank interest rate policies to tackle such a crisis, or a move towards a policy model with an active role for fiscal policies beyond the short run. We will argue that such a change is required in order to stabilise the Eurozone economies in the short run and to deal with inadequate employment performance, asymmetries and imbalances, which have built up over the last two decades, in the medium to long run. Such an alternative policy approach can build on the contributions by Michał Kalecki, particularly those from the 1940s, which have been further developed in modern post-Keynesian macroeconomics.

In order to underline the problems, imbalances and vulnerabilities of the economic development within the Eurozone since its inception, we will start in Section Two with an analysis of the macroeconomic demand and growth regimes, which have dominated the initial member countries (EA-12) up to the Great Financial Crisis and the Great Recession and then after these crises up to the current Covid-19 Crisis. In Section Three, we will then outline some basic lines of Michał Kalecki's economic policy suggestions for macroeconomic recovery and for the management of full employment in the long run. Based on Kalecki's macroeconomics and economic policy suggestions, we will then outline a modern post-Keynesian macroeconomic policy alternative for the Eurozone in Section Four. Section Five will briefly summarise and conclude.

2. Demand and Growth Regimes in the Eurozone

2.1. Demand and Growth Regimes in Finance-Dominated Capitalism

From the Kaleckian/post-Keynesian perspective, different macroeconomic demand and growth regimes have emerged under the conditions of financialisation since the early 1980s, when the capitalist economies were exposed to major changes in the financial sectors, including the liberalisation of financial markets, the development of new financial instruments and an overall increasing role of finance in the operation of the economies (Epstein 2005). From a macroeconomic perspective, these transformations have had important implications for (1) income distribution, (2) investment in capital stock, (3) consumption and (4) the build-up of global and regional (European) current account imbalances (Hein 2012).[1]

---

[1]See also Hein (2019), Hein and Mundt (2012), Stockhammer (2010, 2012, 2015), van Treeck and Sturn (2012), the contributions in Hein, Detzer, and Dodig (2015, 2016), and several others. These macroeconomic features of financialisation have been derived from the broad and extensive literature on changes in the structure, institutions and power relationships in modern capitalism since the early 1980s. Some recent overviews can be found in Guttmann (2016), Palley (2013), Sawyer (2013) and van der Zwan (2014).

With respect to income distribution, financialisation has been associated with increasing profit shares, higher top income shares and rising inequality of household incomes. Moreover, financialisation has coincided with lower investment in the capital stock. This trend emerged as shareholder power vis-à-vis firms and workers increased, shifting firms' objectives from long-run growth to short-term profitability through financial activities. These two first features of financialisation have negatively affected aggregate demand — both directly by decreasing investment, and indirectly by re-distributing income to groups with lower propensities to consume in mostly wage-led economies.[2] Against this background two extreme regimes have developed.

In some countries, the shortfall in aggregate demand was compensated by wealth-based and debt-financed consumption, which has been facilitated by financialisation. Other countries facing rising income inequality and dampened real investment have been relying on net exports to generate growth.[3] As the subsequent analysis will show, these two different growth models have been mirrored by opposed but complementary external account positions of the two country groups. The current account deficits of the debt-financed model have been matched by the current account surpluses of the export-driven growth model. Financialisation contributed to these developments to the extent that the deregulation and liberalisation of international capital markets and capital accounts has allowed current account imbalances to persist and deficits to be financed over longer periods (Hein 2012, chapter 6; Stockhammer 2015).

In what follows, we will cluster the demand and growth regimes of the initial Eurozone member countries, without Luxembourg but including Greece, and the EA-12 as a whole, following a procedure introduced and applied by Dodig, Hein, and Detzer (2016), Hein (2012, chapter 8; 2013, 2019) and Hein, Paternesi-Meloni, and Tridico (2020), among others. First, we will look at the growth contributions of the main demand aggregates, private and public consumption, investment and net exports, which should sum up to real GDP growth. Second, we will examine the sectoral financial balances of the main macroeconomic sectors, the private household sector, the financial and non-financial corporate sectors, the government sector and the external sector, which should sum up to zero. These two sets of indicators will allow us to distinguish between (1) a debt-led private demand boom regime, (2) an export-led mercantilist regime, (3) a weakly export-led regime and (4) a domestic demand-led regime:

The *debt-led private demand boom regime* is characterised by deficits of the private domestic sectors as a whole, which are, one the one hand, driven by corporate deficits and, on the other hand, by negative or close to zero financial balances of the private household sector. The latter implies that major parts of the private household sector have negative saving rates out of current income and finance these deficits by increasing their stock of debt or by decreasing their stock of assets. The deficits of the (private) domestic sectors are mirrored by positive financial balances of the external sector, i.e., current account deficits. Growth is mainly driven by private domestic demand, to

---

[2]Econometric research based on demand-driven post-Kaleckian distribution and growth models has shown that most of the advanced capitalist economies, including the EU-15, tend to be wage-led, that is a falling wage share will dampen aggregate demand and growth (Hartwig 2014; Onaran and Obst 2016; Onaran and Galanis 2014).

[3]For a derivation of these regimes in simulated stock-flow consistent models see Belabed, Theobald, and van Treeck (2018) and Detzer (2018), and for a stylized Kaleckian model see Hein (2018b).

large degree financed by credit, while the balance of goods and services negatively contributes to growth.

The *export-led mercantilist regime* shows positive financial balances of the domestic sectors as a whole that are matched by negative financial balances of the external sector, indicating current account surpluses. There are high growth contributions of the positive balance of goods and services, and thus, rising net exports and current account surpluses, and small or even negative growth contributions of domestic demand.

The *weakly export-led regime* either shows positive financial balances of the domestic sectors, negative financial balances of the external sector, and hence current account surpluses, but negative growth contributions of the balance of goods and services and thus falling net exports and current account surpluses. Alternatively, we may have negative financial balances of the domestic sectors, positive financial balances of the external sector, and hence current account deficits, but positive growth contributions of the balance of goods and services, and thus improving net exports and falling current account deficits.

The *domestic demand-led regime* is characterised by positive financial balances of the private household sector, while the government and, to some extent, the corporate sector are running deficits. The external sector is roughly balanced with only small deficits or surpluses. Domestic demand contributes positively to growth (without being driven by credit-financed private consumption) and there are slightly negative or positive growth contributions of the balance of goods and services.

Our analysis will distinguish average values over two periods: first, the period from the start of the Eurozone in the considered constellation (EA-12) in 2001[4] until the Great Recession in 2009, and second, the period from the start of the Eurozone Crisis in 2010 until 2019, the most recent available data.

2.2. Demand Regimes and Imbalances Within the Eurozone 2001–09

Between 2001 and 2009, Greece, Ireland and Spain were characterised by the debt-led private demand boom regime, with negative financial balances of the private domestic sector as a whole, mainly driven by high deficits of the private household sector (Table 1). The counterpart to the negative financial balances of the domestic sectors was the positive financial balance of the external sector, indicating current account deficits. The debt-led private demand boom countries showed the highest real GDP growth rates among the EA-12 countries. These were mainly driven by the growth contributions of domestic demand, and in particular, of private consumption demand, financed by financial deficits of private households to a large degree. Growth contributions of the balance of goods and services contributed negatively to GDP growth in Greece and Spain, indicating falling net exports and rising current account deficits. This was not the case for Ireland, where both net exports and the growth contribution of the balance of goods and services were positive. The negative current account has thus to be explained by highly negative net cross-border flows of primary incomes, in particular capital incomes.

In the period 2001–09, the export-led mercantilist regime dominated in Austria, Belgium, Germany and the Netherlands (Table 1). All countries were characterised by

---

[4]Greece joined in 2001.

Table 1. Key macroeconomic variables for the economies of the core Eurozone, average annual values for the period 2001–09.

	Export-led mercantilist				Weakly export-led	Domestic demand-led				Debt-led private demand boom		
	Austria	Belgium	Germany	Netherlands	Finland	France	Italy	Portugal	EA-12	Greece	Ireland	Spain
Financial balances of external sector as a share of nominal GDP, per cent	−2.05	−4.20	−4.00	−5.55	−4.91	−0.42	1.04	7.96	−0.63	10.08	2.60	5.61
Financial balances of public sector as a share of nominal GDP, per cent	−2.43	−1.21	−2.44	−1.43	3.01	−3.45	−3.28	−5.19	−2.63	−8.03	−1.58	−1.32
Financial balances of private sector as a share of nominal GDP, per cent	4.47	5.40	6.43	6.98	1.90	3.87	2.24	−2.77	3.22	−2.04	−3.23	−4.29
– Financial balance of private household sector as a share of nominal GDP, per cent	4.87	4.58	5.52	−1.39	−2.32	2.78	2.47	2.00	2.21	−6.77	−6.06	−2.73
– Financial balance of the corporate sector as a share of nominal GDP, per cent	−0.40	0.82	0.91	8.36	4.21	1.08	−0.23	−4.77	1.01	4.73	2.83	−1.56
Real GDP growth, per cent	1.52	1.60	0.53	1.39	1.68	1.19	0.18	0.63	1.04	2.64	3.05	2.36
Growth contribution of domestic demand including stocks, percentage points	1.16	1.44	0.02	1.21	1.60	1.43	0.36	0.51	0.96	2.96	2.66	2.61
– Growth contribution of private consumption, percentage points	0.79	0.60	0.19	0.30	1.23	0.97	0.23	0.64	0.62	2.09	1.49	1.34
– Growth contribution of public consumption, percentage points	0.34	0.42	0.25	0.78	0.35	0.38	0.22	0.38	0.40	0.66	0.62	0.87
– Growth contribution of gross fixed capital formation, percentage points	0.02	0.38	−0.18	0.19	0.22	0.24	0.00	−0.40	0.09	0.59	0.69	0.47
Growth contribution of the balance of goods and services, percentage points	0.35	0.18	0.51	0.17	−0.10	−0.25	−0.18	0.07	0.09	−0.31	0.87	−0.25
Net exports of goods and services as a share of nominal GDP, per cent	3.34	3.85	4.81	7.56	5.52	0.35	0.05	−8.14	1.82	−10.44	12.40	−3.56

Source: European Commission (2019), authors' calculations.

negative balances of the external sector and hence by current account surpluses. These deficits were mirrored by positive financial balances of the domestic sectors as a whole, mainly the outcome of significant surpluses of the private sector. Compared to the rest of the Eurozone, economies of this regime displayed moderate real GDP growth rates, with positive growth contributions of the balance of goods and services, in particular. In the extreme case of Germany, growth was driven almost exclusively by net exports with a close to zero growth contribution of domestic demand. In the case of Finland, we find a weakly export-led regime, with negative financial balances of the external sector, current account and net export surpluses, but negative growth contributions of net exports.

France, Italy and Portugal, as well as the EA-12 as a whole can be classified as domestic demand-led regimes on average over the period 2001–09 (Table 1). These countries were characterised by positive financial balances of the private household sector, while the public sector — and in Italy and Portugal also the corporate sector — were running deficits. Portugal differs from the other countries of this group insofar as its financial balance of the external sector showed high external surpluses and hence current account deficits. Growth rates were modest and mainly driven by domestic demand with slightly positive (Portugal, EA-12) or negative (Italy, France) growth contributions of the balance of goods and services.

The emergence of the two extreme macroeconomic growth regimes under financial-isation, the debt-led private demand boom regime and the export-led mercantilist regime, implied large current account imbalances at the global as well as Eurozone level, as shown in Figure 1 (see also Hein 2012, chapters 6 and 8, 2019). These imbalances were driven, on the one hand, by high growth contributions of domestic demand, fuelled in particular by increasing indebtedness of the private household sector in debt-led private demand boom countries, providing expanding markets for the export-led mer-cantilist economies. On the other hand, stagnating unit labour cost growth and low inflation rates in the export-led mercantilist countries depressed domestic demand and also improved price competitiveness of these countries.

When the Great Financial Crisis and then the Great Recession hit in 2007–09 — first in the USA and then in the European debt-led private demand boom countries — these crises were quickly transmitted to the export-led mercantilist economies, and also to the domestic demand-led economies, through the international trade and the financial con-tagion channel. Initially, expansionary fiscal policy measures were applied, also in the Eurozone. But when the crisis turned into a Eurozone Crisis in 2010, starting in Greece and then affecting Ireland, Portugal and Spain, the Eurozone responded by turning towards austerity policies. The necessary financial rescue packages for these countries, as well as a gradual extension of the ECB towards a guarantor of government debt of Eurozone member countries, were linked with the enforcement of 'structural reforms' in the labour market and fiscal expenditure cuts. Furthermore, new agreements to contain government deficits and debt for all Eurozone member countries were estab-lished (De Grauwe 2012; Dodig and Herr 2015; Hein 2013).[5]

---

[5]For detailed analysis of the crisis processes in individual countries, see for example the contributions in Arestis and Sawyer (2012) and in Hein, Detzer, and Dodig (2016).

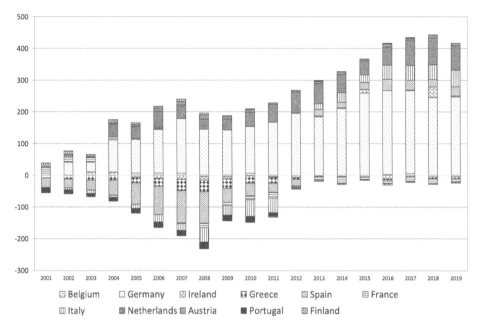

Figure 1. Current account balance in core Eurozone countries, 2001–19 (in bn euros).

Source: European Commission (2019), authors' representation.

2.3. Demand Regimes, 'Rebalancing' and Stagnation à la Eurozone 2010–19

The restrictive economic policy responses towards the Eurozone crisis have contributed to another recession in the EA-12 in 2012/13 and to a weak recovery in international comparison (Figure 2). EA-12 growth has been lagging behind other non-Eurozone developed capitalist economies, for which the recovery has also been weak in historical perspective.[6] In particular, growth contributions of investment, which had been very modest already in the period 2001–09, even declined on average over the period 2010–19, turning negative in some countries (Spain, Italy, Greece, Portugal) (Table 2). Financial balances of the corporate sectors turned positive in all the countries we are examining. Corporate saving thus exceeded corporate investment — a phenomenon of finance-dominated capitalism (Hein 2012, Chapter 3).[7]

Furthermore, the weak recovery of the EA-12 has been highly asymmetric, with Germany growing at a well above average rate and the crisis countries in the periphery, Greece, Italy and Portugal at considerably below average rates (Table 2).[8] Additionally, this period has been associated with a considerable shift in demand and growth regimes.

The former debt-led private demand boom countries with high external deficits have undergone substantial transformations and have turned towards export-led mercantilist or weakly export-led regimes. Spain and Greece significantly improved their current

---

[6]It should also be noticed that even in the first period we are considering, the financial balances of the corporate sectors had been positive in several Eurozone countries.

[7]The phenomenon of weak investment and growth has given rise to re-emergence of a debate on 'secular stagnation' (Summers 2014, 2015; Hein 2016).

[8]The extremely high growth rates for Ireland seem to be driven by severe accounting problems in a country with a high relevance of foreign owned companies (Joebges 2017).

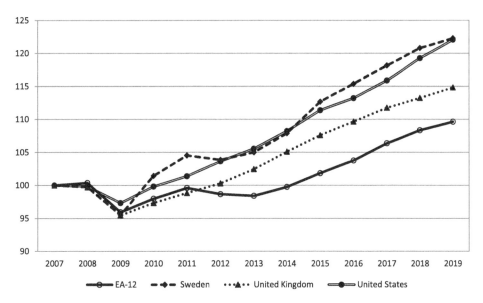

Figure 2. Real GDP in selected OECD countries and the Eurozone (EA-12), 2007–19, 2007 = 100.
Source: European Commission (2019), authors' representation.

accounts. On average over the period 2010–19, Spain saw negative and Greece only slightly positive financial balances of the respective external sectors. Ireland continued with positive financial balances of the external sector, i.e., current account deficits, again dominated by the deficit in the cross-border flows of primary incomes. The reduction of the external deficits was the result of the substantial deleveraging of the private sectors, whose financial balances turned positive in each of the countries, associated with a collapse in consumption and investment demand. While public sector deficits stabilised the economies up to 2012/13, austerity measures implemented in response to the Eurozone Crisis then forced Ireland, Spain and Greece to decrease their public deficit considerably, turning them even into surpluses in Ireland and Greece. On average over the period 2010–19, however, the public financial balances remained deeply negative in each of the countries. The impact of the financial and economic crisis, and in particular the austerity measures implemented when the Eurozone crisis hit, caused negative growth in Greece and only very weak positive growth in Spain on average over 2010–19 (Table 2). Growth contributions of domestic demand collapsed, turned deeply negative in Greece, and growth was exclusively driven by the balance of goods and services. Ireland saw much higher growth in the statistics, due to accounting conventions and the activities of multinationals, which was driven to large extent by net exports. Summing up, therefore, Spain and, with some reservations because of the accounting problems, Ireland shifted towards export-led mercantilist regimes during the period 2010–19. Greece, on average over the period, turned to weakly export-led, combining a negative current account with positive growth contributions of net exports, with a tendency towards export-led mercantilist towards the end of this period.

From the domestic demand-led economies in the first period, also Italy and Portugal moved towards an export-led regime, export-led mercantilist in the case of Italy and weakly export-led for Portugal with a tendency towards export-led mercantilist in the

Table 2. Key macroeconomic variables for the economies of the core Eurozone, average annual values for the period 2010–19.

	Export-led mercantilist							Weakly export-led			Domestic demand-led	
	Ireland	Spain	Austria	Germany	Nether-lands	Italy	EA-12	Belgium	Greece	Portugal	France	Finland
Financial balances of external sector as a share of nominal GDP, per cent	3.77	−1.41	−2.15	−7.24	−8.82	−0.94	−2.75	−0.76	1.74	0.20	0.81	1.08
Financial balances of public sector as a share of nominal GDP, per cent	−6.55	−6.03	−1.65	0.18	−1.65	−2.83	−2.53	−2.69	−4.92	−4.76	−4.06	−1.80
Financial balances of private sector as a share of nominal GDP, per cent	3.88	7.44	3.80	7.05	10.46	3.77	5.31	3.44	3.18	4.56	3.25	0.72
– Financial balance of private household sector as a share of nominal GDP, per cent	1.77	0.89	2.50	5.27	2.80	1.24	2.77	1.90	−5.53	2.68	3.09	−2.83
– Financial balance of the corporate sector as a share of nominal GDP, per cent	2.10	6.55	1.31	1.78	7.66	2.53	2.54	1.55	8.72	1.88	0.16	3.55
Real GDP growth, per cent	6.31	1.03	1.57	1.96	1.45	0.22	1.34	1.54	−1.98	0.76	1.35	1.23
Growth contribution of domestic demand including stocks, percentage points	3.62	0.34	1.25	1.74	0.92	−0.16	1.01	1.57	−3.01	0.25	1.36	1.61
– Growth contribution of private consumption, percentage points	0.64	0.27	0.49	0.73	0.33	0.05	0.43	0.79	−1.67	0.44	0.55	0.75
– Growth contribution of public consumption, percentage points	0.12	0.04	0.14	0.38	0.13	−0.09	0.18	0.15	−0.52	−0.17	0.29	0.18
– Growth contribution of gross fixed capital formation, percentage points	2.65	−0.05	0.53	0.56	0.36	−0.12	0.32	0.57	−1.16	−0.11	0.39	0.37
Growth contribution of the balance of goods and services, percentage points	3.10	0.69	0.20	0.21	0.53	0.39	0.34	−0.03	1.03	0.50	−0.01	−0.26
Net exports of goods and services as a share of nominal GDP, per cent	21.38	2.48	3.33	6.25	9.73	1.78	3.53	0.71	−2.75	−0.88	−1.03	−0.65

Source: European Commission (2019), authors' calculations.

second half of the period 2010–19. Both countries generated high private sector financial surpluses, in particular driven by the corporate sector, indicating weak investment (Table 2). The public sector could exert its stabilising function, accepting higher deficits, only until 2009/10; then the public deficit started shrinking. The foreign sector balances decreased significantly, turning negative in Italy, and remaining only slightly positive in Portugal on average over the period. Nevertheless, both countries have seen positive current accounts since 2013. Overall, Portugal and Italy witnessed below EA-12 average growth in the period 2010–19, due to the crisis and the following austerity policies. Growth was mainly driven by the balance of goods and services with weakly positive, in the case of Portugal, or even negative growth contributions of domestic demand in the case of Italy.

France, the third domestic demand-led economy in the period 2001–09, remained so also in the period 2010–19, with slightly positive external sector financial balances, financial surpluses of the private (household) sector, and negative financial balances of the public sector (Table 2). In the 2007–09 crisis, high public deficits contributed to stabilise the economy relatively quickly, so that France could reach EA-12 average growth in the 2010–19 period. Growth continued to be mainly driven by domestic demand with small negative growth contributions of the balance of goods and services.

The initial export-led mercantilist economies Austria, Germany and the Netherlands remained so in the period 2010–19. The financial deficit of their external sectors, hence current account surpluses, rather increased on average over the period, and allowed the private sector surpluses to rise — partly also due to weak private investment — and the government sector to consolidate and to move towards financial surpluses, too (Table 2). On average over the period, however, government financial balances remained slightly negative in Austria and the Netherlands and became positive only in Germany. These economies recovered relatively quickly from the 2007–09 crisis, initially benefiting from the recovery of the world economy through the external trade channel, and achieved above average EA-12 growth on average over the period 2010–19. Relative growth contributions of net exports remained considerable.

From the export-led mercantilist countries of our first period, Finland and Belgium have moved towards a domestic demand-led regime in the period 2010–19. However, Belgium is still classified as weakly export-led, because the financial balance of the external sector remained negative on average, whereas in Finland it turned positive (Table 2). Growth contributions of net exports were negative in both countries, and growth was exclusively driven by domestic demand. In Belgium GDP growth was slightly above EA-12 average, and in Finland it was slightly below.

Summing up, with the exception of Belgium and Finland, we have seen a shift of towards export-led mercantilist or weakly export-led regimes in the core Eurozone. This has also meant that the regime of the EA-12 as a whole has moved from domestic demand-led towards export-led mercantilist (Table 2). Financial balances of the external sector have turned negative, financial balances of the public sector are still negative on average over 2010–19, but with a tendency to be balanced, and the private sector, both households and corporate, generated high surpluses. Growth was driven to a considerable degree by net exports.

This shift towards export-led mercantilism and the 'rebalancing à la Eurozone' can also be seen in Figure 1. Whereas the current account of the EA-12 as a whole had been roughly balanced before the start of the Eurozone crisis, such that we only had internal current account imbalances, these imbalances have now been externalised. Most of the EA-12 countries have been running current surpluses during the recent years, with the exception of Belgium, Finland, France and Greece with slight deficits. Therefore, the core Eurozone, as one of the largest economic and monetary areas in the world, has become a free rider of aggregate demand generated in the rest of the world. On the one hand, this lack of internal demand generation has generated stagnation tendencies in the developed capitalist world as a whole. On the other hand, this export-led mercantilist regime has contributed to global imbalances and the related tendencies towards over-indebtedness in those economies providing the counterpart current account deficits. This is a problem in particular for those countries that are unable to finance these deficits by issuing debt in their own currencies, in particular the relatively faster growing emerging market economies. For countries that are able to go into debt in their own currency, the current account deficits may nonetheless face political limits, as recently observed in the case of the USA.

The turn towards an export-led mercantilist regime has thus not only been harmful for the EA-12, since it has meant weak recovery after the crises 2007–09, low growth and the associated unemployment problems, in particular in the Eurozone periphery. It also faces serious external risks related to the implied global imbalances. Therefore, what is required is the return towards a domestic demand-led regime, which will need an alternative approach towards macroeconomic management and policies, not only in a situation of a deep recession, like the current Covid-19 Crisis, but also in the medium to long run, which has to overcome the problems and limitations summarised in the introduction to this paper. For this purpose, we will first go back to the basic ideas proposed by Michał Kalecki in order to achieve and maintain full employment in the mid-1940s at the end of World War II, and then we will explain how these considerations have been further developed and applied to the problems of the Eurozone by modern post-Keynesians/Kaleckians.

3. Kalecki's Economic Policy Suggestions for Achieving and Maintaining Full Employment

Kalecki (1954, 1971), one of the founding fathers of post-Keynesian economics (Hein and Lavoie 2019), is well known as the co-inventor of the 'principle of effective demand' in macroeconomics, together with Keynes (1936).[9] In fact, Kalecki (1933) had proposed his 'principle of effective demand' even earlier than Keynes, however, initially published in Polish. Different from Keynes, Kalecki included the role of income distribution into the very basics of his principle of effective demand, with the profit share being mainly determined by mark-up pricing in oligopolistic or monopolistic markets dominating the industrial and service sectors of the advanced capitalist economies. Firms usually hold excess capacity, and changes in demand will rather lead to changes in the rate of

---

[9]See Hein (2018c) for a recent comparison of Kalecki's and Keynes's – as well as Marx's – principle of effective demand. For a recent intellectual biography of Kalecki, see Toporowski (2013, 2018). For an excellent introduction into Kalecki's economics, see Sawyer (1985), and for macroeconomic textbooks based on Kalecki's economics, see Bhaduri (1986) and Łaski (2019). For further references on Kaleckian economics, including further intellectual biographies, see Hein (2014, Chapter 5).

capacity utilisation than to changes in prices, which tend to remain constant because of constant unit variable costs and constant mark-ups in pricing in the short run. Aggregate demand is mainly determined by investment, which can be financed independently of prior saving by means of credit generated endogenously by the banking and financial sector, which does not have to obtain reserves or deposits before lending. Investment is mainly affected by expected demand and by firms' internal means of finance, which will impact their creditworthiness in incompletely competitive financial markets — Kalecki's (1937) 'principle of increasing risk'. Equilibrium domestic demand tends to be 'wage-led', i.e., raising the profit share will depress domestic demand, because the propensity to consume out of wages is higher than out of profits, and investment is mainly determined by sales (expectations) and not by real unit wage costs. Government deficit expenditures as well as domestic export surpluses each raise equilibrium aggregate demand and the volume of profits.

According to Sawyer (2015), against this theoretical background, Kalecki presented a clear and compelling macroeconomic policy strategy to reach and maintain full employment in several publications between 1943 and 46, when he was based at the Oxford University Institute of Statistics, and then at the International Labour Office in Montreal. In the wellknown 'Three ways to full employment', Kalecki (1944) assumes a closed economy with elastic labour supply. The three ways to full employment that he discusses are:

1. Government deficit spending on public investment (schools, hospitals, highways) and on subsidies to mass consumption (family allowances, reduction of indirect taxes, subsidies to keep down prices of necessities),
2. Stimulating private investment through reductions in the interest rate or through lowering income taxes.
3. Redistribution of income from higher to lower income classes.

Kalecki (1944, 1945) does not consider the second way—namely, relying on the stimulation of private investment by means of interest rate and tax cuts—very promising and abandons it for two reasons. First, it is an indirect method that relies on positive responses of entrepreneurs, which may be blocked by depressed expectations in an economic recession. Second, even if lowering interest rates and/or tax rates stimulates investment and thus aggregate demand in the very short run, the capacity effect will then dampen investment again if there is no adequate increase in autonomous demand. Therefore, further interest rate and tax cuts will be required to sustain investment at a higher level, which, obviously, faces serious limits. Consequently, Kalecki (1944) proposes a combination of the first and the third way, i.e., government deficit spending and progressive income re-distribution.

Regarding government deficit spending, Kalecki (1944) explains that there will not be any crowding out of private demand if there are unemployed resources and if interest rates are kept low. First, any initial deficit will partly finance itself through higher incomes and higher tax revenues. Second, also the remaining budget deficit will finance itself, too, because it generates additional saving of an equal amount through the income effect which can fund the deficit. From the national income accounting identities for a closed economy:

$$G + I + C_\Pi + C_W = T_\Pi + \Pi + T_W + W = T_\Pi + C_\Pi + S_\Pi + T_W + C_W + S_W \qquad (1)$$

with G representing government expenditures, I private investment, C_Π and C_W private consumption out of profits and wages, T_Π and T_W taxes on profits and on wages, W wages net of taxes, Π profits net of taxes, and S_Π and S_W private saving out of profits and wages, it follows:

$$S = I + G - T \qquad (2)$$

with $S = S_\Pi + S_W$ as private saving and $T = T_\Pi + T_W$ as total taxes. Gross (net) private saving is thus always equal to the government deficit plus gross (net) investment:

> (W)hatever is the general economic situation, whatever the level of prices, wages or the rate of interest, any level of private investment and Budget deficit will always produce an equal amount of saving to finance these two items. (Kalecki 1944, p. 41)

If this additional saving by the private sector is not creating demand for bonds issued by the government in order to fund the deficit, but rather for liquidity, imposing upward pressure on interest rates in government bonds markets, central banks have to step in and prevent interest rates from rising. Therefore, ' ... the rate of interest may be maintained at a stable level however large the Budget deficit, given proper banking policy' (Kalecki 1944, p. 42).

Permanent government deficits raise the issue of a potential burden of government debt. However, Kalecki (1944) argues that national debt cannot be a burden to society as a whole, because it only constitutes internal transfers between those holding government debt and those paying taxes — who can be the same economic units. Furthermore, in an expanding economy, interest payments will not rise out of proportion with tax revenues at given tax rates. Therefore, there is no need for raising tax rates to service government debt. However, should taxation be applied in order to bring the government debt-GDP ratio down, f.e. in the course of the recovery from a war or a deep recession,[10] Kalecki (1943a, 1944) proposes taxes on wealth, both on financial and real assets.

Government deficit expenditures find a limit when scarcity of labour and/or capital stock will emerge and a full employment or full utilisation inflation barrier is reached:

> In order to avoid inflation the Government must, therefore, be careful not to push their deficit spending beyond the mark indicated by full utilization of labour and equipment. (Kalecki 1944, p. 43)

If the capital stock is too low for full employment, as it may occur in backward countries, the focus of government activities should also be on expanding productive capacities.

Government deficit spending within the outlined limits will also stabilise private investment and prevent violent cyclical fluctuations. Besides, private investment should be regulated by tax rates with the following target:

> Private investment must be at a level adequate to expand the capacity of equipment pari passu with the increase in working population and productivity of labour, i.e., proportionately to full employment output. (Kalecki 1944, p. 47)

---

[10]We thank Malcolm Sawyer for clarifying this issue in private communication.

Regarding the type of government expenditure, Kalecki (1944) argues that it should be guided by social priorities and hence not exclusively be focused on public investment, but also include public consumption and subsidies to private consumption. Of course, government investment is possible and useful, too, and state-owned enterprises should invest in desired areas where there is a lack of private investment, i.e., social housing.

Government deficit expenditure should be complemented by the third way to full employment, the redistribution of income, according to Kalecki (1944), shifting disposable income to low income households with a higher propensity to consume. For this purpose, he advocates progressive taxation. In order to avoid negative effects on investment, he proposes a 'modified income tax', exempting re-invested profits from (progressive) taxation (Kalecki 1943a) or a wealth tax on financial and real assets. Furthermore, redistribution of market incomes can be achieved by real wages growing faster than productivity, or nominal wage growth exceeding productivity growth plus the inflation rate. At full employment, however, attempting re-distribution by wage policies would require higher taxes on profit income in order to prevent inflation due to excess demand. Alternatively, or in combination with tax increases, Kalecki suggests price controls in order to squeeze profits when wages are rising. In the absence of such measures, nominal wage growth would have to be limited to the sum of labour productivity growth and inflation, in order to prevent the latter from rising.

While a combination of government deficit expenditures and re-distribution may generate and sustain full employment, Kalecki (1943a) in 'Political aspects of full employment' is well aware of the potential resistance from 'economic experts' closely connected with banking and industry against such a policy. This will occur although higher government deficits raise capitalists' profits after taxes, as can be derived from the accounting equation (1) (see also Kalecki 1954, Chapter 3, 1971, Chapter 7):

$$\Pi = I + C_\Pi + G - T - S_W \qquad (3)$$

> The reasons for the opposition of 'industrial leaders' to full employment achieved by government spending may be subdivided into three categories: (i) dislike of government interference in the problem of employment as such; (ii) dislike of the direction of government spending (public investment and subsidizing consumption), (iii) dislike of the social and political changes resulting from the *maintenance* of full employment. (Kalecki 1943b, pp. 349–350, emphasis in the original)

The first motive is related to the social function of 'sound finance': Avoiding government deficits for full employment makes the level of employment dependent on business confidence — and gives capitalists political power. The second motive means that public investment should be strictly confined to areas that do not compete with private investment. This implies resistance against nationalisation of transport and public utilities. Subsidising consumption is rejected, because it contradicts the rule that 'you should earn your bread in sweat' (Kalecki 1943a, p. 351). The third motive means that 'the "sack" would cease to play its role as a disciplinary measure' (Kalecki 1943b, p. 351). Workers would become more self-conscious and the power of capitalists would be undermined. Capitalists would favour discipline in the factories and 'political stability' over profits.

Kalecki (1943a) concedes that in post-war economies, or in deep recessions, governments' responsibility for full employment may be acknowledged, also by capitalists and their 'experts'. But still, conflict will prevail over what type of government deficit expenditure should be applied and for how long. First, capitalists would prefer indirect stimuli for private investment (interest rate and tax cuts) over government expenditure. And if government expenditure is accepted, the focus should be on investment, not subsidising consumption. Second, capitalists would insist that measures should be confined to the slump and would resist permanent public deficit spending to sustain full employment. From this a 'stop and go policy' and a 'political business cycle' would emerge:

> The regime of the political business cycle would be an artificial restoration of the position as it existed in nineteenth century capitalism. Full employment would be reached only at the top of the boom, but slumps would be relatively mild and short-lived. (Kalecki 1943a, p. 355)

Of course, Kalecki rejects the regime of the political business cycle and rather advocates the combination of long-term government deficit expenditures for public investment, public consumption and subsidising private consumption in combination with progressive income taxation, wealth taxes and other measures of redistribution. In order to achieve this beyond the short run, he holds that full employment capitalism will have to develop new social and political institutions which reflect the increased power of the working class and requires 'fundamental reform' without specifying what exactly this implies in his writing in the 1940s. Kowalik (2004, p. 48) explains that the late 'Kalecki would most probably say, that the essence of "crucial reform" was successful governance of overall demand', as it happened in the period of what is now called the 'golden age' of capitalism in the third quarter of the 20th century. Kalecki and Kowalik (1971, p. 467) had argued that '(t)here will then be a paradoxical situation: a "crucial reform" imposed on the ruling class may stabilise the system, temporarily at least'. Of course, when the 'crucial reform' is reversed, as in the late 1970s, early 1980s, with the liberalisation of labour and financial markets and the monetarist turn of macroeconomic policies, stagnation tendencies and high unemployment are back on the agenda — and they have stayed since then. Extending Kalecki's (1943a) notion of a 'political business cycle', Steindl (1979) then called this 'stagnation policy' or 'stagnation as a political trend'.[11]

4. A Kaleckian/Post-Keynesian Policy Mix for the Eurozone

Kalecki's full employment policy proposal from the 1940s implies a macroeconomic policy mix, which has inspired modern post-Keynesian macroeconomics, both in general (i.e., Hein and Stockhammer 2010; Arestis 2013; Hein 2017) and more specifically in its application to the Eurozone (Hein, Truger, and van Treeck 2012; Arestis and Sawyer 2013; Hein and Detzer 2015a, 2015b; Hein 2018a).

Introducing such a policy mix to the Eurozone with the aim of establishing a stable domestic demand-led regime, avoiding the problems inherent to the debt-led private demand boom and export-led mercantilist regimes dominating up to and after the

---

[11]For an elaboration on Steindl's notion of stagnation as a political trend and its application to stagnation policies in the Eurozone, see Hein (2018a).

crises 2007–09, would mean to overcome the limitations and problems of the NCM applied in the Eurozone, as outlined in the introduction.[12] This means that the lender of last resort problem for Eurozone member state government needs to be solved, the focus on monetary policy as the only stabilising policy at the Eurozone level needs to be overcome, and unsustainable current account imbalances have to be avoided. For such a policy along Kaleckian/post-Keynesian lines ex ante 'horizontal coordination' among monetary, fiscal and wage policies is of utmost importance, as is the 'vertical coordination' of decentralised member state policies in the areas of fiscal and wage policies in the case of the Eurozone. Furthermore, these coordinated demand management policies will have to be supplemented by effective regional and industrial policies in order to facilitate the sustainable catch-up of the Eurozone periphery with respect to the core countries and to overcome limitations given by the capital stock in these countries — as suggested by Kalecki (1944). However, space limitations do not allow us to elaborate extensively on the latter.[13]

At the centre of a Kaleckian/post-Keynesian coordinated macroeconomic policy mix are fiscal policies, which should assume responsibility for real stabilisation at non-inflationary full employment levels of economic activity and also for a more equal distribution of disposable income in the short and in the long run. Fiscal policies can also contribute to catching up productivity growth in the periphery and thus to rebalancing the Eurozone internally, if they are targeted towards public investment in these countries improving productivity growth and the capacity to export.

Extending equation (2) to the open economy, adding nominal exports (X) and imports (M), ex post the excess of private saving over private investment at a given level of economic activity and employment has to be absorbed by the excess of nominal exports over nominal imports (including the balance of primary income and the balance of income transfers, thus the current account balance) plus the excess of government spending over tax revenues:

$$S - I = X - M + G - T \qquad (4)$$

Since the current export-led mercantilist regime has to be overcome, the current accounts of member countries and the Eurozone as a whole should be roughly balanced in the long run (X–M = 0). Therefore, as recommended by Kalecki (1944) and also by Lerner's (1943) concept of functional finance, government deficits (D) have to permanently take up the excess of private saving over private investment in order to maintain a desired level of economic activity and employment:[14]

$$D = G - T = S - I \qquad (5)$$

Government deficit spending should be on government consumption and investment, guided by social and development priorities in the member countries.

As argued by Kalecki (1944) and shown by Domar (1944), permanent government deficits will not lead to the explosion of public debt. With a long-run constant government deficit-nominal GDP ratio (D/Y^n), the government debt-nominal GDP ratio (B/Y^n) will

---

[12]This section is based on Hein (2018a). For more extensive elaborations of the approach see Hein and Detzer (2015b).
[13]See Hein and Detzer (2015b) for a broader review.
[14]Of course, if the private sector is in deficit and the current account is balanced, the government sector has to be in surplus.

converge towards a constant value in the long run, given by the ratio of the deficit-GDP ratio and nominal GDP growth ($\hat{Y}^n$):

$$\frac{B}{Y^n} = \frac{\dfrac{D}{Y}}{\hat{Y}^n} \tag{6}$$

Furthermore, if we distinguish the government deficit in a primary deficit (D') and government interest payments on the stock of debt (iB), equation (6) turns to:

$$\frac{B}{Y^n} = \frac{\dfrac{D'}{Y^n}}{\hat{Y}^n - i} \tag{7}$$

Therefore, nominal interest rates below nominal GDP growth will even make a primary deficit consistent with a long-run constant government debt-nominal GDP ratio.[15] It will thus prevent government debt services from redistributing income from the average taxpayer to the rich government bondholders, which would be detrimental to aggregate demand. Government deficit spending will thus need the assistance of the central bank, guaranteeing government debt and keeping interest rates below GDP growth, as will be explained in more detail further below.

Apart from this permanent role of government deficits and debt, which also supplies a safe haven for private saving and thus stabilises financial markets, counter-cyclical fiscal policies — together with automatic stabilisers — should stabilise the economy in the face of (also country-specific) aggregate demand shocks. From these considerations, we get the following requirements for fiscal policies:

$$D = D_L + D_S(Y^T - Y), \quad D_S > 0 \tag{8}$$

with D_L as permanent government deficit (or surplus), which is required to keep output at non-inflationary full employment target (Y^T) in the long run, according to equation (5), and D_S as the reaction parameter in the case of short-run deviations of output from full employment target. Fiscal policies would thus also have to prevent inflationary pressure generated by demand exceeding full employment levels, as recommended by Kalecki (1944).

Furthermore, also following Kalecki (1944), governments should apply progressive income taxes and relevant wealth, property and inheritance taxes, as well as social transfers, which aim at redistribution of income and wealth in favour of low income and low wealth households. On the one hand, this will reduce the excess of private saving over private investment at non-inflationary full employment levels (equation 5) and thus stabilise aggregate demand. On the other hand, redistributive taxes and social policies will improve automatic stabilisers and thus reduce fluctuations in economic activity.

Applying this general approach to the Eurozone could either aim at a relevant federal EU/Eurozone budget with a EU/Eurozone fiscal authority issuing debt, which will then be accepted by the ECB as collateral, as for example proposed by Bibow (2016). However, this would require major institutional changes, which might be difficult to obtain in the

---

[15]For recent derivations of this condition in Kaleckian distribution and growth models driven by autonomous and deficit financed government expenditure growth, see Dutt (2020), Hein (2018d) and Hein and Woodgate (2020).

short to medium run.[16] Alternatively, a revamped Stability and Growth Pact for the coordination of national fiscal policies should be considered, which should focus on long-run expenditure paths for non-cyclical government spending — a variable which member state government can indeed control, different from government deficits (Hein, Truger, and van Treeck 2012). The sum of these expenditure paths should be geared towards stabilising aggregate demand in the Eurozone at non-inflationary full employment levels with a roughly balanced current account with the rest of the world. For each Eurozone member state this would mean that, on average over the cycle and with the long-run net tax rate in each member country given, the path for non-cyclical government expenditure should be targeted at generating a long-run or 'structural' government deficit/surplus as required in equation (5). Automatic stabilisers plus discretionary counter-cyclical fiscal policies could then be applied to fight short-run demand shocks, both aggregate (symmetric) and country-specific (asymmetric) shocks (equation 8).

Instead of the current 'one-size-fits-all' coordination with respect to target or maximum government deficit- and debt-GDP ratios, this new type of coordination of member countries' fiscal policies implies country-specific government deficit-GDP ratios, given by the long-run national private sector financial balances. It would also lead to country-specific long-run government debt-GDP ratios, depending on the respective government deficit-GDP ratios and the nominal GDP growth trends (equation 6). The expenditure paths for non-cyclical public sector spending of each member country could be coordinated and monitored by the European Commission in the context of the European Semester.

Such a coordination of national fiscal policies, together with the recently announced efforts at the EU level (see introduction) should contribute to overcoming the Covid-19 Crisis. It should also boost aggregate domestic demand for the Eurozone as a whole in the medium to long run, contribute to overcoming the export-led mercantilist regime and the long-run stagnation tendencies by stimulating also private investment and domestic demand. In order to avoid or to overcome the re-emergence of undesirable internal current account imbalances, non-price competitiveness of catching-up countries within the Eurozone needs to be improved, decreasing the income elasticity of their imports and increasing the income elasticity of their exports, by means of industrial, structural and regional policies. Government expenditures should thus be focussed on public investment and be linked with a European industrial and regional policy strategy aiming at the sustainable catch-up of the periphery with respect to the core. Furthermore, this would have to be integrated into a strategy of ecological modernisation — like the European Green Deal. For such catching-up processes, perfectly balanced current accounts between member states cannot be expected and, therefore, the rules for fiscal policy co-ordination outlined above would have to be modified.[17] Catch-up countries should have a persistent tendency to grow faster than the more mature countries, which, *cet. par.*, will make their imports grow faster than their exports. Therefore, with the Eurozone as a whole running a balanced current account with the rest of the world, internally there would be a tendency for catch-up member countries to run

---

[16]Furthermore, it is not clear, how such an approach should contribute to rebalancing the Eurozone. For a discussion and comparison with what is proposed here, see Hein and Detzer (2015b).
[17]See Hein and Detzer (2015b) for a more detailed derivation of the conditions.

current account deficits, and for more mature countries to run current account surpluses. These current account deficits and surpluses should be tolerated and taken into account in the coordination of fiscal policies. Target long-run public sector financial balances in the catch-up countries can hence be somewhat lower than implied above in equation (5), i.e., allow for higher government deficits (or lower government surpluses). Target long-run public sector financial balances of mature countries can be somewhat higher, i.e., aim at lower government deficits (or higher government surpluses). The pre-condition for this is, of course, that higher growth in the catch-up countries can be sustained — and is not driven by financial or housing market bubbles as prior to the 2007–09 crises. Therefore, the direction and the use of the capital inflows into catch-up current account deficit countries should be part of an integrated European industrial and regional development strategy for the periphery. This should include the efficient regulation of and intervention in capital flows to avoid bubble growth, on the one hand, and the promotion of 'high road' development strategies, on the other hand. These strategies should make use of public investment, both national and European, in infrastructure and education, as well as public development banks and funds (i.e., the European Investment Bank, EIB, and the European Investment Fund, EIF, etc.) to support private investment in the respective countries.

Regarding monetary policy, the ECB should give up targeting inflation and should instead (continue) targeting low real interest rates in financial markets. A slightly positive long-term real rate of interest, below long-run real GDP growth, or a nominal long-term interest rate above the rate of inflation but below nominal GDP growth (equation 9), seems to be a reasonable target. Real financial wealth will be protected against inflation, but redistribution of income in favour of the productive sector will be favourable for investment in the capital stock, aggregate demand and employment. Furthermore, the central bank has to act as a 'lender of last resort' during liquidity crises and should stabilise financial markets using other tools than the short-term interest rate. These include the definition of credit standards for refinancing operations with commercial banks, the implementation of reserve requirements for different types of assets, and even credit controls in order to channel credit into desirable areas and to avoid credit-financed bubbles in certain markets. Most importantly, the ECB should not only act as a lender of last resort for the banking system, but also unconditionally guarantee the public debt of Eurozone member states. The ECB as a lender of last resort for member state governments would allow these governments to issue debt in their 'own currency' again, and it would thus reduce the pressure imposed by financial markets, in line with Kalecki's consideration regarding the interest rate stabilising role of the central bank. The ECB could simply announce that it will intervene unconditionally in secondary government bond markets and provide unlimited liquidity, as soon as the nominal rate of interest on government bonds (i_j) for member country j shows a tendency to exceed the long-run growth rate of nominal GDP of the respective country, i.e., the sum of real GDP growth ($\hat{Y}_j$) plus the rate of inflation ($\hat{p}_j$), thus maintaining in the long run:

$$\hat{p}_j \leq i_j \leq \hat{Y}_j + \hat{p}_j \tag{9}$$

This would imply country-specific caps on nominal interest rates on government bonds in the respective countries. It reliefs governments from running primary surpluses in order to stabilise government debt-GDP ratios, with restrictive effects on aggregate demand, and provides the conditions for fiscal policies of the member states to stimulate aggregate demand in the respective countries and for the Eurozone as a whole.

In line with Kalecki's considerations, wage and incomes policies should accept responsibility for nominal stabilisation, that is for stable inflation rates, in particular when full employment is reached, but may also affect income distribution. As an orientation, nominal wages (w) should rise according to the sum of long-run average growth of labour productivity ($\hat{y}_j$) in the national economy j plus the target rate of inflation for the Eurozone as a whole ($\hat{p}^T$):

$$\hat{w}_j = \hat{y}_j + \hat{p}^T \tag{10}$$

In the case of actual inflation rates being below the target, such a wage norm would also raise the labour income share during the resulting adjustment process. In the long run, implementing such a wage norm in each of the member states would contribute to equal inflation rates across the Eurozone, and it would prevent mercantilist strategies of individual countries based on nominal wage moderation.

To achieve the nominal wage growth targets, a high degree of wage bargaining co-ordination at the macroeconomic level and organised labour markets with strong trade unions and employer associations seem to be necessary conditions. Government involvement in wage bargaining may be required, too. In particular, Eurozone-wide minimum wage legislation could be helpful for providing a floor to nominal stabilisation at the macroeconomic level, apart from its usefulness in terms of containing wage inequality (Schulten 2012). Furthermore, legal extensions of wage bargaining agreements throughout an entire industry or sector and other extension mechanisms, as well as public sector bargaining setting the pattern for private sectors, could be helpful for effective wage bargaining coordination.

In principle, the European Union and the Eurozone have developed some institutions for the implementation of such a policy mix with the Macroeconomic Dialogue, the European Semester and the financing institutions for regional and industrial policies, such as the EIB and the EIF. In the current Covid-19 Crisis, the establishment of further institutions and plans are on the agenda, as outlined in the introduction to this paper. However, this institutional framework needs to be linked with the Kaleckian/post-Keynesian macroeconomic and development policies outlined above, aiming at establishing stable full employment domestic demand-led regimes in the member states and in the Eurozone as a whole.

5. Conclusions

We have argued that the current Covid-19 Crisis has hit the Eurozone in a highly fragile situation, with a weak and asymmetric recovery from the Great Financial Crisis, the Great Recession and the following Eurozone Crisis. These crises have also revealed the weaknesses of the macroeconomic policy institutions and strategies of the Eurozone based on the NCM. In order to illustrate these weaknesses and the fragilities of macro-economic development in the core Eurozone, the EA-12, we have applied a Kaleckian/post-Keynesian analysis of the demand and growth regimes to the EA-12 countries, up to and then in the course and after the Eurozone crisis. We have shown that the internal imbalances within the EA-12 in the first period, with the polarisation of current account deficit debt-led private demand boom countries, on the one hand, and current account surplus export-led mercantilist countries, on the other hand, have been externalised in the second period. Most of the countries of the core Eurozone and the EA-12 as a whole have now turned export-led mercantilist. The EA-12 has thus not only seen a weak recovery from the previous crises in international comparison, it has also contributed to sustained global current account imbalances, and it is highly vulnerable with respect to turbulences of world demand.

Since the neglect of any active and expansionary long-run role of fiscal policy inherent in the NCM and the turn towards austerity policies in the course of the Eurozone crisis have mainly contributed to this development, we have then turned towards Kalecki's macroeconomic policy proposals for achieving and maintaining full employment in a capitalist economy. Kalecki's suggestions of government deficit expenditures, in combination with re-distribution policies in favour of labour and low-income households, assisted by central banks targeting low interest rates, have been applied to the Eurozone by modern Kaleckian/post-Keynesians. We have outlined such a macroeconomic policy mix, complemented by adequate regional and industrial policies, which can be (partly) based on current institutions. It should contribute to a more rapid recovery from the Covid-19 Crisis and to a medium- to long-run non-inflationary full employment domestic demand-led regime, on the one hand, and to sustainable catching-up of the periphery of the Eurozone with respect to the more mature centre, on the other hand. Whether the implementation of such a policy mix would be equivalent to a 'crucial reform' in the sense of Kalecki and Kowalik (1971) may need further discussion.

Acknowledgements

For helpful comments, we are grateful to Daniel Detzer, Ryan Woodgate and to the participants in the online Poznań Conference on Kalecki and Kaleckian Economics in the 21st Century, 24–26 September 2020. We have also benefitted from the comments and suggestions of an anonymous referee. Remaining errors are ours, of course.

Disclosure Statement

No potential conflict of interest was reported by the author(s).

References

Arestis, P. 2013. 'Economic Theory and Policy: A Coherent Post-Keynesian Approach.' *European Journal of Economics and Economic Policies: Intervention* 10 (2): 243–255.
Arestis, P., and M. Sawyer. 2011. 'The Design Faults of the Economic and Monetary Union.' *Journal of Contemporary European Studies* 19 (1): 21–32.
Arestis, P., and M. Sawyer, eds. 2012. *The Euro Crisis*. Basingstoke: Palgrave Macmillan.
Arestis, P., and M. Sawyer. 2013. *Economic and Monetary Union Macroeconomic Policies. Current Practices and Alternatives*. Basingstoke: Palgrave Macmillan.

Belabed, C., T. Theobald, and T. van Treeck. 2018. 'Income Distribution and Current Account Imbalances.' *Cambridge Journal of Economics* 42 (1): 47–94.

Bhaduri, A. 1986. *Macroeconomics: The Dynamics of Commodity Production.* Basingstoke: Macmillan.

Bibow, J. 2016. 'Making the Euro Viable: The Euro Treasury Plan.' *European Journal of Economics and Economic Policies: Intervention* 13 (1): 72–86.

De Grauwe, P. 2012. 'The Governance of a Fragile Eurozone.' *Australian Economic Review* 45 (3): 255–268.

Detzer, D. 2018. 'Inequality, Emulation and Debt: The Occurrence of Different Growth Regimes in the Age of Financialization in a Stock-Flow Consistent Model.' *Journal of Post Keynesian Economics* 41 (2): 284–315.

Dodig, N., E. Hein, and D. Detzer. 2016. 'Financialisation and the Financial and Economic Crises: Theoretical Framework and Empirical Analysis for 15 Countries'. In *Financialisation and the Financial and Economic Crises: Country Studies*, edited by E. Hein, D. Detzer, and N. Dodig, 1–41. Cheltenham: Edward Elgar.

Dodig, N., and H. Herr. 2015. 'Current Account Imbalances in the EMU: An Assessment of Official Policy Responses.' *Panoeconomicus* 62 (2): 193–216.

Domar, E. 1944. 'The "Burden of the Debt" and National Income.' *American Economic Review* 34 (4): 794–828.

Draghi, M. 2012. 'Speech by Mario Draghi, President of the European Central Bank at the Global Investment Conference in London, 26 July.' http://www.ecb.europa.eu/press/key/date/2012/html/sp120726.en.html.

Dutt, A. K. 2020. 'Autonomous Demand Growth, Distribution, and Fiscal and Monetary Policy in the Short and Long Runs.' In *Economic Growth and Macroeconomic Stabilization Policies in Post-Keynesian Economics, Essays in Honour of Marc Lavoie and Mario Seccareccia, Book Two*, edited by H. Bougrine and L.-P. Rochon, 16–32. Cheltenham: Edward Elgar.

ECB. 2012. 'Technical Features of Outright Monetary Transactions, Press Release, 6 September.' https://www.ecb.europa.eu/press/pr/date/2012/html/pr120906_1.en.html.

ECB. 2020. 'Monetary Policy Decisions, Press Release, 30 April.' https://www.ecb.europa.eu/press/pr/date/2020/html/ecb.mp200430~1eaa128265.en.html.

Epstein, G. A. 2005. 'Introduction: Financialization and the World Economy.' In *Financialization and the World Economy*, edited by G. A. Epstein. Cheltenham: Edward Elgar.

European Commission. 2019. *Annual Macro-Economic Database (AMECO)*, November. https://ec.europa.eu/info/business-economy-euro/indicators-statistics/economic-databases/macro-economic-database-ameco/ameco-database_en#database.

European Commission. 2020a. *European Economic Forecast.* Brussels: European Commission.

European Commission. 2020b. 'Jobs and Economy During the Coronavirus Pandemic.' https://ec.europa.eu/info/live-work-travel-eu/health/coronavirus-response/jobs-and-economy-during-coronavirus-pandemic_en.

European Commission. 2020c. *The EU Budget Powering the Recovery Plan for Europe.* Brussels: European Commission.

Guttmann, R. 2016. *Finance-Led Capitalism: Shadow Banking, Re-Regulation, and the Future of Global Markets.* Basingstoke: Palgrave Macmillan.

Hartwig, J. 2014. 'Testing the Bhaduri–Marglin Model with OECD Panel Data.' *International Review of Applied Economics* 28 (4): 419–435.

Hein, E. 2012. *The Macroeconomics of Finance-Dominated Capitalism – And Its Crisis.* Cheltenham: Edward Elgar.

Hein, E. 2013. 'The Crisis of Finance-Dominated Capitalism in the Euro Area, Deficiencies in the Economic Policy Architecture and Deflationary Stagnation Policies.' *Journal of Post Keynesian Economics* 36 (2): 325–354.

Hein, E. 2014. *Distribution and Growth After Keynes: A Post-Keynesian Guide.* Cheltenham: Edward Elgar.

Hein, E. 2016. 'Secular Stagnation or Stagnation Policy? Steindl After Summers.' *PSL Quarterly Review* 69 (276): 3–47.

Hein, E. 2017. 'Post-Keynesian Macroeconomics Since the Mid-1990s – Main Developments.' *European Journal of Economics and Economic Policies: Intervention* 14 (2): 131–172.

Hein, E. 2018a. 'Stagnation Policy in the Eurozone and Economic Policy Alternatives: A Steindlian/Neo-Kaleckian Perspective.' *Wirtschaft und Gesellschaft* 44 (3): 315–348.

Hein, E. 2018b. 'Inequality and Growth: Marxian and Post-Keynesian/Kaleckian Perspectives on Distribution and Growth Regimes Before and After the Great Recession.' In *Inequality: Trends, Causes, Consequences, Relevant Policies. International Papers in Political Economy*, edited by P. Arestis and M. Sawyer, 89–137. Basingstoke: Palgrave Macmillan.

Hein, E. 2018c. 'The Principle of Effective Demand – Marx, Kalecki, Keynes and Beyond.' In *The Routledge Handbook of Heterodox Economics: Theorizing, Analyzing, and Transforming Capitalism*, edited by T.-H. Jo, L. Chester, and C. D'Ippoliti, 84–100. Abingdon: Routledge.

Hein, E. 2018d. 'Autonomous Government Expenditure Growth, Deficits, Debt and Distribution in a Neo-Kaleckian Growth Model.' *Journal of Post Keynesian Economics* 41 (2): 316–338.

Hein, E. 2019. 'Financialisation and Tendencies Towards Stagnation: The Role of Macroeconomic Regime Changes in the Course of and After the Financial and Economic Crisis 2007–09.' *Cambridge Journal of Economics* 43 (4): 975–999.

Hein, E., and D. Detzer. 2015a. 'Post-Keynesian Alternative Policies to Curb Macroeconomic Imbalances in the Euro Area.' *Panoeconomicus* 62 (2): 217–236.

Hein, E., and D. Detzer. 2015b. 'Coping with Imbalances in the Euro Area: Policy Alternatives Addressing Divergences and Disparities Between Member Countries.' *Wirtschaft und Management, Schriftenreihe zur wirtschaftswissenschaftlichen Forschung und Praxis* (22) (1): 13–50.

Hein, E., D. Detzer, and N. Dodig, eds. 2015. *The Demise of Finance-Dominated Capitalism: Explaining the Financial and Economic Crises*. Cheltenham: Edward Elgar.

Hein, E., D. Detzer, and N. Dodig, eds. 2016. *Financialisation and the Financial and Economic Crises: Country Studies*. Cheltenham: Edward Elgar.

Hein, E., and M. Lavoie. 2019. 'Post-Keynesians Economics.' In *The Elgar Companion to John Maynard Keynes*, edited by R. W. Dimand and H. Hagemann. Cheltenham: Edward Elgar.

Hein, E., and M. Mundt. 2012. 'Financialisation and the Requirements and Potentials for Wage-Led Recovery – A Review Focussing on the G20.' In *Conditions of Work and Employment Series No. 37*, 540–546. Geneva: ILO.

Hein, E., W. Paternesi-Meloni, and P. Tridico. 2020. 'Welfare Models and Demand-Led Growth Regimes Before and After the Financial and Economic Crisis.' *Review of International Political Economy*, advance access, https://doi.org/10.1080/09692290.2020.1744178.

Hein, E., and E. Stockhammer. 2010. 'Macroeconomic Policy Mix, Employment and Inflation in a Post-Keynesian Alternative to the New Consensus Model.' *Review of Political Economy* 22 (3): 317–354.

Hein, E., A. Truger, and T. van Treeck. 2012. 'The European Financial and Economic Crisis: Alternative Solutions from a (Post-)Keynesian Perspective.' In *The Euro Crisis*, edited by P. Arestis and M. Sawyer, 35–78. Basingstoke: Palgrave Macmillan.

Hein, E., and R. Woodgate. 2020. 'Stability Issues in Kaleckian Models Driven by Autonomous Demand Growth – Harrodian Instability and Debt Dynamics.' In *FMM Working Paper 55/ 2020*. Duesseldorf: Hans Boeckler Foundation.

IMF. 2020. *World Economic Outlook. The Great Lockdown*. Washington, DC: IMF.

Joebges, H. 2017. 'Crisis Recovery in a Country with a High Presence of Foreign Owned Companies – The Case of Ireland.' In *IMK Working Paper 175*. Duesseldorf: Hans Boeckler Foundation.

Kalecki, M. 1937. 'The Principle of Increasing Risk.' *Economica* 4 (16): 440–447.

Kalecki, M. 1943a. 'Political Aspects of Full Employment.' *The Political Quarterly* 14 (4): 322–330. Reprinted in *Collected Works of Michał Kalecki, Vol. I, Capitalism: Business Cycles and Full Employment*, edited by J. Osiatynski, 347–356. Oxford: Clarendon Press, 1990.

Kalecki, M. 1943b. 'The Burden of the National Debt.' *Bulletin of the Oxford University Institute of Statistics* 5 (5): 76–80. Reprinted in *Collected Works of Michał Kalecki, Vol. VII, Studies in*

Applied Economics 1940–1967, Miscellanea, edited by J. Osiatynski, 163–167. Oxford: Clarendon Press, 1997.

Kalecki, M. 1944. 'Three Ways to Full Employment.' In *The Economics of Full Employment*, edited by Oxford University Institute of Statistics. Oxford: Basil Blackwell. Reprinted in *Collected Works of Michał Kalecki, Vol. I, Capitalism: Business Cycles and Full Employment*, edited by J. Osiatynski, 357–376. Oxford: Clarendon Press, 1990.

Kalecki, M. 1945. 'Full Employment by Stimulating Private Investment?' *Oxford Economic Papers* NS-7 (1): 83–92. Reprinted in: *Collected Works of Michał Kalecki, Vol. I, Capitalism: Business Cycles and Full Employment*, edited by J. Osiatynski, 377–386. Oxford: Clarendon Press, 1990.

Kalecki, M. 1954. *Theory of Economic Dynamics*. London: Allen and Unwin.

Kalecki, M. 1971. *Selected Essays on the Dynamics of the Capitalist Economy, 1933–1970*. Cambridge: Cambridge University Press.

Kalecki, M. 1990 [1933]. 'Essay on the Business Cycle Theory.' In *Collected Works of Michał Kalecki, Vol. I, Capitalism: Business Cycles and Full Employment*, edited by J. Osiatynski, 66–108. Oxford: Clarendon Press.

Kalecki, M., and T. Kowalik. 1991 [1971]. 'Observations on the "Crucial Reform".' In *Collected Works of Michał Kalecki, Vol. II, Capitalism: Economic Dynamics*, edited by J. Osiatynski, 467–476. Oxford: Clarendon Press.

Keynes, J. M. 1973 [1936]. *The General Theory of Employment, Interest, and Money*. In *The Collected Writings of J.M. Keynes, Vol. 7*, edited by E. Johnson and D. Moggridge. London: Macmillan.

Kowalik, T. 2004. 'Kaleckian Crucial Reform of Capitalism and After.' In *Kalecki's Economics Today*, edited by Z. L. Sadowski and A. Szeworski, 42–50. London: Routledge.

Lerner, A. P. 1943. 'Functional Finance and the Federal Debt.' *Social Research* 10 (1): 38–51.

Łaski, K. 2019. *Lectures in Macroeconomics: A Capitalist Economy Without Unemployment*. Edited by J. Osiatynski and J. Toporowski. Oxford: Oxford University Press.

Onaran, Ö, and G. Galanis. 2014. 'Income Distribution and Growth: A Global Model.' *Environment and Planning A: Economy and Space* 46 (10): 2489–2513.

Onaran, Ö, and T. Obst. 2016. 'Wage-led Growth in the EU15 Member-States: The Effects of Income Distribution on Growth, Investment, Trade Balance and Inflation.' *Cambridge Journal of Economics* 40 (6): 1517–1551.

Palley, T. I. 2013. *Financialization: The Economics of Finance Capital Domination*. Basingstoke: Palgrave Macmillan.

Sawyer, M. 1985. *The Economics of Michał Kalecki*. Armonk, NY: M.E. Sharpe.

Sawyer, M. 2013. 'What is Financialization?' *International Journal of Political Economy* 42 (4): 5–18.

Sawyer, M. 2015. 'Addressing the 'Great Recession' Using Kalecki's Macroeconomic Analysis.' In *Michał Kalecki in the 21st Century*, edited by J. Toporowski and L. Mamica, 198–211. Basingstoke: Palgrave Macmillan.

Schulten, T. 2012. 'European Minimum Wage Policy: A Concept for Wage-led Growth and Fair Wages in Europe.' *International Journal of Labour Research* 4 (1): 85–104.

Steindl, J. 1979. 'Stagnation Theory and Stagnation Policy.' *Cambridge Journal of Economics* 3 (1): 1–26.

Stockhammer, E. 2010. 'Income Distribution, the Finance-Dominated Accumulation Regime, and the Present Crisis.' In *The World Economy in Crisis – the Return of Keynesianism?*, edited by S. Dullien, E. Hein, A. Truger, and T. van Treeck, 63–86. Marburg: Metropolis.

Stockhammer, E. 2012. 'Financialization, Income Distribution and the Crisis.' *Investigación Económica* 71 (279): 39–70.

Stockhammer, E. 2015. 'Rising Inequality as a Cause of the Present Crisis.' *Cambridge Journal of Economics* 39 (3): 935–958.

Summers, L. A. 2014. 'U.S. Economic Prospects: Secular Stagnation, Hysteresis, and the Zero Lower Bound.' *Business Economics* 49 (2): 65–73.

Summers, L. A. 2015. 'Demand Side Secular Stagnation.' *American Economic Review: Papers and Proceedings* 105 (5): 60–65.

Toporowski, J. 2013. *Michał Kalecki: An Intellectual Biography, Volume I: Rendezvous in Cambridge, 1899–1939*. Basingstoke: Palgrave Macmillan.

Toporowski, J. 2018. *Michał Kalecki: An Intellectual Biography, Volume II: By Intellect Alone, 1939–1970*. Basingstoke: Palgrave Macmillan.

van der Zwan, N. 2014. 'Making Sense of Financialization.' *Socio-Economic Review* 12 (1): 99–129.

van Treeck, T., and S. Sturn. 2012. 'Income Inequality as a Cause of the Great Recession? A Survey of Current Debates.' In *Conditions of Work and Employment Series No. 39*. Geneva: ILO.

The Relevance of Kalecki for Financial Capitalism of the 2020s

Jerzy Osiatyński ⓘ

ABSTRACT

The paper focuses on four critical differences between capitalism of the Keynes-Kalecki times and the present-day financial capitalism. The first follows from the wholesale globalisation and liberalisation of financial and capital markets which drastically changed the nature of political opposition against full employment. The second results from changes in income and wealth distribution and in access to basic public services like health, education, and social security. The third is the evolution of the Schumpeterian entrepreneurial innovators to financial rent-seekers and speculators. The fourth relates to the question whether economic dynamics and business fluctuations are of Kaleckian nature, i.e. resulting from the feedback between the income generating effect, and the productive capacity augmenting effect, of private investment in fixed capital, or are they of Minskian financial instability nature. And if the latter is true, what is the room for any countercyclical policy that Keynes and Kalecki recommended. The essay ends with the question on how to include the Minskian financial instability of the present-day capitalism into Kalecki's canonical profit equation on which his theory of economic dynamics and business fluctuations is founded.

The most obvious and important difference between the capitalist system studied by Kalecki and that of our times is the emergence of globalisation from the wholesale liberalisation of financial and capital markets. Government counter-cyclical intervention proposed by Keynes and Kalecki applied to a market economy which, as a rule, operated below full capacity use of factors of production, even in the boom phase of the cycle. Among other characteristic features of the modus operandi of that economy are (i) sovereign money, (ii) no constitutional, international treaty or restrictions of a similar nature on the permissible upper limit for ratios of government deficit and public debt to GDP, and (iii) no similar restrictions on central banks financing government spending.

For Kalecki, political opposition to permanent full employment was of a domestic nature. It came from 'business leaders' supported by small and large rentier interests that could be negatively affected should inflationary pressure appear in the boom phase of the cycle. He wrote: 'In this situation a powerful alliance is likely to be formed between big business and rentier interests, and they would probably find more than one economist to declare that the situation was manifestly unsound' (1943 [1990], p. 355). The policy instrument used by this alliance and supporting economists and politicians was the doctrine of 'sound finance', the aim of which was to make governments return to a balanced budget. The political function of this instrument was 'to make the level of employment dependent on the state of confidence' (1943 [1990], p. 350).

With the end of the 'golden age' of capitalism, the rise of financial capitalism in our time has restored the dominant position of the doctrine of 'sound finance' and the 'state of confidence' in economic and political argument, albeit in a modified form. The role of the block of interests formed by domestic big capital, rentiers and their supporting academic economists and politicians has been much strengthened by the globalisation of financial markets and their speculative trading,[1] and the 'sound finance' doctrine has been augmented by the concept of the 'natural rate of unemployment'.

In the absence of sovereign money, when rigid constitutional and similar limits on debt-financed public spending are in force, and when the cost of public debt servicing is determined by global financial markets, there is very limited room remaining for the counter-cyclical and full employment policies recommended by Kalecki and Keynes (except for military and similar spending). Only in three well-known cases do these limitations not apply: (i) when the country is sovereign with respect to the supply of its money by a central bank (e.g., the UK case); (ii) when the central bank notes of a given country and its government securities denominated in these notes are the world reserve currency (the US Dollar case); (iii) when nearly all government debt is owned by the country's residents (as, e.g., in Japan).

A second difference relates to the income redistributive policy instrument that was Kalecki's 'third way to full employment' (1944 [1990]). The changes over the past few decades in the functional distribution of income and wealth have had significant consequences on economic dynamics and social cohesion. Since these economic and political consequences have already attracted much attention, I shall not discuss them here. Instead, I shall merely offer a brief comment on Kalecki's 'third way to full employment'.

In the *Theory of Economic Dynamics*, Kalecki relaxed the assumption that 'workers spend what they earn' and introduced worker savings into his analytical model. This complicated his formal argument but did not affect its conclusions (see Kalecki 1954 [1991], p. 243). However, significant and long-lasting income transfers may with time decreasingly stimulate output and employment, giving rise to an increasing propensity to save among low-income households, and thus weakening the multiplier effects of a change in any autonomous component of aggregate demand. In this case, the stimulating (or at least stabilising) impact of *monetary* transfers to low-income households would gradually be weakened. However, this is not necessarily the case for transfers *in kind* to those households (neglecting their substitution effect), and one might speculate that Kalecki would probably recommend a corresponding change in the structure of those transfers.

Let me note in passing that increased household incomes, including monetary transfers, increase the bankability and creditworthiness of those households, thus enabling their 'deficit spending'—a question to which I shall return later.

---

[1] In 1972, James Tobin proposed taxing these operations, chiefly foreign exchange speculations, but his idea encountered large opposition, and the 1984–90 Swedish attempt to introduce such a tax failed, among other reasons because it could not work if introduced in a single country or in a few countries only.

A third difference, which I have already discussed elsewhere (see Osiatyński 2015, 2019a, 2019b), relates to the pattern of behaviour of business leaders. In the tradition of Kalecki, Steindl (1952, 1990) and his followers, business leaders were above all Schumpeterian innovative entrepreneurs. They earned profits thanks to introducing new products and technologies, and by opening new markets. This made them different to capitalist rent-seekers, who earned profits mainly from financial transactions and the related wealth gains. Under the financial capitalist system, however, the Schumpeterian 'would-be innovators' are dominated by financial rent-seekers, Moreover, they face the choice between expected profitability from investment in new productive capacity, or in financial speculation, and may often opt for the latter (thus strengthening the stagnation tendencies that have recently reappeared in mature capitalism in the past two decades or so).

When the power of rentiers increases and entrepreneurs are guided also by the wealth effects of their financial investment, these effects become an important co-determinant of the course of the business cycle and economic dynamics. If, however, instability and the cyclical development of present-day financial capitalism are generated by factors that operate in financial and capital markets rather than—or as well as—by factors operating in the real sphere of the economy, to what extent are instability and business fluctuations Minskian rather than Kaleckian in nature? (see Osiatyński 2019a, p. 315).

This inherent instability of financial capitalism, which brought well-earned recognition to Hyman Minsky (1986, 1992), is the essence of the fourth key difference between the capitalist system of the Kalecki and Keynes period on the one hand, and present-day global financial capitalism. What macroeconomic analytical framework do we need to study an economy in which speculation in financial and capital markets dominates investment in expanding productive capacity? To what extent are business fluctuations and the financial instability of the system generated by the factors defined by Minsky, and/or by Kalecki? In Minsky's 'financial theory of investment', as in Keynes's theory, the prime source of a business crisis lies in the disruptions in financial markets due to alternating waves of optimism and pessimism which, in turn, are transferred to the real sphere of the economy. In line with Minsky's 'financial Keynesianism', investments determine the volume of income needed to service the debt, and the volume of output and employment is, in a way, debt-determined.

What is the difference between Minsky's theory of fluctuations in the financial markets and Kalecki's theory of business fluctuations? For Kalecki, the business cycle is an inherent feature of the process of investing in fixed capital assets and it takes place in the real sphere of the economy. Its prime cause is the time lag between the income effect of investment, which operates during the course of investment construction, and its supply effect, which appears as soon as the investment project is put into operation and starts to impair the profitability of the capital stock acquired by previous generations. Kalecki's theory of the business cycle (similar to Tinbergen's 1937 *Schiffbauzyklus* on which it was patterned) is embedded precisely in this feedback between the income and the supply effect of investment. But his theory also requires that the period of fluctuations is roughly constant and that the oscillations are neither dampened nor explosive. The former is secured by the time lag between an investment decision and the completion of an investment project, and the latter by random shocks of normal frequency. Notwithstanding his 'principle of increasing risk' and the ownership of private capital determining the bankability of an individual entrepreneur (and therefore an important co-determinant of investment decision-making), for Kalecki financing investment was not a prime cause of cyclical fluctuations, although it might inhibit private investment if increased demand for credit was not accompanied by a sufficiently flexible policy of the central bank aimed at preventing a rise in the long-term rate of interest.

The world of Kalecki is neither that of Minsky, nor of present-day financial capitalism. When explaining instability and fluctuations in financial markets, Minsky did not expect a steady period of these fluctuations, nor their regular amplitude. However, if the course of the business cycle and of financial crises is primarily decided by global financial markets, and by the mechanism of business downturns as discussed by Minsky rather than by Kalecki, then we face at least two challenges. The first relates to economic policy-making and the second to economic theory.

Empirical studies of oscillations in financial markets provide no evidence of any regularity with respect to their duration or amplitude. While the average duration of the cycle in the real sphere of the economy from the years of Kalecki and Keynes until the mid-1970s was 6–8 years, that of present-day fluctuations in financial markets is rather of quarterly dimension and their amplitude is very volatile. Considering the time span between the appearance of the first symptoms of a financial crisis and the first effects of any counter-cyclical policy, which may also have a quarterly dimension, is it not the case that the short duration of financial market fluctuations undermines the potential of any counter-cyclical policy? And is it not also the case that it undermines it, not because of the supposed changes in the shape of the Phillips curve, but rather because the time span of financial market oscillations and the time lag between the start and the effects of even the most appropriate counter-cyclical policy measures are of the same length? And what if the former is of a shorter time span than the latter? (see Osiatyński 2019b, p. 54).

The question for post-Kaleckian economic theory is this: How are we to modify Kalecki's canonical profit equation, and the resulting equation of determinants of the business cycle-cum-trend, under the present-day capitalist system in such a way that this equation would bring together the factors that determine the course of business fluctuations in the real sphere of the economy with those that determine the instability of financial markets, and the feedback between the former and the latter? I do not have an answer to this question, nor even an intuition as to how Kalecki might have approached it. Towards the end of his life Kalecki wrote that he thought his investment decision function was 'the central *piéce de résistance* of economics' and that he tried to improve it all his life (see Kalecki 1968 [1991], p. 435). Needless to say, in the financial capitalism of the 2020s, this challenge becomes even more difficult.

Finally, let me draw your attention to a possible extension of Kalecki's canonical profit equation that may shed some new light on the determinants of economic growth. Let me start by recalling his profit equation and some relations that follow from it. For his stylised open economy, operating below full employment of factors of production, his profit equation takes the form:

$$P = IP + (G - T) + (EX - IM) - (YH - CP)$$
$$P = IP + D + NE - SH \tag{1}$$

where P represents profits, IP is private investment, G is government spending, T are taxes net of government subsidies to firms and households, EX is export, IM is import, YH is household income net of taxation, CP is household consumption, D is the consolidated general government deficit, NE is net export and SH represents household savings. After manipulating (1) we get:

$$SH - (IP{-}P) = D + NE$$
$$(SH + P){-}IP = D + NE \tag{2}$$

$$NPS = D + NE \tag{3}$$

where SH + P represents private saving, SP, and SP—IP represents net private savings, NPS, which by definition must be equal to the sum D + NE.

When intended private savings are greater than intended private investment, SP > IP, (and assuming equilibrium of the balance of foreign trade, NE = 0), in line with (2) the disequilibrium between intended private savings and intended private investment must be matched by a positive deficit in the general government balance, i.e., D > 0. Otherwise the ex post equilibrium between actual savings and investment would not be reached through changes in the rate of interest, the rise of which would stimulate private saving and reduce private investment, and whose fall would have the reverse effect (as stipulated by mainstream economics in both Kalecki's and our own times). Instead, the equilibrium would be reached through the income channel, i.e., when SP > IP, through reduction of output and employment, and thereby of profits and household incomes from which savings can be made.

Kalecki's key concern was about what happens when intended private investment necessary to achieve and maintain full employment is insufficient compared to intended private savings which reduce aggregate effective demand. From the point of view of a government policy-maker, Kalecki's concern may be phrased as the following question: given the balance of foreign trade, what is the volume of net public borrowing (i.e., of the primary budget deficit) necessary to secure and maintain full employment?

In line with Kalecki's argument, rising private savings, whether of worker households, or from profits, depress aggregate demand, private investment and the economic dynamics of the system. By contrast, when consumption is debt-financed, it performs a similar function to that of debt-financed government spending. This macroeconomic relationship has long been noticed and examined. However, debt-financed consumption is not the only factor that can operate in this direction to this end.

In a Kaleckian analysis, the argument is expressed in terms of *Gross Domestic Product*, which is assumed to represent disposable income, and the multiplier effects are estimated at a given proportion of private savings to GDP, sp = SP/Y, where SP represents in fact private domestic saving and by definition it is calculated as SP = IP + D + NE (see e.g., Łaski 2019, p. 58). However, NE does not represent all incomes and expenditures of the rest-of-the-world (the ROW) sector. The current account of the balance of payments includes also the balance of incomes earned by residents abroad and of incomes earned by non-residents in the host country, and the same applies to the balance of property incomes of residents and non-residents. The latter two balances add to the aggregate disposable incomes of households, the corporate sector, and the government, and therefore to their respective sectoral consumption, investment and saving. Therefore, in a stock-flow consistent Kaleckian multi-sector model, it is more appropriate to express the argument in terms of *Gross National Product* (GNP), or Gross Disposable Income. If the flow-of-funds analytical framework is used, the net balance of each sector will find its reflection in its net lending/borrowing position and the potential gap between the intended investment of non-financial corporate investment and its internal saving may be covered by the net lending of the government, the household, as well as the ROW sectors. This approach at the same time helps to shed some light on factors of total disposable income growth. Preliminary results of the enquiry presently underway by Ms. Jolanta Zięba (co-author of our early estimates of GDP multipliers in Poland and the Czech Republic, see Łaski, Osiatyński, and Zięba 2010, 2012) show that in Poland, for instance, in the last decade the gap between the intended investment of the corporate sector and its intended savings was covered not only by household deficit spending, but also by the ROW sector, and that this debt-financing to a certain extent allowed for some decline in government deficits (in relation to GNP). Our study, however, is still at an early stage.

This may prove a promising extension of Kalecki's profit equation for empirical studies. When we consider, however, on the one hand that there are obvious limits to household borrowing (since households—unlike governments—cannot and must not issue their own money to pay for their debts, and household debt can give rise to speculative credit-driven bubbles), and on the other hand that in the medium and long run the ROW balance should be in equilibrium (lest there are balance of payments crises giving rise to sovereign crises), then we see that one way or another we are back to Kalecki's canonical profit equation, and government debt financing as possibly the most important instrument of full employment policies. Therefore I conclude my contribution to this conference by leaving open for us all the question much discussed by Malcolm Sawyer and others about how to trim the financial globalisation of our times to make it serve a full employment market economy that would be liberal and social-democratic at the same time.

Disclosure Statement

No potential conflict of interest was reported by the author.

ORCID

Jerzy Osiatyński ⓘ http://orcid.org/0000-0001-5539-2556

References

Kalecki, M. 1943 [1990]. 'Political Aspects of Full Employment.' In *Collected Works of Michał Kalecki, Vol. 1*, edited by J. Osiatyński. Oxford: Clarendon Press.

Kalecki, M. 1944 [1990]. 'Three Ways to Full Employment.' In *Collected Works of Michał Kalecki, Vol. 1*, edited by J. Osiatyński. Oxford: Clarendon Press.

Kalecki, M. 1954 [1991]. 'Theory of Economic Dynamics: An Essay in Cyclical and Long-Run Changes in Capitalist Economy.' In *Collected Works of Michał Kalecki, Vol. 2*, edited by J. Osiatyński. Oxford: Clarendon Press.

Kalecki, M. 1968 [1991]. 'Trend and the Business Cycle.' In *Collected Works of Michał Kalecki, Vol. 2*, edited by J. Osiatyński. Oxford: Clarendon Press.

Łaski, K. 2019. *Lectures in Macroeconomics. A Capitalist Economy Without Unemployment*, edited by J. Osiatyński and J. Toporowski. Oxford: Oxford University Press.

Łaski, K., J. Osiatyński, and J. Zięba. 2010. 'The Government Expenditure Multiplier and its Estimates for Poland in 2006–2009.' The Vienna Institute for International Economic Studies Working Paper, No. 63.

Łaski, K., J. Osiatyński, and J. Zięba. 2012. 'Fiscal Multipliers and Factors of Growth in Poland and the Czech Republic in 2009.' National Bank of Poland Working Paper No. 117.

Minsky, H. P. 1986. *Stabilizing an Unstable Economy*. New Haven: Yale University Press.

Minsky, H. P. 1992. 'The Financial Instability Hypothesis.' Working Paper No. 74, Levy Economics Institute of Bard College.

Osiatyński, J. 2015. 'Ekonomia Michała Kaleckiego.' In M. Kalecki, *Kapitalizm – dynamika gospodarcza i pełne zatrudnienie*, edited by K. Łaski, and J. Osiatyński. Warsaw: iTON Society.

Osiatyński, J. 2019a. 'Kazimierz Laski's *Lectures in Macroeconomics* Under Financial Capitalism.' *European Journal of Economics and Economic Policies: Intervention* 16 (3): 302–317.

Osiatyński, J. 2019b. 'Spory o mikroekonomiczne podstawy makroekonomii po Kaleckim i Keynesie.' In *Metaekonomia tom II. Perspektywa makroekonomiczna*, edited by T. Kwarciński, and A. Wincewicz-Price. Krakow: Copernicus Center Press.

Steindl, J. 1952. *Maturity and Stagnation in American Capitalism*. Oxford: Basil Blackwell.

Steindl, J. 1990. *Economic Papers 1941–88*. Houndmills: Macmillan.

Debt Management and the Fiscal Balance

Jan Toporowski

ABSTRACT

This paper presents a method for integrating debt management into fiscal policy using principles derived from the work of Kalecki. It proposes dividing the government budget into a functional budget containing taxes and expenditure that may affect expenditures in the non-financial economy, and a financial budget containing taxes on wealth and higher incomes that do not affect expenditures in the real economy but do affect the liquidity of wealth portfolios. This gives the government two more or less independent instruments to manage economic growth and government debt. The respective balances between the functional and financial budgets then affect the fiscal multiplier showing how cases of expansionary fiscal contraction, contractionary fiscal expansion, expansionary financial instability, and deflationary financial instability may arise. The analysis applies to domestically financed debt.

1. Introduction

The management of government debt plays a key role in public finance. But discussion of it is, on the whole, driven by political economy considerations. On the one hand, fiscal conservatives regard any government debt as a drain on future resources and thus to be avoided. On the other hand, Keynesians tend to dismiss concerns about government borrowing by arguing that the future growth assisted by debt-financed fiscal stimulus will allow the debt to be repaid. The conservative argument may be true of foreign borrowing, and even perhaps of domestic borrowing under a gold standard, but it is certainly not true of domestic borrowing in a credit economy. The Keynesian case depends on assumptions about the fiscal multiplier that need more than just assertions that this ratio will be sufficient. Both cases need a more careful analysis of the principles and methods of government debt management and its effect on macroeconomic dynamics: the conservative case to show the resource constraints on government debt in a credit economy; and the Keynesian case to show the effective connections between government debt and the fiscal multiplier. This paper provides such an analysis of domestic debt financed using fiscal principles derived from the work of Michał Kalecki.

2. Debt management and the fiscal balance

The government's budget may be divided into a functional or effective budget, and a financial budget. The functional or primary budget contains all government expenditures in the real economy (the provision of public services, welfare payments and subsidies to economic activities) together with their financing by taxes on incomes, excluding profits and rents, and on trade in the economy. The financial budget contains, on the expenditure side, the servicing of government debt and, on the income side, taxes on wealth, including financial assets, and taxes on profits and rents:

> Fiscal budget = Functional balance + Balance of financial operations
>
> Functional budget = Government taxation of incomes and trade – Government expenditure on goods, services and welfare transfer payments
>
> Balance of financial operations = Government taxation of assets (real and financial) rents and profits – Government expenditure on debt interest

The balance of the functional, or effective, budget may be called the primary balance. But it is perhaps slightly misleading to call this balance the primary balance, since this term is normally reserved for the fiscal balance *excluding* debt servicing but including taxes on assets, profits and rents. The functional balance is more obviously the economically effective one, because it is through this balance that incomes and expenditures are affected, for example through Keynesian fiscal stimulus or fiscal deflation. The financial budget merely affects the liquidity of private sector portfolios and preferences about the composition of those portfolios, rather than macroeconomic variables such as income, expenditure and employment.

This may be illustrated by Michał Kalecki's proposal for deficit spending to maintain a high level of employment by means of a fiscal deficit, but with the annual cost of servicing government debt paid for by a wealth tax, or capital levy, or a tax on profits, with appropriate deductions for investment, equal to the servicing required in that fiscal year. These taxes will, in general, fall upon wealthy individuals. But the money will be returned to them in proportion to their holdings of government bonds.[1] If the financial budget is balanced, so that the tax to pay the cost of servicing the debt is returned to the wealthy in the form of interest payments on the bonds, then the money in the portfolios of the wealthy remains the same, and the money markets can be relied upon to redistribute this liquidity in accordance with individual preferences.

A crucial advantage of this kind of taxation is that it does not affect the incentives to invest, in the sense that the liability for a tax on wealth depends on the overall value of the portfolio of assets of the wealthy, and not on the share of industrial assets in that portfolio. In the case of the profits tax, the calculation is a little more complicated. But a deduction for business investment can be calibrated in such a way as to maintain the

---

[1] If full employment is maintained by government spending financed by borrowing, the national debt will continuously increase. This need not, however, involve any disturbances in output and employment, if the interest on the debt is financed by an annual capital tax. The current income, after payment of capital tax, of some capitalists will be lower and of some higher ... but their aggregate income will remain unaltered. (Kalecki 1943 [1990], p. 348; see also Toporowski (2020) forthcoming)

A wealth tax, or capital levy as a means of covering the debt costs of a government, has a long record of support among economists such as David Ricardo, Otto Bauer, Joseph Schumpeter, J. A. Hobson, as well as Keynes and Kalecki.

calculated profitability of particular projects.[2] Kalecki's proposal of setting the financial balance at zero therefore represents a sustainable debt position that allows the government to engage in deficit financing of its functional or effective budget, while at the same time keeping up payments on its debt with a neutral effect on the liquidity of private sector portfolios.

3. Debt management and the fiscal multiplier

Dividing up the fiscal budget into a functional budget that affects the real economy, and a financial budget that just maintains debt payments and the liquidity of the financial system overcomes the dilemma that makes fiscal policy ineffective, namely, whether the fiscal budget is to be used for macroeconomic management (the Keynesian position) or for debt management. By splitting the fiscal budget, the government can have two independent instruments that can be used to target the macro-economy and government debt, satisfying the Tinbergen Rule of an independent instrument for every target of economic policy. In this case, the targets are economic growth, using the instrument of the functional budget, and financial stability (debt management), using the instrument of the government's financial operations.

This feature of the budget arrangement can be illustrated by considering a situation in which the financial balance (of wealth taxation and financial operations) is positive and greater than the functional fiscal deficit. This is the 'expansionary fiscal contraction' that made a brief appearance in policy discussions a couple of years ago.[3] Because the financial budget is positive and its balance is greater than the functional deficit, the government has an overall surplus with which to pay off some portion of its debt, at the same time as stimulating the economy with its functional deficit. In effect, monetary resources are being transferred from rentier capitalists (who are paying more in taxes than they are receiving back in interest on government debt and repayments) to entrepreneurs who are receiving as profits the amount of the functional fiscal deficit. In effect, the liquidity of rentier capitalists is modestly reduced by the difference between the financial budget surplus (which is taxed away from rentiers), and the overall fiscal surplus that is returned to holders of government bonds in the process of paying off the national debt.[4]

(*Ex post*, of course, the overall budget cannot have an overall surplus, since any excess of total revenue over total expenditure can only be transferred to the financial account, there to buy in and cancel government debt, or to buy in other assets and, in this way, expand the balance sheet of the government. This is further discussed below.)

Somewhat more common than this 'expansionary fiscal contraction' is what may be called a 'contractionary fiscal expansion'. This may be used to describe a situation in which the financial budget of a government is in deficit, and a part of that deficit is financed by running a surplus in the functional budget. This kind of fiscal outcome typically results from considerations of 'supply-side economics', in which wealth taxes are

---

[2]Such taxes can finance a growing debt service in a way that is 'harmless in the sense that it will have no repercussions on output and employment (Kalecki 1943 [1997], p. 163).

[3]See Nuti (2015) for a summary of the controversy around the fiscal multiplier.

[4]Cf. 'capital taxation is perhaps the best way to stimulate business and reduce unemployment. It has all the merits of financing state expenditure by borrowing, but it is distinguished from borrowing by the advantage of the state not becoming indebted' (Kalecki 1937 [1990], p. 325).

deemed to act as a disincentive to business enterprise and are therefore reduced. At the same time, attempts at reducing government expenditure in the functional budget are frustrated by the overall surplus in the functional budget that reduces the overall profitability of business and thereby moves the economy into recession. Unless the surplus in the functional budget exceeds the deficit in the financial budget, the overall government budget remains in deficit, so that government debt continues to rise, with a growing financing requirement. Thus, efforts at stimulating economic growth through reduction of wealth taxation fail.

Slow growth and rising government debt are not the only consequences of such 'supply-side' policies. Since governments are contractually obliged to service their national debt, the deficit in the financial balance is in effect covered by the transfer of financial resources from the real (non-financial) economy into the portfolios of the wealthy asset-holders. The implication of a deficit in a government's financial balances is rising liquidity in the portfolios of the wealthy. This rising liquidity makes the financial system less stable, as the overall situation of slow economic growth and rising government debt keeps the wealthy on the look-out for more assured returns in other assets and currencies, no matter how delusory those returns may turn out to be.

Two further possible outcomes may be identified. One is what may be called 'expansionary financial instability', whereby the government operates with a deficit on the functional budget and a further deficit on its financial budget, so that there is an even larger overall fiscal deficit. The government would have two means of financing such an expansionary policy. One would be through monetisation of the overall deficit, using central bank credit to pay for the functional and financial deficits. The outcome of this would be rising liquidity in the financial system, and the bank accounts of big businesses that would benefit disproportionately (with higher profit margins) from the deficit spending in the functional budget. Excess liquidity would drain off into asset markets or foreign currency in the event of any alarm in the financial system, for example over growing government indebtedness or an increasing (credit) money supply.

The other means of financing the overall fiscal deficit is through increasing the circulation velocity of existing monetary resources by issuing of bills or longer-term government bonds. These transfer otherwise 'idle' balances into circulation in the real economy. However, financing a deficit by means of bill issue entails rolling over increasing quantities of governments bills. Reliance on long-term bond issues runs the risk of having to raise the interest rates on those bonds to effect the portfolio adjustment necessary to absorb the bonds. This can be avoided by means of what is called in the markets 'operation twist'—issuing short-term bills and using the proceeds to buy in long-term bonds. But this would have to be done on such a scale as to raise the price of government bonds, and thereby lower their yields. With a given bank balance sheet, it is easy to show that a government, relying on the central bank to maintain its official policy rate in the money markets, can also control the long-term rate of interest on its bonds. But the transactions involved increase the velocity of circulation of existing bank deposits.

A sale of government bonds to the public is paid for by a transfer of bank deposits held by the public to the account of the government. If this sale cannot be effected without raising the rate of interest on the bonds, then the government can issue short-term bills at or just slightly above the central bank's policy rate of interest. These will be readily bought up by banks because such bills are a liquid addition to a bank's balance sheet. Effectively, the bills are swapped for bank deposits, which the government then swaps for its own bonds in the secondary market. Given a certain preference for holding government bonds (nowadays the main influence on this preference is the regulations prescribing the amount of government bonds that institutional investorspension funds and insurance companies—must hold against their given liabilities; see Toporowski 2010), holders of financial securities will now have bank deposits to exchange for new bonds issued by the government at its preferred rate of interest.[5]

With government borrowing, the usual monetary circulation is that the government borrows bank deposits from the public, which deposits are then returned to the public in the course of government expenditure on public services and welfare payments, and payments on government debt (Toporowski 2020). With government financial operations along the yield curve, such as 'operation twist', this 'financial circulation' of money is augmented by additional exchange of the public's bank deposits for Treasury bills issued by the government, and the government's return of those bank deposits to the public in exchange for government bonds. As the price of government bonds rises, the government issues new government bonds in exchange for bank deposits, to be then returned to the public with government expenditure. Whereas simple government borrowing to finance its expenditure requires two exchanges of bank deposits (at bond issue and then at government expenditure), operations along the yield curve require at least three exchanges of bank deposits: the government acquiring bank deposits in exchange for Treasury bills; the government returning the bank deposits to the public in exchange for government bonds from the secondary market; and the government then re-acquiring the bank deposits. The same bank deposits may therefore undergo three exchanges in order to control long-term interest rates. This is in addition to the two exchanges when the government simply borrows in order to finance expenditure.

The aim of such operations is, of course, the issue of government debt at the longest possible maturity, in order to fix the rate of interest on that debt and minimise the amount of rolling over (issue of new debt to repay maturing debt) of debt. However, while the issue of long-term debt may extend the average maturity of government debt, control of the terms of that issue may require reduction of that average, through the issue of bills. In addition to reducing the average maturity of government debt, the issue of bills puts government financing at the mercy of any possible future change in short-term interest rates; hence the term used in Keynes's and Kalecki's time to describe such financing by means of bill issue as 'floating debt'.

Control of the conditions of government borrowing through operations along the yield curve or debt management was familiar to Keynes and Kalecki, who routinely commented on war finance and the debt problems of governments in inter-war Europe. However, such control has been ignored in recent monetary economics, in which debt management is reduced to the issue of government paper in the primary market.[6] Without such control, the financial markets readily become disorderly. The challenge of maintaining order in the markets is, of course, greater when both the financial and the functional budgets are operating in deficit.

---

[5]Cf. Kalecki (1944 [1990]) in which he suggests that control of long- and short-term interest rates may be achieved through the issue of bills and bonds in similar proportions.
[6]An exception here is Allen (2018). See Toporowski (2019).

A fourth outcome is the Mecca of fiscal conservatives in which the government operates an overall fiscal surplus, on both the financial and functional accounts. The fiscal
surplus reduces the overall rate of profit and drains liquidity from the non-financial
economy, resulting in recession. At the same time, the financial surplus exacerbates
the conditions of financial instability, as the government taxes wealth portfolios more
than it is obliged to pay to holders of those portfolios, at the same time as that
surplus, and the surplus on the functional account, is applied to buy in government
bonds or to buy other assets. The concentration of corporate liquidity in wealth portfolios, at the same time as risk-free government bonds or bills are becoming scarcer, also
threatens government control of interest rates: an over-issue of bonds, to maintain the
long-term rate of interest, in order to invest in short-term securities (either directly or
through the central bank), would reinforce downward pressure on short-term interest
rates.

The possible outcomes are summarised in Table 1.

Functional budget balance	Financial balance	Overall balance (ex ante)	Macroeconomic outcome
Deficit	Surplus	Surplus or balance	Expansionary fiscal contraction
Surplus	Deficit	Deficit	Contractionary fiscal expansion
Deficit	Deficit	Large deficit	Expansionary financial instability
Surplus	Surplus	Surplus	Deflationary financial instability

The analysis in this paper applies in the case of borrowing in domestic financial markets.
The situation is, of course, considerably more problematic in the case of foreign borrowing. A fundamental advantage of domestic financing of government debt, as opposed to
foreign borrowing, is that *domestic borrowing keeps financial resources within the
economy*. Domestic borrowing merely recycles (increases the circulation velocity of)
existing money stocks, redistributing them among the wealthy who hold the largest monetary stocks. It fixes government borrowing on terms that the government itself determines, through the central bank's control over domestic interest rates. At the same
time, the central bank's open market operations allow that bank to control the liquidity
of the portfolios of the wealthy, so that government bonds may be 'rolled over', limiting
payments out of the financial budget to interest payments. With such government borrowing, it is not future generations of taxpayers paying the cost of government expenditure today but future generations of taxpayers paying future generations of government
bond-holders. Servicing government debt by means of taxes on wealth and adjusted taxes
on profits means future generations of the wealthy paying future generations of the
wealthy (Toporowski 2020).

4. Conclusion

The debt management operations of the government should not be viewed in isolation
from taxes on wealth and profits. Combined with such taxation, debt management can
be an independent instrument to manage the portfolios of the wealthy in such a way
as to maintain the stability of the capital market and assure financing of fiscal deficits.

This fiscal–financial analysis suggests that economic stagnation in rich countries is not
so much a failure of Keynesianism as a sign that the wealthy do not pay their dues

towards servicing government debt and, as a result, governments' financial resources are diverted from fiscal stimulus of the real economy towards financial circulation. At the same time, the financial instability that plagues poor countries may be because government debt is insufficiently domestic and the wealthy are, as in richer countries, insufficiently taxed to pay for debt servicing. A financial budget servicing government debt from taxes on wealth and profits that do not affect incomes and expenditures in the economy allows government to manage its debts without compromising the economic goals set for fiscal policy in the functional budget.

A further conclusion from this analysis concerns the apportionment of taxes among different wealth and income classes. With rising government debt and annual debt service commitments, such a system of debt management implies that the incidence of taxation needs to be adjusted in a progressive direction to maintain the balance in the financial operations budget. If this is not done and the financial budget is in deficit, then the redistribution from taxpayers to bond-holders becomes regressive and the fiscal stance becomes contractionary, even if the overall fiscal balance is in deficit. This may be a factor in the recent differing assessments of the fiscal multiplier.

In sum, a disaggregation of the government's budget identifying a financial budget balance is critical not only for the financing of government debt but also for the effectiveness of fiscal policy. A financial budget deficit diverts expenditure from the functional budget to financial circulation. So, whether it is the functional fiscal deficit or the total amount of non-debt expenditure that determines the value of the fiscal multiplier, the effectiveness of fiscal stimulus is reduced by the deficit in the financial balance. It requires little reflection to show that 'supply-side' policies, such as reducing taxes on wealth, profits and luxury consumption, have contributed to a decline in the fiscal multiplier and the economic efficiency of government finances.

Acknowledgements

This is an extended version of 'Debt Management and the Fiscal Balance', *Policy Note* 2020/5, Levy Economics Institute of Bard College, July 2020, pp. 1–4. I am grateful to Robert Jump and Enrico Pulieri for discussion of some of the issues in this paper.

Disclosure statement

No potential conflict of interest was reported by the author.

References

Allen, W. A. 2018. *The Bank of England and the Government Debt Operations in the Gilt-Edged Markets, 1928–1972.* Cambridge: Cambridge University Press.

Kalecki, M. 1937 [1990]. 'A Theory of Commodity, Income and Capital Taxation.' In *Collected Works of Michał Kalecki Volume I Capitalism: Business Cycles and Full Employment*, edited by J. Osiatyński. Oxford: The Clarendon Press.

Kalecki, M. 1943 [1990]. 'Political Aspects of Full Employment.' In *Collected Works of Michał Kalecki Volume I Capitalism: Business Cycles and Full Employment*, edited by J. Osiatyński. Oxford: The Clarendon Press.

Kalecki, M. 1943 [1997]. 'The Burden of the National Debt.' In *Collected Works of Michał Kalecki Volume VII Studies in Applied Economics 1940-1967 Miscellanea*, edited by J. Osiatyński. Oxford: The Clarendon Press.

Kalecki, M. 1944 [1990]. 'Three Ways to Full Employment.' In *Collected Works of Michał Kalecki Volume I Capitalism: Business Cycles and Full Employment*, edited by J. Osiatyński. Oxford: The Clarendon Press.

Nuti, D. M. 2015. 'Michał Kalecki's Capitalist Dynamics from Today's Perspective.' In *Michał Kalecki in the 21st Century*, edited by J. Toporowski, and Ł Mamica. Basingstoke: Palgrave Macmillan.

Toporowski, J. 2010. 'A Theory of Capital Rationing.' *Working Paper* No. 166, Department of Economics, School of Oriental and African Studies, University of London.

Toporowski, J. 2019. 'Open Market Operations.' In *The Oxford Handbook of the Economics of Central Banking*, edited by D. G. Mayes, P. L. Siklos, and J.-E. Sturm, 436–453. Oxford: Oxford University Press.

Toporowski, J. 2020. 'The Transfer Theory of Government Debt: What Keynes Learned from Kalecki.' In *Essays in Honour of Sheila Dow*, edited by P. Hawkins, and I. Negru, forthcoming. Abingdon, UK: Routledge.

Kalecki and Marx Reconnected

Peter Kriesler ⓘ and Joseph Halevi

ABSTRACT
The paper considers the nature that Kalecki's contributions represent a significant contribution to the Marxist tradition. While we argue that the underlying method of both Marx and Kalecki — their vision of society and its dynamics — and much of their analysis is fundamentally the same, differences arise because of the development of capitalism and the different stages of society each is analysing. For Kalecki, developed capitalist economies have reached a stage of capital accumulation where the existing capital stock is sufficient to employ all the economy's labour. Associated with this is the rise of imperfectly competitive firms. The economic dynamics of capitalism have evolved as a result, with growth and employment being determined by different factors.

1. Introduction

In this paper, we examine the relationship between Kalecki and Marx in terms of their analysis of capitalist economies. In some ways, it is a sequel to a paper we published in ROPE 30 years ago, 'Kalecki, Classical Economics and the Surplus Approach'. That paper examined the relationship between Kalecki's work and that of classical economics and the surplus approach (Halevi and Kriesler 1991). In this paper, we go further by developing the analysis to consider Kalecki's relation to Marx and the contributions of some of the main classical Marxist economists, especially those associated with the Second International.

Given Kalecki's introduction to economics through the works of Rosa Luxemburg and Tugan-Baranovski, and his subsequent interest in Marxian theory, it is not surprising to find that these writers exerted an important influence on him.[1] That their influence never left him is apparent throughout his career, and in his explicit discussions of their work throughout his life. We argue that, due to this influence, Kalecki's writings maintained essentially Marxist elements, and that his work should be regarded as contributing to the Marxist legacy.

The Marxian aspect of Kalecki's analysis, however, is not universally recognised. For instance, in their influential two volume *A History of Marxian Economics 1929–1990*,

---

[1] For a discussion of Kalecki's background see Toporowski (2013). For the relationship between the works of Kalecki and Rosa Luxemburg see Harcourt and Kriesler (2014).

Howard and King (1992) provide a definitive history of Marxian economics, covering the major contributors. However, Kalecki's contributions are not considered as part of this tradition. This, we believe, has led to important problems in their version of Marxian economics. Some examples follow.

It was due to the exclusion of Kalecki that they could claim: 'Despite the fact that Marxian economists were better-equipped than mainstream theorists to deal with crisis theory, it was from the ranks of the latter that the most notable intellectual development occurred namely, Keynes's *General Theory*' (Howard and King 1992, p. xii).

Moreover, in the section on 'Marxists on Keynes', which discusses the reactions to and reviews of *The General Theory* by Marxian economists, no mention is made of Kalecki's very important review which, although it was published originally in Polish, had been translated and published in English in 1982 (Kalecki 1936). Similarly, the important contribution of Kalecki to crisis theory and his independent 'discovery' of many of the important 'Keynesian' ideas are neglected.[2] On p. 101 of volume 2, they clearly state that Kalecki is a post-Keynesian whereas Baran and Sweezy are both regarded as Marxists. Later a Kaleckian reformulation of Marxian analysis of effective demand is seen as the basis of 'an integration of Marxian and Keynesian theory' (1992, p. 105).

In the chapter on 'Monopoly Capital', despite his pioneering contributions, Kalecki is only mentioned in the conclusion as a European alternative approach (see 1992, pp. 123–124). The chapter on 'The Permanent Arms Economy' makes no mention of Kalecki's posthumously published 'Observations on the "Crucial Reform"' (Kalecki and Kowalik 1971). Similarly, there is nothing on the discussion of development, and only a brief mention in the chapter on the 'Political Economy of Socialism', despite Kalecki's significant contributions to these areas.

By contrast, if we consider the major contributors to Marxist economic analysis in the second half of the 20th century, Baran, Sweezy and Dobb all acknowledge Kalecki's Marxism as well as the importance of his contributions to Marxist economic theory. Baran and Sweezy's work on monopoly capital is a fundamental development of Marxian theory, as acknowledged by Howard and King. In *Monopoly Capital*, Baran and Sweezy's most important contribution, there is an acknowledgment to the great debt they owe to Kalecki (Baran and Sweezy [1966] 1968, p. 66).

Dobb specifically addresses the question of the relevance of Kalecki's price analysis to the labour theory of value:

> ... one might say that, while the classical Marxian explanation for the emergence of surplus-value continues to apply to modern capitalism, as to its earlier stage, the influence of monopoly enters in as an additive element in the stage of monopoly capitalism. (Dobb 1973, pp. 269–270)

While agreeing with these authors, we argue further that the underlying method of both Marx and Kalecki — their vision of society and its dynamics — and much of their analysis is fundamentally the same, with differences mainly arising because of the development of capitalism and the different stages of society each is analysing, which is the theme of the next section.[3]

---

[2]For a comparison of the ideas of Kalecki and Keynes see Kriesler (1997).
[3]Sawyer (1985) reaches similar conclusions.

2. Differences Between Marx and Kalecki

Both Marx and Kalecki understood the importance of historical development of the economic forces shaping society. As a result, changes in capitalism as it develops and evolves meant that they were looking at capitalism in different stages of that development so that the factors determining output, growth and employment at the stage of development of capitalism when Kalecki was writing were different to the factors which determined these in Marx's time.

Kalecki explicitly discusses these issues in 'Econometric model and historical materialism' (Kalecki 1965, p. 301) where he provides a summary of Marx's method:

> Historical materialism considers the process of the development of a society as that of productive forces and productive relations (the base) which shape all the other social phenomena such as government, culture, science and technology etc. (the superstructure). There is a feedback effect involved here, the superstructure influencing the base as well.

As long as productive relations and the availability of natural resources remain unchanged, the economy will not be subject to structural change, and so economics and econometrics can model society in terms of functional relationships. Kalecki's analysis of historical materialism stresses the interplay of continuity in economic relations interrupted by discontinuities brought about by changes in productive relations. Structural change brings with it new social institutions and, as 'the institutional framework of a social system is a basic element of its economic dynamics' (Kalecki 1970, p. 111), this has important implications for the analysis of economic society. In other words, Kalecki shared with Marx the view as to why economies change and, as a result, different economic systems require different economic analyses, though their general methods remain the same.

This also explains one of their important differences. The new stage of development of capitalism, since Marx's time, requires additional analysis. In particular, the level of capital accumulation with its concurrent advancement of large corporations and the monopoly element of production led to profound changes to the dynamics of employment and growth, which are reinforced by the concomitant development of the financial sector. For Kalecki, the important difference in the determination of employment and growth between the early less developed competitive stage of capitalism and the later monopoly stage is that in the latter stage, with a relative abundance of capital and with large oligopolistic firms, investment is a double-edged sword. While in the short run investment increases effective demand, which is important in reducing today's unemployment, at the same time it increases capacity and productivity, which increases the problem of generating full employment in the future. In early capitalism, in contrast, while insufficient effective demand is rarely a problem, insufficient capital is. As a result, the effect of investment is unambiguously positive in its ability to increase capacity, and by increasing the size of the capital stock, enable it to employ more workers.[4]

Kalecki is analysing a later stage of capitalism characterised by the relative abundance of capital stock and by a change in the nature of competition towards a more oligopolistic

---

[4]Kalecki (1960). Kaldor makes similar arguments in differentiating Marxian and Keynesian unemployment. See Kaldor (1960) and Kriesler (2013).

structure of industry. This means that the imperative analysed by Marx, whereby competitive pressures forced capitalists to invest in order not to lose out in the competitive struggle, was eroded. As this was no longer the case, investment became part of the capitalists' expenditure decision — and reinvestment of profits could no longer be guaranteed. As is discussed below, this is important in explaining differences between Kalecki and Marx on the nature of the realisation problem.

According to Kalecki, developed capitalist economies have reached a stage of capital accumulation where the existing capital stock is sufficient to employ all the economy's labour. Associated with this is the rise of imperfectly competitive firms. The economic dynamics of capitalism have evolved as a result, with growth and employment being determined by different factors. Unemployment is the result of unused capacity resulting from insufficient effective demand. For both Keynes and Kalecki the major problem with capitalist economies is the underutilisation of capital. The solution to the problem is to increase effective demand via some exogenous means, such as government expenditure, or exports etc. In contrast, earlier stages of capitalist development had not reached that level of capital accumulation. So, the size of the capital stock is not sufficient to employ all the labour. In other words, even if there were no excess capacity, there would not be full employment of labour. The crucial problem is the shortage of productive capacity. Although Marx argued that unemployment was also the result of the dynamics of new investment, which was intentionally designed to replace labour due to 'the labour displacing nature of technological change' (Junankar 1982, p. 77).

Two other important differences between Marx and Kalecki arise as a result of these changes in capitalism. The first relates to what is known in the literature as the realisation problem. According to Marx, after surplus value has been created in the production process, it needs to be realised through exchange — the goods need to be sold. Marx pointed to the potential for overproduction or underconsumption resulting in unsold output whose surplus value could, therefore not be realised. For Marx, this shortage in demand could only come from consumption. This is because of the dynamics under the competitive phase of capitalism which forces capitalists to invest all their surplus or lose out in the competitive struggle. As Marx famously stated: 'Accumulate, accumulate! that is Moses and the prophets' (Marx 1867, Chapter 24). However, as has been noted, the development of capitalism weakened this imperative and investment became a decision capitalists made dependent on their current economic environment amongst other factors. Consumption, by contrast, as it was mainly determined by income is a relatively stable component of demand. Volatility comes from investment. As a result, both Kalecki and Keynes highlighted a lack of investment as the main source of insufficient demand (See, for example Kalecki 1968).

The second important difference relates to the role of the reserve army of the unemployed (aka the industrial reserve army). Both Marx and Kalecki saw the vital role which unemployment served within capitalist economies — and both argued that without it, fundamental problems would arise. For Marx, the main function of the reserve army was to put downward pressure on wages, forcing them to the level of the cost of production of workers — in other words, to subsistence. For Kalecki this was not their main role as, for reasons discussed below, he denied the inverse relation between wages and profits, so reductions in wages were not conducive to the accumulation process. Rather, for

Kalecki, unemployment served the role of disciplining workers, preventing them from 'getting out of hand' and reinforcing the power and position of capitalists (Kalecki 1943).

3. Kalecki and Marxism

The definition of what is Marxism depends upon the historical period under consideration. Today Marxism is mostly an academic subset of bourgeois social disciplines. In the decades covered by Kalecki's life Marxism had a rather limited presence in academia and especially in economics. In Kalecki's times Marxism was still viewed as the analytical and also ideological framework informing the movement to change the present state of things.

In an absolutely natural and self-evident way Kalecki's intellect and ensuing contributions fall within the category of Marxism. In his life span he covered and addressed three major areas: (a) the dynamics of the capitalist economy, which means the laws of motion of the system, (b) the economics of socialist planning, not planning in general, (c) the developing economies and intermediate regimes. Reading his work, the specific historical characteristics of each system are clearly laid out something which would be rare among bourgeois economists. In this respect Kalecki is also the most important economic thinker of the 20th century since he has been the only one to have captured the three forms which, in historical sequence, define the world economic system.

The capitalist economy is analysed by Kalecki as a regime characterised by oligopolistic firms and governed by the problem of effective demand in relation to profits. He therefore takes off from where the great Marxian debates at the beginning of the 20th century were leading to. And he also addressed them (see his paper on Tugan-Baranovski and Rosa Luxemburg, Kalecki 1967) and identified critical junctures in the arguments of one of the most relevant theoretician of the Social Democratic movement in German speaking Europe, Rudolf Hilferding. Indeed, those early debates eventually flowed into the view that the capitalist economy would be dominated by cartels. That position was best developed by Hilferding who had a great influence on Lenin's conception of state monopoly capitalism and imperialism. Although Hilferding saw cartels as engaging in big battles, first national then global, for market domination, the core of his thinking was that cartels, when all accounts would be settled, were essentially stable. Production will be planned by cartels' requirements thereby eliminating the issue of disproportionalities which Hilferding saw as the main cause of crises. Even financial circulation would be regulated by cartels. Hence for Hilferding cartels bring about a stable system without crisis. Kalecki challenged Hilferding's position in an important paper published in Poland in 1932 (Kalecki 1932). There he showed that the economy is not wholly cartelised but that it may be divided into a cartelised and competitive sector. He then pointed out that the investment in cartelised sectors is more unstable due to the unused capacity that goes with a system of large corporations. He concluded that in a cartelised economy investment fluctuates more than in a competitive one. By bringing in the question of effective demand from a profit perspective Kalecki made a definite advance over the traditional divisions among Marxian analyses between crises of overproduction/underconsumption, crises of disproportionalities and crises caused by a falling rate of profits (Halevi 1992).

Kalecki's works were always historically grounded, which ought to be the hallmark of any Marxist analysis. To verify this, it is worth comparing Kalecki's writings before WW2 with those written after the war. The 1930s are seen as a trendless period with the system drifting toward war through the business upswing in Nazi Germany, see the title of his 1935 paper ('The essence of the business upswing' Kalecki 1935). Also, the issue of wages is seen in the historical context of the 1930s where the argument about wages was cast in terms of reducing them as a way to bring about an increase in employment. Here Kalecki performed a true theoretical innovation in the very centre of a Marxian analysis, which was until then based on a strict inverse relation between profits and wages. He showed that a reduction in wages would bring about an increase in unemployment. The crucial contradiction is within capital itself and it is expressed by the conflict between capacity and investment. He never believed that such a contradiction could be normally solved:

> We can see that the question, 'what causes periodic crises?' could be answered briefly: the fact that investment is not only produced, but also producing. Investment considered as expenditure is the source of prosperity, and every increase of it improves business and stimulates a further rise of investment. But at the same time every investment is an addition to capital equipment, and right from birth it competes with the older generation of this equipment. The tragedy of investment is that it causes crisis because it is useful. Doubtless many people will consider this theory paradoxical. But it is not the theory which is paradoxical, but its subject — the capitalist economy. (Kalecki 1936–37, p. 554)

In one of his last theoretical essays, published in 1968 (Kalecki 1968a), Kalecki reiterated the point that the basic conflict is between capacity and investment, since he showed that, under rather general conditions, plausible combinations of the level of the stock of capital and the degree of monopoly may engender a chronic underutilisation of equipment. In other words the economy may be stuck in a persistent form of crisis as appropriate to the regime of monopoly capital, the chief propeller of which is military spending and imperialism. Interestingly, on the issue of imperialism, Kalecki, in the posthumously published paper with Kowalik 'On the Crucial Reform' (Kalecki and Kowalik 1971) rejoined the position of the German Social democratic leader Karl Kautsky, who before WW1 argued that there was a tendency towards a form of super-imperialism through an equilibrium between the major powers that later clashed in the Great War. For Kalecki post 1945 super-imperialism is not the result of an entente between different powers but arises from the dominance acquired by the United States over the other capitalist powers after 1945.

To sum up, Kalecki's view of the world, sustained by his analysis, was that (a) the capitalist economy based on monopoly capital was stagnation prone and subject to crises and therefore required military spending and actual imperialism, (b) socialist economies had to be based on central physical planning of investment, (c) developing economies and intermediate regimes required an alliance with the socialist countries in order to carry out their reforms. He saw them squarely in the spirit of the Bandung Conference of 1955.

As was stated by the late Professor Kazimierz Łaski during the launching in London of Jan Toporowski's first volume on Kalecki's life, the new crisis of socialism in Poland killed him.

3.1. On Class Struggle

Kalecki's analyses have both implicit and explicit implications for the orientation of class struggle. Given that in a system of oligopolistic capitalism wage reductions would increase unemployment, the labour movement should not fall into the trap of that old anti-working class bourgeois idea. This position comes out clearly at the end of the theoretical section of his 1939 pamphlet *Real and Money Wages,* first published in Polish, where he stated that those who advocate wage cuts to cure unemployment are not friends of labour. Also his 1943 'Political Aspects of Full Employment' contains a labour led institutional struggle since it is affirmed that if the capitalist system could not accommodate itself to a state of full employment, it would have to be replaced by another form of social organisation. The issue of class and political relations acquired in Kalecki an explicit dimension throughout the 1950s and the 1960s in conjunction with the Cold War and the Vietnam War. This culminated in the 1971 *Kyklos* paper 'Class Struggle and the Distribution of National Income' and in the historical-theoretical-political contribution with Kowalik.

In the 1950s, Kalecki wrote two essays on the American economy, one comparing it with the pre-war period (Kalecki 1956) and one dealing with the situation of the 1950s decade (Kalecki 1955). In both it emerged that gross accumulation was expanding more than consumption demand on account of government expenditure and US trade surpluses, the latter were still prevalent in US external trade. Government expenditure financed military spending, and this absorbed the potential unemployment. A table showed how in the US the number of unemployed in the 1930s had been replaced by a very large increase in military personnel, namely, by people that otherwise would have been jobless (Kalecki 1956, p. 280). Kalecki concluded that on the whole, the American economy was stagnation prone but that it was unlikely to fall into a crisis because military expenditures held that tendency in check. In this context he pointed out that the real wages of American workers were rising at the same rate as labour productivity. This, he observed, along with the ideological role of the Press, eliminated what he termed as the lively working class radicalism of the 1930s in America. The US war against Vietnam — engendering a vast military expenditure — prompted Kalecki to analyse the role and position of big business in it (Kalecki 1967a). The fact that military Keynesianism was securing a high level of employment with wages rising with labour productivity vexed Kalecki in relation to the acceptance by the industrial working class of that state of affairs. The theme is addressed in the paper with Kowalik, which not by chance, had been sent to, and published in, the economic quarterly of the Communist Party of Italy, *Politica ed Economia.* Starting from the characterisation of the modern form of super-imperialism, Kalecki and Kowalik critically discussed the issue attempting to identify points and forces breaking the rules.

The question of how to break the rules is central also in his paper on class struggle and income distribution (Kalecki 1971). This essay can be directly connected to his *Real and Money Wages* of 1939. There non-competitive conditions transformed a reduction in wages into a further fall in demand for wage goods thereby increasing unemployment. In the 'class struggle' essay, a spectacular increase in wages will expand employment and capacity utilisation in the wage goods sector, leaving total profits unchanged but with their internal composition shifted towards the wage goods sector. Labour unions and supporting political parties in parliaments should devise fiscal and normative means to facilitate the above process. This, in essence, would amount to preventing businesses from raising prices when wage growth alters the relation between wages and productivity in workers' favour.

The theoretical novelty and importance of the 1971 essay consists in its joining Marx's schemes of reproduction with oligopolistic structures. It also showed that, whether under competition or under oligopoly, an increase in wages does not reduce profits, but brings about a change in their sectoral composition. This is an inescapable logical conclusion stemming from Marx's own model. It stands on a par with Rosa Luxemburg's, also arrived at through study of Marx's schemes, where the surplus may not find an outlet within the schemes themselves so that it will have to be realised by other means, chiefly through imperialism. Luxemburg, Kalecki, Baran, Sweezy and Magdoff represent a definite Marxist train of thought, particularly valid in the age of the large corporations. These nowadays encompass both the traditional oligopolies like those in steel, autos, etc., as well as the newest branches like computers and the wholly monopolised technological platforms that operate through them.

Kalecki's analysis of class conflict differs from that of Marx because the conditions regarding the articulation of class relations under monopoly capital are fundamentally different from those prevailing under competition. We consider classical competition, unlike neoclassical perfect competition, to be a valid representation of the conditions prevailing during most of 19th century capitalism in England, which was taken by Marx to be the representative case for the illustration of the general features of capital accumulation and distribution. Under classical competition there always exists an inverse relation between the wage rate and the rate of profits. Hence if wages rise, the share and the rate of profits fall. This approach forms the kernel of Marx's theory of the business cycle. Moreover, he applied it to the discussion of the struggle for higher wages that came up at the First Socialist International in London where Marx clashed with citizen Weston, a British trade unionist. Marx's harsh and not justified polemic against John Weston centred on the question tabled by the latter to the General Council as an item of discussion, namely, whether the material progress of the working class can be helped by wage increases. Marx's response became the booklet *Value, Price, and Profit* (Marx 1865). Weston argued that wage increases are passed onto prices and therefore they cannot help in improving the conditions of the workers. Let us now see how Marx replied to that assertion.

Weston, like Kalecki, argued in terms of increases in money wages. Marx replied by looking at wage variations in terms of labour values, that is, in terms of the quantity of labour time spend by the workers in producing commodities and by the quantity of labour time that is needed to produce the wage goods making up the workers' wages. He argued that an increase in wages is tantamount to an increase in the amount of total labour time spent in production that the workers claw back from the unpaid part of labour time. The value of commodities is determined by the relative quantities of labour time needed to produce them. Hence a rise in wages simply changes the way in which the labour time spent by the worker is distributed between wages and surplus labour. Thus for Marx an increase in money wages does not affect prices, which are determined by relative quantities of labour time bestowed in production, but only the distribution of income. According to Marx variations in wages are themselves endogenous to the cyclical process of accumulation regulated by the Reserve Army of Labor. Given that Marx took a Ricardian view about prices and competition, his conclusions logically follow. The path taken by Kalecki is different. He started from money wages and then showed that their variations may impact on prices differently according to a specific set of circumstances. In the case of a wage cut, as in the 1939 essay, if perfect competition prevailed prices would fall in the same proportion as the fall in wage costs. Hence nothing will change. However, in the more general case of a less than proportional fall in prices, real effective demand will fall and a wage cut will yield a higher level of unemployment. In the 1971 paper a 'spectacular' increase in wages will not change the level of total profits but will only shift their sectoral distribution towards the wage goods sector. The existence of unused capacity, a structural phenomenon under modern oligopolistic capitalism, will then make possible the activation of a wage and employment multiplier. Hence under modern conditions an increase in money wages leads to an improvement of the material conditions of the workers provided unions and labour parties are strong enough to prevent those increases from being whittled away through higher prices.

Kalecki's theory of the relation between variations in money wages, prices, and effective demand leads to a more dialectical view of capitalism than in Marx's own times. It must be pointed out that in 1932 Kalecki published[5] an article critical of Eugene Varga, who was the chief economist of the Communist Third International and a personal advisor to Stalin. In the wake of the Great Depression, Varga had argued that capitalism would find a way out of the crisis, since both the fall in wages brought about by mass unemployment and the fall in prices of capital goods, engendering also a fall in the organic composition of capital, would restore the rate of profit thereby uplifting capital accumulation. In the paper 'Is a "Capitalist" Overcoming of the Crisis Possible?' (Kalecki 1932a), Kalecki argued that a proportional fall in wages and prices would not have much impact upon the cost of production. By contrast, if wages decline more than prices the outcome would be an increase in unwanted inventories in the consumption goods sector. Furthermore, the rate of profit would not be increased by a decline in the prices of the capital goods, supposedly reducing the organic composition of capital. Indeed, if profits fall because output has fallen more than prices, the value of capital per unit value of output would rise thereby pushing the rate of profits downward. Thus, the system has very limited chances of finding its natural way out of the crisis, except in the case of a wartime boom.

4. Conclusion

This paper has considered some of the connections between the works of Marx and Kalecki. It has argued that they employ the same fundamental framework in examining the dynamics of capitalist economies. Differences between their analysis are the result of the development of capitalism from Marx's time. However, despite these theoretic differences, their methods are essentially the same.

---

[5]In the Polish journal, *Socialist Review*.

Acknowledgments

This paper was presented at the Poznań (Virtual) Conference on Kalecki and Kaleckian Economics September 24–26, 2020. We would like to thank the organisers Louis-Philippe Rochon, Marcin Czachor and Gracjan R. Bachurewicz for inviting us, and the participants for their comments. We would also like to thank Geoff Harcourt and Raja Junankar for their helpful suggestions.

Disclosure Statement

No potential conflict of interest was reported by the author(s).

ORCID

Peter Kriesler ⑩ http://orcid.org/0000-0003-1207-3875

References

Baran, P., and P. Sweezy. 1968 [1966]. *Monopoly Capital: An Essay on the American Economic and Social Order*. Middlesex: Pelican Books.

Dobb, M. 1973. *Theories of Value and Distribution Since Adam Smith*. Cambridge: Cambridge University Press.

Halevi, J. 1992. 'Kalecki and Modern Capitalism.' *Monthly Review* 44 (2): 42–52. Reprinted in Halevi et al. 2016: 133–140.

Halevi, J., G. Harcourt, P. Kriesler, and J. Nevile. 2016. *Post-Keynesian Essays from Down Under Vol I Essays on Keynes, Harrod and Kalecki*. Houndsmill: Palgrave Macmillan.

Halevi, J., G. Harcourt, P. Kriesler, and J. Nevile. 2016a. *Post-Keynesian Essays from Down Under Vol IV Essays on Theory*. Houndsmill: Palgrave Macmillan.

Halevi, J., and P. Kriesler. 1991. 'Kalecki, Classical Economics and the Surplus Approach.' *Review of Political Economy* 3 (1): 79–92. Reprinted in Halevi et al. 2016: 177–190.

Harcourt, G. C., and P. Kriesler. 2014. 'Michał Kalecki and Rosa Luxemburg on Marx's Schemes of Reproduction: two Incisive Interpreters of Capitalism.' In *The Legacy of Rosa Luxemburg, Oskar Lange and Michał Kalecki Volume 1*, edited by R. Bellofiore, E. Karwowska, and J. Toporowski. Houndsmill: Palgrave MacMillan. Reprinted in Halevi et al. 2016: 254–264.

Howard, M. C., and J. E. King. 1992. *A History of Marxian Economics Volume II, 1929–1990*. Princeton: Princeton University Press.

Junankar, P. N. 1982. *Marx's Economics*. Oxford: Philip Allan Publishers.

Kaldor, N. 1960. 'The Characteristics of Economic Development.' In his *Essays on Economic Stability and Growth*. London: Duckworth.

Kalecki, M. 1932. 'The Influence of Cartelization on the Business Cycle.' *Polska Gospodarcza* 13 (43): 932–933. Translated in Collected Works Volume I: 56–59.

Kalecki, M. 1932a. 'Is a "Capitalist" Overcoming of the Crisis Possible?' *Przeglad Socjalistyczny* (2): 44. Translated into English in Works Volume 1: 48–53.

Kalecki, M. 1935. 'The Essence of the Business Upswing.' *Polska Gospodarcza* (16): 1320–1324. Reprinted in Collected Works Volume 1: 188–194.

Kalecki, M. 1936. 'Some Remarks on Keynes's Theory.' *Ekonomista* (3): 18–26. Translated and published as Targetti. F and B. Kinda-Hass (1982) 'Kalecki's Review of Keynes's *General Theory*.' *Australian Economic Papers* 21 (39): 245–253. Reprinted in Collected Works Volume 1: 223–232.

Kalecki, M. 1936–37. 'A Theory of the Business Cycle.' *Review of Economic Studies* 4 (2): 77–97. Reprinted in Collected Works Volume 1: 529–584.

Kalecki, M. 1939. *Money and Real Wages*. Reprinted in English in Collected Works Volume 2: 21–50.

Kalecki, M. 1943. 'Political Aspects of Full Employment.' *The Political Quarterly* 14 (4): 322–331. Reprinted in Collected Works Volume 1: 347–356.

Kalecki, M. 1955. 'The Impact of Armaments on the Business Cycle after the Second World War.' In *Collected Works Vol 2*. 351–373.

Kalecki, M. 1956. 'The Economic Situation in the United States as Compared to the Pre-War Period.' *Ekonomista* (3): 3–13. Reprinted in Collected Works Volume 7: 279–286.

Kalecki, M. 1960. 'Unemployment in Underdeveloped Countries.' *Indian Journal of Labour Economics* 3 (2): 59–61. Reprinted in Collected Works Volume 5: 3–5.

Kalecki, M. 1965. 'Econometric Model and Historical Materialism.' In *On Political Economy and Econometrics: Essays in Honour of Oskar Lange*, edited by S. Stuart. Oxford: Pergamon Press. Reprinted in Collected Works Volume 7: 301–307.

Kalecki, M. 1967. 'The Problem of Effective Demand with Tugan-Baranovsky and Rosa Luxemburg.' *Ekonomista* (2): 241–249. Reprinted in Collected Works, vol. 2: 451–458.

Kalecki, M. 1967a. 'Vietnam and US Big Business.' *Polityka* 11. Reprinted in Collected Works Volume 7. 292–297.

Kalecki, M. 1968. 'The Marxian Equations of Reproduction and Modern Economics.' *Social Science Information* 7 (6): 73–79. Reprinted in Collected Works, Volume 2: 459–466.

Kalecki, M. 1968a. 'Trend and Business Cycles Reconsidered.' *The Economic Journal* 78 (310): 263–276. Reprinted in Collected Works Volume 2: 191–202.

Kalecki, M. 1970. 'Theories of Growth in Different Social Systems.' *Scientia; Rivista Di Scienza* (105): 1–6. Reprinted in Collected Works Volume 4: 111–117.

Kalecki, M. 1971. 'Class Struggle and Distribution of National Income.' *Kyklos* 24 (1): 1–9. Reprinted in Collected Works Volume 2: 96–103.

Kalecki, M., and T. Kowalik. 1971. 'Observations on the "Crucial Reform".' *Politica ed Economia* (2–3): 190–196. Reprinted in Collected Works Volume 2: 467–476.

Kriesler, P. 1997. 'Keynes, Kalecki *and The General Theory*.' In *A 'Second Edition' of The General Theory Volume 2*, edited by G. C. Harcourt and P. A. Riach. London: Routledge. Reprinted in Halevi et al 2016: 81–104.

Kriesler, P. 2013. 'Post-Keynesian Perspectives on Economic Development and Growth.' In *Oxford Handbook of Post-Keynesian Economics Volume 1: Theory and Origins*, edited by G. C. Harcourt and P. Kriesler. Oxford: Oxford University Press.

Marx, K. 1865. *Value, Price, and Profit*. https://www.marxists.org/archive/marx/works/download/pdf/value-price-profit.pdf.

Marx, K. 1867. *Capital Volume, 1*. Chapter 24 available online: https://www.marxists.org/archive/marx/works/1867-c1/ch24.htm.

Osiatynski, J., ed. 1990. *Collected Works of Michał Kalecki Volume 1 Capitalism: Business Cycles and Full Employment*. Oxford: Clarendon Press.

Osiatynski, J., ed. 1991. *Collected Works of Michał Kalecki Volume 2 Capitalism: Economic Dynamics*. Oxford: Clarendon Press.

Osiatynski, J., ed. 1993. *Collected Works of Michał Kalecki Volume 4 Socialism: Economic Growth and Efficiency of Investment*. Oxford: Clarendon Press.

Osiatynski, J., ed. 1993a. *Collected Works of Michał Kalecki, Volume 5 Developing Economies*. Oxford: Clarendon Press.

Osiatynski, J., ed. 1997. *Collected Works of Michał Kalecki Volume 7 Studies in Applied Economics 1940-1967 Miscellanea*. Oxford: Clarendon Press.

Sawyer, M. 1985. *The Economics of Michał Kalecki*. London: Macmillan.

Toporowski, J. 2013. *Michał Kalecki: An Intellectual Biography Volume 1: Rendezvous in Cambridge 1899-1939*. London: Palgrave Macmillan.

Personal Income Distribution and Progressive Taxation in a Neo-Kaleckian Model: Insights from the Italian Case

Maria Cristina Barbieri Góes ⓘ

ABSTRACT
This paper develops a stylized short-run neo-Kaleckian model incorporating personal income inequality and income taxes. The main goal is to investigate how changes in income taxes and personal income distribution affect output growth. The theoretical discussion of the stylized model is then empirically assessed using data for Italy retrieved from the Survey of Household Income and Wealth published by the Bank of Italy. The empirical analysis confirms both the heterogeneity of the propensities to consume of Italian households and the dominance of absolute income effects in the Italian consumer behavior that assures the negative trade-off between inequality and aggregate demand. More specifically, it is shown that, overall, Italians are still income constrained, not allowing for a compensation of the demand-depressing effects of raising inequality via debt and wealth-based consumption. Likewise, it is argued that decreasing personal income inequality via progressive income tax reforms would have positive effects on aggregate demand, utilization, and growth.

1. Introduction

Topics related to income distribution and growth have emerged both in the media and in academia since the Great Recession. From then on, several important events shaped the path of the political and economic debate. Even mainstream strands in economics brought topics related to financial instability, inequality, taxation, and stagnation back to the center of discussions, albeit lacking realism in their methodology and consistency on the theoretical ground.

Considering heterodox strands, more specifically the post-Keynesian research agenda, we can argue that the topic of distribution and growth is no novelty, being inclusively one of its commonalities among different strands (Lavoie 2014, p. 36). Increasing discrepancies within wages and the rising inequality (particularly in Western developed countries) pushed for the incorporation of personal income distribution in Kaleckian models. Despite these amendments, the explicit inclusion of interpersonal inequality with heterogeneous propensities to consume has yet not been discussed within a post or neo-

Kaleckian macro model framework. In addition, the connection between the personal dimension of inequality and taxation has also not been made yet.

In line with this gap in the post-Keynesian literature, the first goal of this paper is to develop a stylized neo-Kaleckian model incorporating personal income inequality and income taxes. Accordingly, it seeks to investigate how changes in income taxes and personal income distribution affect output growth in the stylized model. Since it is assumed that the result of the model depends on the behavior of the propensities to consume by quintiles as well as on the dominance of absolute income effects after redistribution, the second research goal of this work is to investigate the relationship between rising interpersonal income inequality and aggregate consumption.

Section 2 presents a brief literature review of post-Keynesian growth models, shortly discussing the incorporation of personal income inequality and reviewing the integration of taxation in these models. Section 3 proposes an extension of the neo-Kaleckian model developed by You and Dutt (1996) which includes both personal income inequality as well as income taxation. Section 4 empirically assesses inequality, consumption patterns, as well as debt and wealth-based consumption in Italy. Finally, Section 5 assesses the results of the stylized model in light of the country case study of Italy presented in Section 4, summarizing the main findings and drawing some policy implications.

2. Growth Models, Personal Income Inequality, and Taxation

2.1. Personal Income Inequality

The most important feature of neo-Kaleckian models, pioneered by Rowthorn (1981) and Dutt (1984, 1987), is that within a private closed economy, aggregate demand, capital accumulation, and growth are wage-led. In this regard, a redistribution towards wages would have a positive impact on capacity utilization, capital accumulation, and (assuming away saving out of wages) also on the rate of profit. The second generation of Kaleckian models, proposed by Bhaduri and Marglin (1990) and Kurz (1990), advocated for the incorporation of the profit-share in the investment equation, giving rise to the distinction between wage or profit-led demand and growth regimes.[1]

The labor-capital conflict of the 1970s shaped the political economy and inspired the research agenda of post-Keynesian economics, motivating the rise of both neo and post-Kaleckian models, which (until recently) were centered on functional income distribution (Palley 2016). However, these models were not restricted to the dichotomies between wages and profits and capitalists and workers. Trends related to the dominance of finance starting in the late 1970s, such as increasing discrepancies within wages, rising inequality (particularly in Western developed countries), and, more recently, the extreme rise in top income and wealth shares (Piketty and Saez 2003; 2007), have pushed for the incorporation of several amendments into Kaleckian models.

One example is the inclusion of a distinction between industrial and financial capitalists. A pioneering attempt was done by Dutt (1989, 1992), adopting a three classes model framework with workers, that receive wages, capitalists, that receive profits, and rentiers, that receive interest income. Lavoie (1995) also proposed the incorporation of monetary

---

[1] A similar result had been reached by Blecker (1989) extending the canonical neo-Kaleckian model by an external sector.

variables into a Minsky-Steindl model with real interest rates as an exogenous distributive variable. More recently, Hein (2006, 2007) constructed an augmented version of Lavoie's 'Minsky–Steindl' model, which explicitly introduces the effects of debt and debt payments as well as interest rate variations both on short and long-run equilibria. The impact of rentiers' class has also been empirically assessed. Onaran, Stockhammer, and Grafl (2011) make a distinction between rentier and non-rentier profit shares using US data (1962–2007). Hein and Schoder (2011) estimate the propensity to save out of rentiers' and wage income for the US and Germany (1960–2007).

Another example is the incorporation of different types of workers (i.e. supervised and non-supervised). A distinction between overhead labor and variable labor already appears in Rowthorn (1981) and later is followed up by Lavoie (1995, 1996). More recent models have done so by including a class of managers that affect the behavior of the firm and its growth path (see Lavoie 2009; Dutt 2012; Palley 2015; Tavani and Vasudevan 2014). Palley (2014), for instance, includes the management class combining managers and capitalists in one single group, leading to a two-class model in which the top-income group receives both wage and capital income. More recently, Dutt (2016) developed a model with the type of dual distinction used by Palley (2014) also including financiers (following the literature on financialization) and placing them on the top-income group.

Other revisions in Kaleckian growth models integrate the phenomenon of increasing wage dispersion. Carvalho and Rezai (2016) derive the aggregate savings function using a Pareto distribution of wages as a measure of wage inequality in a strictly positive relation to savings out of wages. They argue that '[l]owering wage income inequality always increases aggregate demand due to the paradox of thrift' (Carvalho and Rezai 2016, p. 501). However, Prante (2018) points out that this relation might not always hold. A good example where the strictly positive relation between wage dispersion and savings does not hold could be illustrated by the empirical puzzle arising in the Anglo-Saxon world, where top income shares have increased the most (Atkinson, Piketty, and Saez 2011) especially due to a significant and rising wage dispersion that was accompanied by increasing consumption and decreasing savings.

Finally, considering this empirical puzzle that was closely related to the turmoil of 2007, several further attempts have been made to explain this counter-intuitive trend of rising inequality and increasing consumption. In this regard, some works have been devoted to the incorporation of wealth and debt-based consumption that compensate for the lack of demand arising from the increasing inequality in the US American case (Cynamon and Fazzari 2008 and 2013; Zezza 2008; Barba and Pivetti 2009; Palley 2012, chap. 3; and Van Treeck and Sturn 2012 and 2013). The concept of interdependent social norms of Veblen (1899) and Duesenberry (1959) was also revived and incorporated[2] (see Belabed, Theobald, and van Treeck 2013; Detzer 2016; Kapeller and Schütz 2014; Kapeller and Schütz 2015; Setterfield and Kim 2016; Zezza 2008).

The interconnectedness of the functional and personal dimensions of inequality has also been modeled by Dafermos and Papatheodorou (2015) using a stock-flow consistent

---

[2]The incorporation of the concept of 'expenditure cascades' is modeled by Frank, Levine, and Dijk (2014). For a case study on Germany and the US tracking the relation between inequality and demand and the possible presence of relative income effects and expenditure cascades see Prante (2018).

approach. The authors argue that not only the two aspects of inequality are linked but they both interact with the macroeconomic dynamics through two main stages. First, the factor income shares influence not only consumption due to the different propensities to consume out of each income factor but also investment (through the profitability and utilization rate channels). In turn, the interpersonal distribution also impacts consumption expenditures since factor income is distributed to households with different propensities to consume, as it has been highlighted by some of the amendments revised previously. In this regard, it is possible to argue that splitting income into factors would end up ignoring the dispersion within these factors. Second, the authors point out that economic activity itself affects the bargaining power of workers and the ability of firms to set prices, impacting, in turn, the primary distribution of income and thus the overall interpersonal distribution of income.

In this sense, it is possible to argue that despite these amendments that circumscribe part of the dispersion within factor income, the explicit inclusion of interpersonal inequality with the help of more income groups with heterogeneous propensities to consume could be more efficient to target this issue. Accordingly, Section 3 includes personal inequality as the key distribution feature through heterogeneous propensities to consume out of each income stratum (quintile) in the model. Functional income distribution is only empirically assessed in Section 4.1, focusing on the Italian case tracing a parallel with trends in the personal dimension of inequality.

2.2. Taxation

While the theory on fiscal policy has been more related to the Keynesian tradition, the theory on taxation is based on the works of Kalecki, mainly inspired by his 1937 article (Laramie and Mair 2000). Hence, the main feature of heterodox theory on taxation is the distinction between taxes on labor and on capital and their implications for the determination of output. Several post-Keynesian authors have extended the Kaleckian theory of taxation taking into account the possibility that a shift in taxation may imply a regime shift from wage to profit-led (Blecker 2002; Laramie 1991; Laramie and Mair 1996).

More recently, Obst, Onaran, and Nikolaidi (2017, p. 11) evaluated the effects of progressive tax reforms on growth in a post-Kaleckian model in which a more progressive tax system is characterized by 'taxes on capital increasing while those on labor decreasing'. The authors estimate the effects of government expenditure and taxes (including taxes on labor, capital, and consumption as well as government expenditure) on income distribution and demand. They apply a multi-country model with a Europe-wide multiplier which incorporates the government sector within an open economy context showing that 'a redistributive policy of a 1 per cent point fall in ITR on labour income and a simultaneous 1 per cent point increase in ITR on capital income leads to an increase in EU15 GDP of 1.43 per cent' (Obst, Onaran, and Nikolaidi 2017, p. 32). In addition, they estimate the impact of a combined policy mix (wage policy, public spending, and progressive taxation), finding even stronger GDP growth effects.

Summarizing, all the amendments done within post-Keynesian models include a distinction between taxes on labor and on capital. The existing literature lacks a model including personal income inequality and income taxation impacting the different income strata which allows to analyze the recent trends, namely the fundamental increase in wage dispersion and the significant rise in overall income inequality. In this sense Kaleckian models lag somewhat behind compared to a vast literature that emerged after the publication of "Capital in the XXI Century" (Piketty 2014) and Piketty's extensive work on taxation, in particularly "*Pour une révolution fiscale*"[3] co-authored by Camille Landais and Emmanuel Saez.

From a political and strategic spectrum, we can argue that the sole argument of taxing capital over labor might be unwise since it would require not only unrealistic political will but also power from central governments, that have been gradually losing space since the 1980s. Therefore, despite being desirable and appropriate in terms of growth, focusing only on taxing capital might be a hard task to begin with, as already admitted by Kalecki (1937) himself. In this sense, policies that first strengthen labor, such as increasing their bargaining power and progressive general income taxes, could be more strategical to begin with.

Consequently, we propose to focus on income taxes and personal income inequality, also seeking to fulfill the present gap in the post-Keynesian literature. The next section is dedicated to the incorporation of both interpersonal income inequality as well as income taxation in a neo-Kaleckian model framework and to discuss the implications of income distribution and taxation for output and growth.

3. A Stylized neo-Kaleckian Model with Personal Income Inequality and Income Taxes

Following the short-run model presented by You and Dutt (1996) it is assumed that the capital stock and government expenditures are exogenously given and that the equilibrium in the goods market is due to variations in the capacity utilization rate (u) via changes in the output level (Y), since the capital stock (K) is given in the short run and depreciation is assumed away. Let us consider a closed economy where there is no labor supply constraint and firms operate below full capacity.

Following the Keynesian tradition, the aggregate consumption function can be formalized as follows:

$$C = \left(\sum_i c_i(1 - t_i)y_i \right) Y , \ i = 1, \ldots, 5 \tag{1}$$

where c_i is the propensity to consume out of disposable income of each income quintile. The income share of each quintile is represented by y_i, t_i is the income tax rate that impacts the respective quintile, and Y represents the total output.

We adopt the neo-Kaleckian investment equation without profit-share. This simplification can be justified by the empirical studies that find almost in totality that domestic demand is wage-led. Furthermore, according to the recent study by Onaran and Galanis (2012), Italy can be qualified as wage-led for both domestic and total demand.

---

[3] In the book, Landais, Piketty, and Saez (2011) argue that there is a significant space for the increase in the progressivity of the French income tax system.

Accordingly, investment is determined by animal spirits (α_o) and the level of capacity utilization ($u = Y/K$), which reflects the reaction of investment to changes in demand.

$$I = (\alpha_0 + \alpha_1 u)K \tag{2}$$

Real government expenditure (G) is constant and represented as a portion (γ) of the capital stock (K).

$$G = \bar{G} = \gamma K \tag{3}$$

The goods market equilibrium in the short run with government sector in the closed economy is given by:

$$Y = C + I + G \tag{4}$$

Plugging (1), (2), and (3) into equation (4) we have:

$$Y = \left(\sum_i c_i(1 - t_i)y_i \right) Y + (\alpha_0 + \alpha_1 u)K + \gamma K \tag{5}$$

Normalizing equation (5) by K and solving it for u, we obtain the short-run equilibrium rate of capacity utilization:

$$u^* = \frac{\alpha_0 + \gamma}{1 - \sum_i c_i(1 - t_i)y_i - \alpha_1} \tag{6}$$

Since the rate of capital accumulation in the short run ($g = I/K$) is determined by the rate of capacity utilization, we obtain its short-run equilibrium:

$$g^* = \alpha_0 + \alpha_1 u^* \tag{7}$$

The analysis of the stability condition of the model is a bit more complex than in the canonical neo-Kaleckian model without taxes but can be formalized as follows:

$$\sum_i (1 - c_i)(1 - t_i)y_i > \alpha_1 \tag{8}$$

For the adjustment process to be stable, the savings rate of after-tax income has to be more responsive to shifts in capacity utilization than investment.

Finally, the shifts in the short-run equilibrium can be analyzed through the comparative statics of equation (6) with respect to changes in exogenous variables.

$$\frac{\partial u^*}{\partial \gamma} = \frac{\partial u^*}{\partial \alpha_0} = \frac{1}{1 - \sum_i c_i(1 - t_i)y_i - \alpha_1} > 0 \tag{9}$$

If the stability condition is assumed, an increase in animal spirits (α_0) and/or in government expenditure (γ) would imply an increase in the equilibrium capacity utilization (u), hence on capital accumulation and growth.

$$\frac{\partial u^*}{\partial t_i} = -\frac{(\alpha_0 + \gamma) \sum_i c_i y_i}{\left(1 - \sum_i c_i(1 - t_i)y_i - \alpha_1\right)^2} < 0 \tag{10}$$

In turn, the signal of the partial derivative of u with respect to t_i is always negative, as shown in equation (10) above. Accordingly, we can argue that increasing the tax rate on all of the income quintiles has an overall negative effect on utilization and, subsequently, on the rate of capital accumulation.

Solving the partial derivatives of u with respect to each of the income tax rates that impact each quintile separately, we have that the size of the negative (or positive in case of reduction of the tax rate) impact is ultimately determined by the expression $c_i y_i$, as shown in (11), (12), (13), (14), and (15) below. In other words, the impact of a shift in the tax rate that affects each quintile in terms of utilization and capital accumulation is stronger, the bigger the product of the propensity to consume and the income share of this quintile.

$$\frac{\partial u^*}{\partial t_1} = -\frac{(\alpha_0 + \gamma)(c_1 y_1)}{\left(1 - \sum_i c_i(1 - t_i)y_i - \alpha_1\right)^2} < 0 \tag{11}$$

$$\frac{\partial u^*}{\partial t_2} = -\frac{(\alpha_0 + \gamma)(c_2 y_2)}{\left(1 - \sum_i c_i(1 - t_i)y_i - \alpha_1\right)^2} < 0 \tag{12}$$

$$\frac{\partial u^*}{\partial t_3} = -\frac{(\alpha_0 + \gamma)(c_3 y_3)}{\left(1 - \sum_i c_i(1 - t_i)y_i - \alpha_1\right)^2} < 0 \tag{13}$$

$$\frac{\partial u^*}{\partial t_4} = -\frac{(\alpha_0 + \gamma)(c_4 y_4)}{\left(1 - \sum_i c_i(1 - t_i)y_i - \alpha_1\right)^2} < 0 \tag{14}$$

$$\frac{\partial u^*}{\partial t_5} = -\frac{(\alpha_0 + \gamma)(c_5 y_5)}{\left(1 - \sum_i c_i(1 - t_i)y_i - \alpha_1\right)^2} < 0 \tag{15}$$

Assuming that $c_1 > c_2 > c_3 > c_4 > c_5$ and that these propensities to consume of each quintile do not shift with shifts in income distribution, there would be a dominance of absolute income effects. A redistribution policy through progressive tax reform[4] would have then an overall positive impact and increase consumption at the aggregate level, which would lead to an increase in the output through the capacity utilization (Lavoie 2010) and a subsequent increase in the rate of capital accumulation (which is a function of the rate of utilization), as illustrated in Figure 1. The impact of a such a tax reform can be easily estimated by calculating the separate effects on each of the quintiles as shown in expressions (11), (12), (13), (14), and (15) and by summing up the partial effects on utilization coming from tax shifts. Since we assume here that the propensities to consume are a decreasing function of the income level, it is clear that even with a significantly higher income share at the top, the negative impact of increasing the tax rate at the top could be overcompensated by a decrease in the tax rates in the lower quintiles. Moreover, due to the increase in the aggregate propensity to consume, the size of the multiplier would increase, enhancing the effect of an increase in animal spirits (α_0) and government expenditure (γ).

Therefore, the result of the model after both tax reforms affecting income distribution as well as shifts in income distribution coming from other sources becomes an empirical issue. Ultimately, the adjustment of output and hence capacity utilization towards demand in each period depends on the type of relation between shifts in the

---

[4]A progressive income tax reform can be done in different ways: i. increasing tax rates on higher-income earners; ii. decreasing tax rates on low-income earners; iii. adding more tranches; or iv. introducing a higher threshold for tax breaks at the bottom of the distribution.

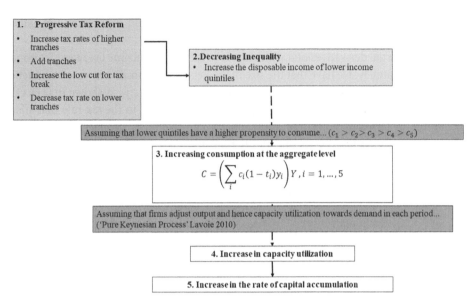

Figure 1. The effects of progressive tax reforms on inequality, utilization, and growth. Source: Author's elaboration.

disposable income of each income stratum (overall inequality) and aggregate consumption. The specific case of Italy concerning inequality and consumption patterns developed in the country are assessed in Section 4.

4. Inequality and consumption patterns in Italy

This section discusses inequality and consumption patterns in Italy[5] to evaluate the behavior of the propensities to consume by quintiles. Section 4.1 discusses recent trends in income inequality. Section 4.2 presents a brief overview drawing some conclusions concerning the shifts in aggregate demand, inequality, and consumer behavior for the years of 1989 and 2014 according to the Italian SHIW. Finally, Section 4.3 analyzes some stylized facts on household consumption and financial behavior, taking into consideration the trends in household debt and wealth.

4.1. Income Inequality Trends in Italy

While in the US the adjusted wage-share decreased around 3.3 percentage points between 1980 and 2017, accompanied by a strong wage concentration at the top culminating in extreme increases in top income shares, in Italy the 7.2 percentage point fall in the adjusted wage share[6] (Figure 2) did not imply a comparable rise in top income shares (Figures 3 and 4). Other European countries (Germany, France, and Spain) presented

---

[5]The choice for the empirical analysis of Italy is justified both by its dissonance in terms of post-crisis recovery as well as by the free availability of the Italian Survey on Household Income and Wealth (SHIW henceforth), which is the only European survey containing data on wealth, consumption, income, and demographic characteristics for every wave. The survey provides information for heads of households, which are defined as a group of individuals related by blood, marriage, or adoption and that share the same dwelling.

[6]For a more in-depth overview of the decline in the wage share in Italy see Stirati (2011). For an overview of the channels which contributed to slow growth and real wages stagnation in Italy see Levrero and Stirati (2005), according to which

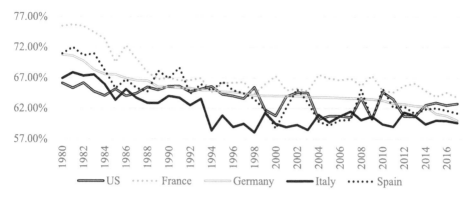

Figure 2. Adjusted wage share as a percentage of GDP at current factor cost in the US, France, Germany, Italy, and Spain (1980–2017). Source: Author's representation, AMECO (2020).

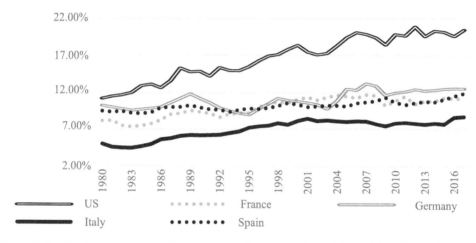

Figure 3. Top 1% income share in the US, France, Germany, Italy, and Spain (1980–2017). Source: Author's representation, WID (2020).

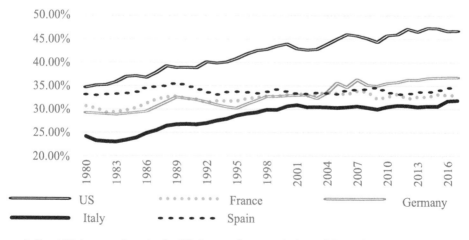

Figure 4. Top 10% income share in the US, France, Germany, Italy, and Spain (1980–2017). Source: Author's representation, WID (2020).

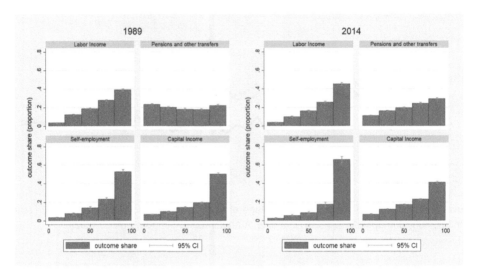

Figure 5. Density histograms: by income types ordered by income quintile in Italy (1989–2014). Source: Author's calculation, SHIW – Bank of Italy (2020).

a stronger decrease, but the level of the wage share in Italy still remains the lowest among the selected European counterparts and the US.

This discrepancy between the US American pattern and the Italian one might have its roots in the peculiar evolution of the distribution of earnings in Italy. Observing the density histograms (Figure 5) of the different income types ordered by income quintiles it is worth stressing a very strong increase in inequality within income from self-employment and individual businesses, a less pronounced increase in the inequality within income from wages, a counter-intuitive increase in inequality within income from pensions and other transfers,[7] and a reduction in inequality within capital income.

Besides explaining the peculiarity of the Italian case, these movements also explain why, despite contributing to the rise in overall inequality measured by the Gini index, the shift away from wages did not always materialize in an increase in the personal dimension of inequality (as illustrated in Figure 6). Simultaneously to the significant increase in the overall level of inequality measured by the Gini as well as the Palma Ratio[8] after the crisis of 1991[9] until 1998, it is possible to verify that the wage share has indeed changed in the opposite direction. However, during the period between 2008–12, we either observe a

---

the redistribution of profits from manufacturing to the service sector (through relative prices mechanisms) contributed to the stagnation of real wages.

[7]This counter-intuitive increase in inequality within income from pensions and other transfers between 1989 and 2014 can be explained by a policy shift particularly related to the 1992 pension reform ('Riforma Amato'). Whereas before 1992 a wage-based system prevailed, afterwards a contribution-based system came to place. For an in-depth review of the inequality profiles that emerged as a consequence of the reforms in the Italian pension system in the last decades see Jessoula and Raitano (2020).

[8]The Palma Ratio is calculated as the share of all income received by the 10 per cent households with highest disposable income divided by the share of all income received by the 40 per cent households with the lowest disposable income.

[9]The crisis initiated in 1991 has its roots in structural and institutional changes related to both economic and political factors. Since then, the Italian economy has begun to experience a long period of decline. In the political sphere, it is possible to highlight the shifts that occurred in the occasion of the corruption scandal that condemned a significant number of Italian politicians in the operation 'Mani pulite' (Clean hands). In the economic sphere, the signature of the Maastricht Treaty in 1992 prevented the possibility of adopting discretionary policies that both boosted the already existing disparities between the member countries and complicated the absorption of shocks, such as the strong devaluation of the Italian Lira. This period was followed by a strong wave of liberalization and flexibilization of the labor

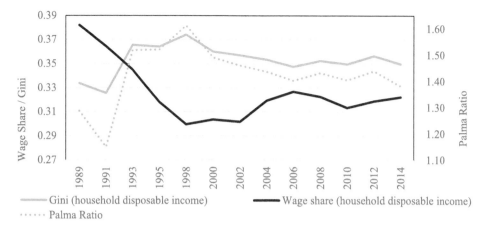

Figure 6. Personal income distribution measured by the Gini and Palma Ratio versus the Wage Share of Italian households to disposable income (1989–2014). Source: Author's calculation, SHIW – Bank of Italy (2020).

decrease in the wage share accompanied by a decrease in the Gini and the Palma Ratio (2008–10), or a positive variation of the Gini concomitant with an increase in the wage share (2010–2).

The period of apparent inversion in the trade-off between the Gini and the Palma Ratio can be explained by the fall in unemployment that was mostly related to precarious jobs, changing the 'economic position of wage earners' (Barba 2013, p. 278). This is clear if we analyze the income percentage shares in households' disposable income by quintiles (Table 1), where it is possible to see that wages have moved to the bottom of the income distribution. Notwithstanding, the substitution of well-paid and protected labor force by precarious labor 'could not fail to translate into a substantial reduction in the wage share' (Barba 2013, p. 279).

4.2. Income Inequality and the Propensity to Consume: A Micro-data Analysis of the Italian Shiws of 1989 and 2014

In order to make an empirical assessment on how consumption, particularly the average propensity to consume (APC henceforth), is impacted by changes in income distribution and to verify if the APC is homogeneous or not across the income distribution, this section relies on data from the Italian SHIW drawing a comparison between the survey from 1989 and the survey from 2014.

The main inference that can be made is that there was clear increase in personal income inequality, measured by the Gini index[10] as well as by the Palma, and the S80/S20 ratios, accompanied by a decrease in the aggregate APC[11] (as illustrated in Table 2).

If we compare the results of 1989 to the last survey of 2014, we can observe that the first three income quintiles lost disposable income shares (Table 3). The first income

---

market that culminated in rising levels of inequality, job precarization and decline in the wage share (Tridico 2015, p. 166).

[10]The income unit to which the calculation refers to here is the household.

[11]The APC is calculated dividing mean consumption by mean disposable income from each year analyzed.

Table 1. Income shares in households' disposable income by quintiles and income type (1989–2014).

	1st Quintile		2nd Quintile		3rd Quintile		4th Quintile		5th Quintile	
	1989	2014	1989	2014	1989	2014	1989	2014	1989	2014
Labor	16.8%	25.0%	41.6%	35.9%	46.2%	35.5%	45.6%	31.2%	33.9%	31.4%
Pensions and other transfers	58.9%	46.6%	31.5%	33.8%	19.8%	30.7%	12.9%	28.4%	8.7%	19.0%
Self-employment and individual businesses	5.1%	4.7%	10.4%	6.9%	13.8%	5.2%	18.2%	9.0%	24.1%	16.2%
Capital	19.2%	23.7%	16.6%	23.5%	20.2%	28.5%	23.3%	31.4%	33.2%	33.5%
Total	100%	100%	100%	100%	100%	100%	100%	100%	100%	100%
Share in total disposable income	7.2%	6.3%	12.1%	12.0%	16.8%	16.6%	23.4%	23.8%	40.5%	41.3%

Source: Author's calculation, SHIW – Bank of Italy (2020).

Table 2. Basic features of the Italian SHIWs of 1989 and 2014.

	1989	2014
Sample	8,269.00	8,151.00
Mean Income	16,807.36	30,570.10
APC	0.76	0.74
Gini	0.33	0.35
Palma Ratio	1.29	1.38
S80/S20 Ratio	5.65	6.52

Source: Author's calculation, SHIW – Bank of Italy (2020).

Table 3. Italian households' average propensities to consume and income shares in total disposable income by quintile (1989–2014).

	1st Quintile		2nd Quintile		3rd Quintile		4th Quintile		5th Quintile	
	1989	2014	1989	2014	1989	2014	1989	2014	1989	2014
Share	7.2%	6.4%	12.2%	12.0%	16.8%	16.6%	23.4%	23.8%	40.5%	41.4%
Δ in %		−11.5%		−1.6%		−1.2%		1.7%		2.1%
Δ in p.p.		−0.8		−0.2		−0.2		0.4		0.9
APC	0.9	1.1	0.9	0.9	0.9	0.8	0.8	0.7	0.7	0.6
Δ in %		21.4%		1.7%		−6.2%		−5.9%		−6.7%

Source: Author's calculation, SHIW – Bank of Italy (2020).

quintile was the one that presented the most significant change. In 1989 its income share was of the magnitude of 7.2 per cent and in 2014 it accounted for 6.4 per cent, registering a loss of 11.5 per cent (−0.8 p.p.) in the period. The second quintile, which had a share of 12.1 per cent in 1989, went slightingly down to 12 per cent (−0.1 p.p.). The third quintile also experienced a mild reduction going from 16.8 per cent to 16.6 per cent (−0.2 p.p.). The fourth and fifth quintiles presented a small increase in their income shares going from 23.4 per cent to 23.8 per cent (+0.4 p.p.) and from 40.5 per cent to 41.3 per cent (+0.9 p.p.) respectively.

Summarizing, the quintiles with the highest propensities to consume lost shares, while the two top quintiles with lower propensities to consume gained shares. Doing a simple arithmetic exercise, it is already possible to conclude that, in this case, the increase in top quintiles' shares with respect to the bottom ones negatively impacted the total APC, proving the dominance of absolute income effects.

In order to better understand the sources of increase in the total Gini index from the first survey to the last one, it is interesting to make an analysis of the decomposition of this index (Table 4) based on the division of the sample into quintiles. In doing so, we can verify to which extent such an increase was caused by an increase in the inequality within (G_h) and between the groups (G_e) that compose the generalized entropy index as well as how the Gini of each quintile evolved. The idea is to capture how income inequality within and between quintiles and the change of the share of each quintile is related to the changes in the aggregate APC $(\sum_i^y *c_i)$ as well as in the APC of each income group (c_i).

In this regard, it is possible to point out that both inequalities within and between the groups have contributed to the general rise in inequality. Another interesting feature is the comparison of the increase in the Gini in the first and third quintiles, together with the decrease in their respective income shares, in relation to what happened to the respective propensities to consume. Whereas in the third quintile the increase in the inequality

Table 4. Gini decomposition by households' income quintile in Italy (1989–2014).

	yi	ci	yi*ci	Gini by quintile	Gh	Ge	Generalized Entropy index	Gini
1989								
1	0.072	0.942	0.068	0.153		0.167		0.334
2	0.122	0.868	0.106	0.059				
3	0.168	0.848	0.143	0.053	0.071		0.238	
4	0.234	0.760	0.178	0.058				
5	0.405	0.661	0.268	0.170				
Σ				0.761				
2014								
1	0.063	1.143	0.073	0.223		0.182		0.350
2	0.120	0.883	0.106	0.059				
3	0.166	0.796	0.132	0.055	0.086		0.268	
4	0.238	0.715	0.170	0.061				
5	0.414	0.617	0.255	0.171				
Σ				0.736				

Source: Author's calculation, SHIW – Bank of Italy (2020).

and decrease in the participation has been translated into a lower propensity to consume (reinforcing the aggregate result), in the first quintile the worsening of the Gini and the reduction of the income share translated into a higher propensity to consume (minimizing the overall decrease in the aggregate APC). Furthermore, a rather constant inequality within the top quintile and its increasing income share translated into lower APC (reinforcing the aggregate result).

Consequently, it is possible to argue that the absolute income hypothesis does not fully explain the Italian results. Despite the confirmation of the existence of a trade-off between inequality (increase in the global Gini index) and APC at the aggregate level, the separate analysis of the different quintiles shows that higher inequality at the bottom quintile resulted in a significantly higher APC, whereas higher inequality within the top quintile resulted in a lower APC of that income group. In other words, the negative trade-off between inequality and APC is inverted in the bottom extreme of the distribution.

Accordingly, it seems that the absolute income effects of a higher overall level of inequality have been partially compensated by relative income effects at the bottom. Figure 7 illustrates exactly this movement with the consumption expenditure functions with respect to the actual income of each of the quintiles (C_1 and C_5 highlighted) as well as their respective shifts (dashed line) and the total effect ($C_{T,1989}$ and $C_{T,\,2014}$).

4.3. Stylized Facts on Household Consumption and Financial Behavior in Italy

The question that remains is how relative income effects could partially (but not fully) compensate for the demand depressing effects of rising inequality on aggregate consumption. As argued by Brown (2004), the answer depends on how constrained consumption decisions are by households' income. In this sense, credit, debt, and wealth might play an important role.

The relation between rising debt and the compensation for increasing inequality has been extensively discussed in the literature for the US American case. Barba and Pivetti (2009) have argued that rising income inequality has been the main source of the rise in debt levels, explaining the puzzle of declining wages coexisting with increasing consumption demand. Cynamon and Fazzari (2013) have also associated inequality, worsening

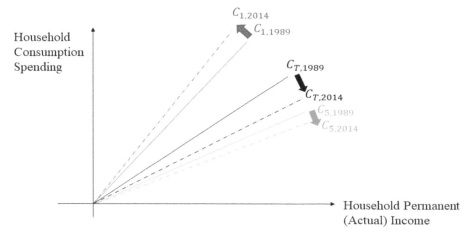

Figure 7. Italian households' consumption spending and the effect of worsening income distribution (1989–2014). Source: Author's elaboration, based on Palley (2010).

relative income, and changing consumption and financial norms with the rise in debt levels in the US. Carr and Jayadev (2015) provide evidence from panel data also for the US that the rising indebtedness of households is related to high levels of inequality as well as relative income effects.

For the Italian case, despite the marginal existence of relative income effects, the dominance of overall demand-depressing effects of rising inequality already indicates that rising indebtedness does not play the same role as in the US American case. Analyzing the level of household debt to the net disposable income ratio (Figure 8), there is a clear upward trend from mid-1990s until 2012. Nevertheless, while Spain and France reached levels comparable to the US, Italy maintains lower debt levels even compared to Germany, despite the strong acceleration in the 2000s. An interesting feature is that, even after the 2007–9 crisis, the ratio of debt to disposable income has kept increasing in Italy, although at a slower pace.

At the micro-level, analyzing the data from the Italian SHIW, it is possible to observe the indebtedness by quintile. It is clear that the increasing average of financial liabilities

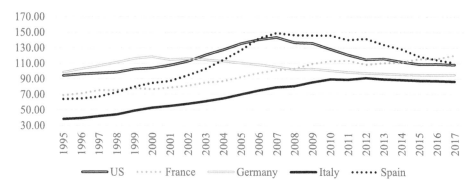

Figure 8. Household debt to net disposable income ratio in the US, France, Germany, Italy, and Spain (1995–2017). Source: Author's representation, OECD (2020).

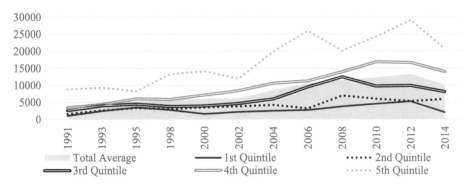

Figure 9. Italian households' average financial liability by quintiles in euros (1991–2014). Source: Author's representation, SHIW – Bank of Italy (2020).

has materialized in all the five quintiles (Figure 9), which have reached a higher average liability level in 2014 compared to the starting point (1991).[12] However, it is evident that the upper quintiles are the ones that pull up the average, also meaning that the ones holding more income and wealth also hold the highest amounts of financial liabilities.

Analyzing Figures 10a, b, c, d, and e it is possible to see the decomposition and the exact period when the growth of financial liabilities accelerated the most in each of the quintiles (ordered by disposable income).[13] The increase in average liabilities in the first quintile (Figure 10a) was concentrated in the period between 2000–12. The interesting feature is that this accelerating trend did not stop after the crisis but rather kept its pace until 2012, which can be related to the need of maintaining a certain basic living standard in face of decreasing income levels. Another peculiar characteristic of the profile of average liability related to the first quintile is the importance of commercial debt and debt towards other families, which, despite being very small, is the highest among all the other income strata. The second quintile (Figure 10b) presented the peak of acceleration between 2006–10. The third quintile (Figure 10c) had the biggest increase in average liability between 2002–8, clearly decreasing after the crisis. The fourth quintile (Figure 10d) had a rather stable accelerating path between 1991–2012. Finally, the fifth quintile (Figure 10e) presented two periods of acceleration between 2002–6, possibly related to the euphoria after the adoption of the Euro, and between 2010–2.

Going back to the macro-level and analyzing the composition of household debt, it is possible to make a distinction between mortgages and consumer credit. In the Italian case, the key component of households' debt is mortgages, accounting for more than 66 per cent of total loans in 2014 (see Figure 11a below). Taking a closer look at this key component mortgage financing in the Mediterranean country is still very low in comparison to other European countries (as illustrated in Figure 11b).

The fact that demand-depressing effects triggered by increasing inequality levels did not significantly shift private households' financial balances in Italy is also discussed in the literature of macro growth regimes. While some European member countries have experienced a debt-led private demand boom regime (Spain, for example) that

---

[12]The analysis of the financial liability is constrained to start in 1991 due the availability of data from the historical files published by the Bank of Italy.
[13]The trend line is a moving average trend referent to the total average of financial liability of each quintile.

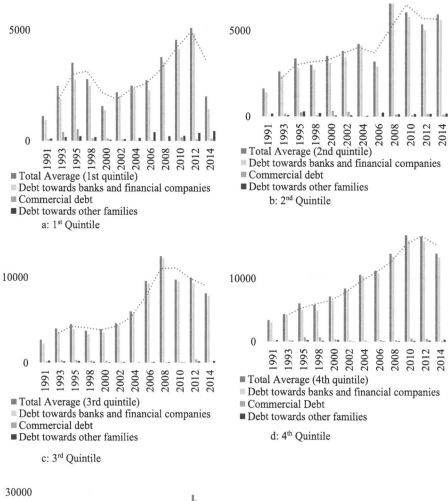

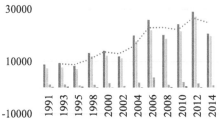

Figure 10. Italian households' average financial liability by quintile and type in euros (1991–2014). (a) 1st Quintile. (b) 2nd Quintile. (c) 3rd Quintile. (d) 4th Quintile. Source: Author's representation, SHIW – Bank of Italy (2020).

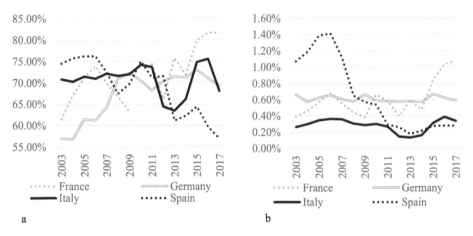

Figure 11. Loans to households for the purchase of houses in France, Germany, Italy and Spain (2003–2017). (a) Total outstanding volume of loans to households for the purchase of houses to total debt ratio. (b) Total outstanding volume of loans to households for the purchase of houses to GDP ratio. Source: Author's calculation, ECB (2020) and EUROSTAT (2020).

compensated the scenario of stagnating income and increasing inequality through current account deficits and debt accumulation, other countries have complementarily developed an export-led mercantilist regime (Germany, for example). Italy (like France and Portugal) was qualified in the literature as an intermediate case, following a domestic-demand led regime in which 'positive financial balances of the private household sector as well as the external sector, and hence, current account deficits' (Dodig, Hein, and Detzer 2015, p. 8) were sustained by negative results run by the government and by the corporate sector. In the Italian case, in particular, Gabbi, Ticci, and Vozella (2014) demonstrate that the largest component of aggregate demand and growth was aggregate private consumption, with a relatively low contribution of stock investments and a balanced current account. In this sense, the authors qualify the growth regime of the country as internal domestic-demand led.

Besides the possible compensation of debt-based consumption, wealth[14] might have also played a role. Barba and Pivetti (2009) and Cynamon and Fazzari (2008) have emphasized the mechanism of rising housing prices functioning as collateral with significant effects on consumption once mortgages holders make use of refinancing schemes to create disposable income (transforming houses in ATM machines).[15] This was, again, especially true in the US (which was extensively analyzed in the literature).

In Italy, however, despite the increase in housing loans pushing the levels of total household debt, housing equity withdrawals did not play a significant role. Regardless of the attempt of the Ministry of Economy and Finance to encourage such recourse in

---

[14]The positive impact of wealth on consumption is discussed by different economic paradigms. As highlighted by Stockhammer, Rabinovich, and Reddy (2018), whereas in the mainstream the positive effect of wealth is related to utility-maximizing behaviour of rational households, in the heterodox literature it is related to financialization, to the role of lenders and to consumption norms. In addition, New Keynesians have argued that the effect of wealth on consumption runs from the channel of wealth functioning as collateral to households that are credit constrained.

[15]For an extensive description of mortgage refinancing in the US see Guttmann (2016).

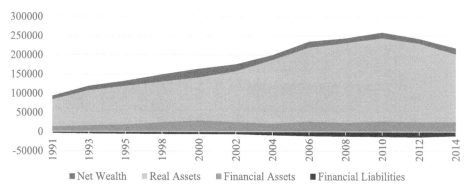

Figure 12. Italian Households' Average Net Wealth by component in euros (1991–2014). Source: Author`s calculation, SHIW – Bank of Italy (2020).

the face of stagnating wages and consumption in 2003, housing equity withdrawals did not successfully boost consumption demand.[16]

The strategy of the Ministry was accurate in what concerns the decomposition of wealth of Italian households, which, according to data from the Italian SHIW, was around 90 per cent concentrated in real assets (as illustrated in Figure 12). However, most of Italian households' real wealth is concentrated in residential properties,[17] that they fear to lose in refinancing schemes, which not only prevented them from incurring in home equity withdrawals but also contributed to the relatively low risk contribution coming from the household sector (IMF 2013).

Besides social norms that shape Italian households' behavior and their reluctance towards mortgage refinancing schemes, the low presence of wealth effects might also be related to the very unequal wealth distribution, as highlighted by Gabbi, Ticci, and Vozella (2014) and illustrated in Figure 13.

Recent econometric studies have also tested the influence of real and financial wealth on Italian households' consumer behavior. Rossi and Visco (1995) have shown that the marginal propensity to consume out of wealth varies between 3 and 3.5 percent. A smaller magnitude of around 2 percent is found by Paiella (2007), Grant and Peltonen (2008), and Guiso, Paiella, and Visco (2005). Slacalek (2009) applies an estimation method based on the sluggishness of aggregate consumption, implying that the long-run MPC (averaged across countries) out of total wealth is 5 cents. In Italy, however, the total wealth effect on the MPC is found to be statistically insignificant. Analyzed separately, neither financial nor housing wealth effects are significantly different from zero (at the 95 percent significance level) in the Mediterranean country.

Summarizing, it is possible to argue that the discussed stylized facts and the literature cannot confirm the existence of significant wealth and debt effects on consumption, despite the increasing trend in indebtedness particularly related to the real estate

---

[16]The main argument behind this attempt is that 'much of the wealth of Italian households is concentrated in the real estate market, and support to consumption could come from the possibility of converting part of this wealth into disposable income' (Ministero dell'Economia e delle Finanze 2003, p. 25, author`s translation).

[17]In 2014, 85 per cent of Italian households' real assets were made up by dwellings, 6 per cent by non-residential buildings, 4 per cent by land, 3 per cent by plant, machinery, equipment, inventories and goodwill and 2 per cent by valuables (Bank of Italy 2014).

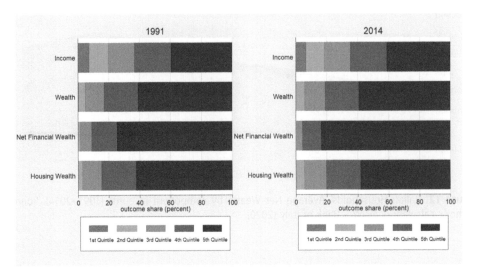

Figure 13. Italian households' wealth by type and quintile (1991–2014). Source: Author's calculation, SHIW – Bank of Italy (2020).

sector in Italy. This can be justified by the very unequal distribution of both financial and real wealth among Italian households (Gabbi, Ticci, and Vozella 2014) as well as by its high concentration on real estate, particularly residential properties that Italian households are skeptical to involve in refinancing schemes or use as collateral (Barba and Pivetti 2009).

5. Conclusions and Policy Implications

In this paper, the evolution of Kaleckian growth models, particularly regarding the incorporation of personal income inequality and taxation, has been briefly reviewed. Despite the amendments done up until now, it has been pointed out that the inclusion of interpersonal inequality with heterogeneous propensities to consume and the connection between the personal dimension of inequality and income taxation has not been touched upon. Therefore, the first goal of this work was to develop a simple neo-Kaleckian model, inspired by You and Dutt (1996), incorporating both personal income inequality as well as income taxes in order to identify how changes in income taxes and personal income distribution affect output and growth.

The result of the model both with respect to tax reforms that affect income distribution and to shifts in income distribution coming from other sources is primarily dependent on the propensities to consume out of each income quintile. These propensities should be heterogeneous and a decreasing function of income levels (following the Keynesian tradition based on Keynes (1936)) for progressive tax shifts to be positive (and vice versa). Thereafter, the model's result was shown to be conditioned by the type of relation between overall inequality and aggregate consumption. In this sense, the strictly negative trade-off between aggregate consumption and inequality has been attached to the dominance of absolute income effects. Accordingly, the second research goal of this work was to verify empirically the behavior of the propensities to consume by quintiles as well as to test the dominance of absolute income effects in Italy.

As demonstrated in Section 4.2, the propensities to consume of Italian households are a decreasing function of their income level. In other words, the propensity to consume out of disposable income is higher in the bottom and lower in the top quintiles. The interesting feature here is that not only the assumption of heterogeneity of the propensities to consume has been confirmed but the dispersion of the APCs of the quintiles has increased in a comparison between the Italian SHIW of 1989 and 2014.

In the Italian case, the worsening of the distribution has implied a decrease in the aggregate APC, confirming the dominance of absolute income effects in the country. In this regard, a redistribution policy would be effective in terms of boosting aggregate demand (through the consumption channel), increasing capacity utilization and growth. Furthermore, as argued in Section 3, the positive effect on the aggregate consumption function would boost the size of the multiplier, also increasing the positive effects of positive shifts in animal spirits and government expenditure. In other words, the adoption of progressive income tax reforms could improve the positive effect of the public-sector component on aggregate demand.

Despite the existence of some minor relative income effects, the stylized facts could not confirm the existence of significant wealth and debt effects on consumption, regardless of the increasing trend of indebtedness (particularly related to the real estate sector). In this sense, the dominance of the absolute income effects was argued to be based on financial and consumption norms that prevent a detachment of the consumer behavior of Italian households from their income budget, thus avoiding the dominance of relative income effects (as occurred in the US case).

Succinctly, it is possible to argue that, in the Italian case, a progressive income tax reform would have a positive effect on aggregate demand, utilization, and growth because of the heterogeneity in the propensities to consume and the dominance of absolute income effects. Moreover, adding more income brackets could also be efficient in the Italian case, given the significant disparities of consumption propensities from one stratum to the other. Furthermore, a redistribution policy would also increase the size of the fiscal multiplier, which was only briefly discussed here. Lastly, a shift towards wages and the abolishment of the neoliberal labor market reforms implemented in Italy could also affect the model positively, decreasing the overall level of inequality and mitigating the harmful scenario raised in the country in terms of youth unemployment, massive emigration flow, and in-work poverty levels.

Acknowledgments

I am most grateful to Eckhard Hein, Dany Lang, Orsola Costantini, Stefano Lucarelli, Ettore Gallo, Vinicius Diniz Moraes, and two anonymous referees for their helpful comments and suggestions on earlier drafts of this article. I would also like to thank the participants of the 22nd FMM Conference in Berlin and the 16th STOREP Conference at the University of Siena. All remaining errors are, of course, my own.

Disclosure Statement

No potential conflict of interest was reported by the author.

ORCID

Maria Cristina Barbieri Góes ⓘ http://orcid.org/0000-0001-8953-5412

References

AMECO. 2020. 'Adjusted Wage Share as a percentage of GDP at current factor cost [ALCD2] in the US, France, Germany, Italy and Spain (1989–2017).' https://ec.europa.eu/economy_finance/ameco/user/serie/ResultSerie.cfm.

Atkinson, A., T. Piketty, and E. Saez. 2011. 'Top Incomes in the Long run of History.' *Journal of Economic Literature* 49 (1): 3–71.

Bank of Italy. 2014. 'Household Wealth in Italy 2013. *Supplements to the Statistical Bulletin* 69.

Bank of Italy. 2020. 'Survey on Household Income and Wealth (Historical Database).' https://www.bancaditalia.it/statistiche/tematiche/indagini-famiglie-imprese/bilanci-famiglie/distribuzione-microdati/index.html.

Barba, A. 2013. 'On the Link Between Functional and Personal Distribution in Italy.' In *Sraffa and the Reconstruction of Economic Theory: Volume One*, edited by E. S. Levrero, A. Palumbo, and A. Stirati, 260–283. London: Palgrave Macmillan.

Barba, A., and M. Pivetti. 2009. 'Rising Household Debt: Its Causes and Macroeconomic Implications—a Long-Period Analysis.' *Cambridge Journal of Economics* 33 (1): 113–137.

Belabed, C., T. Theobald, and T. van Treeck. 2013. 'Income Distribution and Current Account Imbalances.' Duesseldorf: Macroeconomic Policy Institute (IMK) at Hans-Boeckler Foundation, IMK Working Paper No 126.

Bhaduri, A., and S. Marglin. 1990. 'Unemployment and the Real Wage: The Economic Basis for Contesting Political Ideologies.' *Cambridge Journal of Economics* 14 (4): 375–393.

Blecker, R. A. 1989. 'International Competition, Income Distribution and Economic Growth.' *Cambridge Journal of Economics* 13 (3): 395–412.

Blecker, R. A. 2002. 'Distribution, Demand and Growth in neo-Kaleckian Macro-Models.' In *The Economics of Demand-led Growth: Challenging the Supply-Side Vision of the Long Run*, edited by M. Setterfield. Cheltenham, UK: Edward Elgar.

Brown, C. 2004. 'Does Income Distribution Matter for Effective Demand? Evidence From the United States.' *Review of Political Economy* 16 (3): 291–307.

Carr, M. D., and A. Jayadev. 2015. 'Relative Income and Indebtedness: Evidence From Panel Data.' *Review of Income and Wealth* 61 (4): 759–772.

Carvalho, L., and A. Rezai. 2016. 'Personal Income Inequality and Aggregate Demand.' *Cambridge Journal of Economics* 40 (2): 491–505.

Cynamon, B. Z., and S. M. Fazzari. 2008. 'Household Debt in the Consumer age: Source of Growth-Risk of Collapse.' *Capitalism and Society* 3 (2): 1–30.

Cynamon, B. Z., and S. M. Fazzari. 2013. 'Inequality and Household Finance During the Consumer Age.' Levy Economics Institute, Working Paper No.752.

Dafermos, Y., and C. Papatheodorou. 2015. 'Linking Functional with Personal Income Distribution: A Stock-Flow Consistent Approach.' *International Review of Applied Economics* 29 (6): 787–815.

Detzer, D. 2016. 'Financialisation, Debt and Inequality – Scenarios Based on a Stock Flow Consistent Model.' Institute for International Political Economy Berlin, IPE Working Paper, No. 64.

Dodig, N., E. Hein, and D. Detzer. 2015. 'Financialisation and the Financial and Economic Crises: Theoretical Framework and Empirical Analysis for 15 Countries.' FESSUD Studies in Financial Systems No. 110, Berlin School of Economics and Law and Institute for International Political Economy (IPE).

Duesenberry, J. S. 1959. *Income, Saving, and the Theory of Consumer Behavior.* Cambridge, MA: Harvard University Press.

Dutt, A. K. 1984. 'Stagnation, Income Distribution and Monopoly Power.' *Cambridge Journal of Economics* 8 (1): 25–40.

Dutt, A. K. 1987. 'Alternative Closures Again: a Comment on 'Growth, Distribution and Inflation'.' *Cambridge Journal of Economics* 11 (1): 75–82.

Dutt, A. K. 1989. 'Accumulation, Distribution and Inflation in a Marxian-Post Keynesian Model with a Rentier Class.' *Review of Radical Political Economics* 21 (3): 18–26.

Dutt, A. K. 1992. 'Rentiers in Post Keynesian Models.' In *Recent Developments in Post-Keynesian Economics*, edited by P. Arestis, P. and, and V. Chick. Aldershot, UK: Edward Elgar.

Dutt, A. K. 2012. 'Growth, Distribution and Crises.' In *From Crisis to Growth? The Challenge of Imbalances and Debt*, edited by H. Herr, T. Niechoj, C. Thomasberger, A. Truger, and T. van Treeck. Marburg, Germany: Metropolis Verlag.

Dutt, A. K. 2016. 'Growth and Distribution in Heterodox Models with Managers and Financiers.' *Metroeconomica* 67 (2): 364–396.

ECB. 2020. 'Total Outstanding Volume Loans (in Millions of Euros) to Households for Consumption and for House Purchase Excluding Revolving Loans and Overdrafts in France, Germany, Italy and Spain (2003–2017).' https://sdw.ecb.europa.eu/browse.do?node=9691395.

EUROSTAT. 2020. 'Gross Domestic Product at market prices (in millions of euros) in France, Germany, Italy and Spain (2003–17).' https://appsso.eurostat.ec.europa.eu/nui/show.do?dataset=nama_10_gdp&lang=en.

Frank, R. H., A. S. Levine, and O. Dijk. 2014. 'Expenditure Cascades.' *Review of Behavioral Economics* 1: 55–73.

Gabbi, G., E. Ticci, and P. Vozella. 2014. 'Financialisation and the Financial and Economic Crises: The Case of Italy.' FESSUD Studies in Financial Systems No. 23, University of Leeds.

Grant, C., and T. A. Peltonen. 2008. 'Housing and Equity Wealth Effects of Italian Households.' ECB Working Paper No. 857.

Guiso, L., M. Paiella, and I. Visco. 2005. 'Do Capital Gains Affect Consumption? Estimates of wealth Effects from Italian Households Behavior.' Bank of Italy. Economic Research Department, Temi di discussione (Economic working papers) 555.

Guttmann, R. 2016. *Finance-led Capitalism: Shadow Banking, re-Regulation, and the Future of Global Markets*. New York, US: Palgrave Macmillan.

Hein, E. 2006. 'Interest, Debt and Capital Accumulation—A Kaleckian Approach.' *International Review of Applied Economics* 20 (3): 337–352.

Hein, E. 2007. 'Interest Rate, Debt, Distribution and Capital Accumulation in a Post-Kaleckian Model.' *Metroeconomica* 58 (2): 310–339.

Hein, E., and C. Schoder. 2011. 'Interest Rates, Distribution and Capital Accumulation – a Post-Kaleckian Perspective on the US and Germany.' *International Review of Applied Economics* 25: 693–723.

IMF. 2013. *Technical Note on the Financial Situation of Italian Households and non-Financial Corporations and Risks to the Banking System*, Country Report No. 13/348. Washington, US: International Monetary Fund.

Jessoula, M., and M. Raitano. 2020. "Pensioni e Disuguaglianze: una Sfida Complessa, L'equità Necessaria.'.' *Politiche Sociali* 7 (1): 57–76.

Kalecki, M. 1937. 'A Theory of Commodity, Income, and Capital Taxation.' *The Economic Journal* 47 (187): 444–450.

Kapeller, J., and B. Schütz. 2014. 'Debt, Boom, Bust: A Theory of Minsky-Veblen Cycles.' *Journal of Post Keynesian Economics* 36 (4): 781–814.

Kapeller, J., and B. Schütz. 2015. 'Conspicuous Consumption, Inequality and Debt: The Nature of Consumption-Driven Profit-led Regimes.' *Metroeconomica* 66 (1): 51–70.

Keynes, J. M. 1936. *The General Theory of Employment, Interest, and Money*. London, UK: Macmillan.

Kurz, H. D. 1990. 'Technical Change, Growth and Distribution: A Steady-State Approach to 'Unsteady' Growth.' In *Capital, Distribution and Effective Demand: Studies in Classical Approach to Economic Theory*, edited by H. D. Kurz. Cambridge, UK: Polity Press.

Landais, C., T. Piketty, and E. Saez. 2011. *Pour une Révolution Fiscale: un Impôt sur le Revenu Pour le 21 ème Siècle*. Paris: Seuil.

Laramie, A. J. 1991. 'Taxation and Kaleckìs Distribution Factors.' *Journal of Post Keynesian Economics* 13: 583–594.

Laramie, A. J., and D. Mair. 1996. 'Taxation and Kaleckìs Theory of the Business Cycle.' *Cambridge Journal of Economics* 20: 451–464.

Laramie, A. J., and D. Mair. 2000. *A Dynamic Theory of Taxation: Integrating Kalecki Into Modern Public Finance*. Cheltenham, UK: Edward Elgar.

Lavoie, M. 1995. 'Interest Rates in Post-Keynesian Models of Growth and Distribution.' *Metroeconomica* 46 (2): 146–177.

Lavoie, M. 1996. 'Unproductive Outlays and Capital Accumulation with Target-Return Pricing.' *Review of Social Economy* 54 (3): 303–322.

Lavoie, M. 2009. 'Cadrisme Within a Post-Keynesian Model of Growth and Distribution.' *Review of Political Economy* 21 (3): 369–391.

Lavoie, M. 2010. 'Surveying Long-run and Short-run Stability Issues with the Kaleckian Model of Growth.' In *Handbook of Alternative Theories of Economic Growth*, edited by M. Setterfield. Cheltenham, UK and Northampton, MA: Edward Elgar.

Lavoie, M. 2014. *Post-Keynesian Economics: New Foundations*. Cheltenham: Edward Elgar Publishing.

Levrero, E. S., and A. Stirati. 2005. 'Distribuzione del Reddito e Prezzi Relativi in Italia 1970–2002.' *Politica Economica* 21 (3): 401–434.

Ministero dell'Economia e delle Finanze. 2003. *Documento di Programmazione Economico-Finanziaria per gli Anni 2004–2007*. Rome, Italy.

Obst, T., Ö Onaran, and M. Nikolaidi. 2017. *The Effect of Income Distribution and Fiscal Policy on Growth, Investment, and Budget Balance: The Case of Europe*. Greenwich Papers in Political Economy, University of Greenwich.

OECD. 2020. 'Household Debt to Net Disposable Income Ratio in the US, France, Germany, Italy, and Spain (1995–2017).' https://data.oecd.org/hha/household-debt.htm.

Onaran, Ö, and G. Galanis. 2012. 'Is Aggregate Demand Wage-led or Profit-led. National and Global Effects.' *ILO Conditions of Work and Employment Series* 31 (3): 1–51.

Onaran, Ö, E. Stockhammer, and L. Grafl. 2011. 'Financialisation, Income Distribution and Aggregate Demand in the USA.' *Cambridge Journal of Economics* 35: 637–661.

Paiella, M. 2007. 'Does Wealth Affect Consumption? Evidence for Italy.' *Journal of Macroeconomics* 29 (1): 189–205.

Palley, T. I. 2010. 'The Relative Permanent Income Theory of Consumption: A Synthetic Keynes–Duesenberry–Friedman Model.' *Review of Political Economy* 22 (1): 41–56.

Palley, T. I. 2012. *From Financial Crisis to Stagnation: The Destruction of Shared Prosperity and the Role of Economics*. New York: Cambridge University Press.

Palley, T. I. 2014. 'A Neo-Kaleckian-Goodwin Model of Capitalist Economic Growth: Monopoly power, Managerial Pay and Labour Market Conflict.' *Cambridge Journal of Economics* 38 (6): 1355–1372.

Palley, T. I. 2015. 'The Middle Class in Macroeconomics and Growth Theory: A Three-Class neo-Kaleckian-Goodwin Model.' *Cambridge Journal of Economics* 39 (1): 221–243.

Palley, T. I. 2016. 'Inequality and Growth in Neo-Kaleckian and Cambridge Growth Theory.' Duesseldorf: Macroeconomic Policy Institute (IMK) at Hans-Boeckler Foundation, IMK Working Paper No. 167.

Piketty, T. 2014. *Capital in the Twenty-First Century*. Cambridge, MA: Harvard University Press.

Piketty, T., and E. Saez. 2003. 'Income Inequality in the United States, 1913–1998.' *The Quarterly Journal of Economics* 118 (1): 1–41.

Piketty, T., and E. Saez. 2007. 'How Progressive is the US Federal tax System? A Historical and International Perspective.' *Journal of Economic Perspectives* 21 (1): 3–24.

Prante, F. J. 2018. 'Macroeconomic Effects of Personal and Functional Income Inequality: Theory and Empirical Evidence for the US and Germany.' *Panoeconomicus* 65 (3): 289–318.

Rossi, N., and I. Visco. 1995. 'National Saving and Social Security in Italy.' *Ricerche Economiche* 49 (4): 329–356.

Rowthorn, B. 1981. *Demand, Real Wages and Economic Growth*. North East London, UK: Polytechnic.

Setterfield, M., and Y. Kim. 2016. 'Debt Servicing, Aggregate Consumption, and Growth.' *Structural Change and Economic Dynamics* 36: 22–33.

Slacalek, J. 2009. 'What Drives Personal Consumption? The Role of Housing and Financial Wealth.' *The BE Journal of Macroeconomics* 9 (1): Art. 37.

Stirati, A. 2011. 'Changes in Functional Income Distribution in Italy and Europe.' In *The Global Economic Crisis: New Perspectives on the Critique of Economic Theory and Policy*, edited by E. Brancaccio, and G. Fontana. London, UK: Routledge.

Stockhammer, E., J. Rabinovich, and N. Reddy. 2018. 'Distribution, Wealth and Demand Regimes in Historical Perspective. USA, UK, France and Germany, 1855–2010.' Duesseldorf: Macroeconomic Policy Institute (IMK) at Hans-Boeckler Foundation. IMK Working Paper No. 14.

Tavani, D., and R. Vasudevan. 2014. 'Capitalists, Workers and Managers: Wage Inequality and Effective Demand.' *Structural Change and Economic Dynamics* 30: 120–131.

Tridico, P. 2015. 'From Economic Decline to the Current Crisis in Italy.' *International Review of Applied Economics* 29 (2): 164–193.

Van Treeck, T., and S. Sturn. 2012. *Income Inequality as a Cause of the Great Recession?: A Survey of Current Debates*. Geneva: ILO, Conditions of Work and Employment Branch.

Van Treeck, T., and S. Sturn. 2013. 'The Role of Income Inequality as a Cause of the Great Recession and Global Imbalances.' In *Wage-led Growth: An Equitable Strategy for Economic Recovery*, edited by E. Stockhammer. London, UK: Palgrave Macmillan.

Veblen, T. 1899. *The Theory of the Leisure Class*. Hazleton, PA: the Pennsylvania State University, Electronic Classics Series Publication.

WID. 2020. 'Top 1% income share in the US, France, Germany, Italy, and Spain (1989–2009); Top 10% income share in the US, France, Germany, Italy, and Spain (1989–2009).' http://www.wid.world.

You, J., and A. K. Dutt. 1996. 'Government Debt, Income Distribution and Growth.' *Cambridge Journal of Economics* 20 (3): 335–351.

Zezza, G. 2008. 'US Growth, the Housing Market, and the Distribution of Income.' *Journal of Post Keynesian Economics* 30 (3): 375–401.

Gender Issues in Kaleckian Distribution and Growth Models: On the Macroeconomics of the Gender Wage Gap

Eckhard Hein

ABSTRACT
We introduce a gender wage gap into basic one-good textbook versions of the neo-Kaleckian distribution and growth model for a developed capitalist economy and examine the effects of improving gender wage equality on income distribution, aggregate demand, capital accumulation and productivity growth. For the closed economy model, reducing the gender wage gap has no effect on the profit share, and a gender equality-led regime requires the propensity to save out of female wages to fall short of the propensity to save out of male wages. For the open economy model, this condition is modified by the effects of improved gender wage equality on exports, and – through changes of the profit share – on domestic demand. Finally, for the open economy with productivity growth we find an unambiguously expansionary effect of narrowing the gender wage gap on long-run equilibrium capital accumulation and productivity growth if the demand growth regime is gender equality-led. A gender equality-burdened demand growth regime, however, may generate different long-run effects of improving gender wage equality on capital accumulation and productivity growth: expansionary, intermediate or contractionary.

1. Introduction

Post-Keynesian models of distribution and growth, and Kaleckian models in particular, have historically focused on the class division of society. The analysis has been concerned with the distribution of income (and partly wealth) between capital and labour and on the relationship of the distribution between profits and wages with capital accumulation and economic growth.[1] In some contributions, a distinction has been made between direct labour and overhead labour, thus allowing for differentiation of the working class into managers and workers.[2] Then, explicitly introducing finance, interest and credit into post-Keynesian models of distribution and growth has led to the distinction of the capitalist class into creditors and debtors,[3] or into rentiers/shareholders, on the one hand, and corporations run by managers, on the other hand, when the focus turned

---

[1] See, for example, Blecker and Setterfield (2019, Chapters 3–4), Hein (2014, Chapters 4–8) and Lavoie (2014, Chapter 6).
[2] See, for example, Lavoie (1995a, 1996, 2009) and Rowthorn (1981).
[3] See, for example, Hein (2008, 2014, Chapter 9) and Lavoie (1995b).

towards the macroeconomics of finance-dominated capitalism.[4] In the latter context, and in order to explain different demand and growth regimes in finance-dominated capitalism, and the debt-led private demand boom regime in particular, several models have been proposed allowing for a division of the working class into high and low wage earners, the latter emulating consumption behaviour of the former financed by increasing indebtedness.[5] Whereas these developments have involved a broad range of researchers in the post-Keynesian academic community, a smaller group of authors, so far, has been concerned with integrating gender issues into post-Keynesian/Kaleckian macroeconomic models thus linking two heterodox schools of thought, post-Keynesian economics and feminist economics.[6]

These approaches have included the reproduction of labour into macroeconomic models, focusing on the disproportional share of women as compared to men in unpaid reproductive and care work (Braunstein, van Staveren, and Tavani 2011, 2020). Most feminist post-Keynesian macroeconomic models have examined the effects of gender inequality on growth for developing countries, further taking into account the specific structural features of these economies, like a dual production structure, segregated labour markets, the balance-of-payments constraint, and partly also the role of economic policies (Blecker and Seguino 2002; Seguino 2010, 2012, 2020; Seguino and Braunstein 2019).[7] Recently, Onaran (2015) and Onaran, Oyvat, and Fotoupoulo (2019) have integrated several of these features into a more general gendered macroeconomic model on Kaleckian grounds, which has then also been estimated for the UK. This model integrates three dimensions of inequalities – functional income distribution between wages and profits, gender inequality, and wealth concentration, and their interactions. It includes the impact of fiscal policies, in particular the effects of government spending on social and physical infrastructure, as well as different types of taxation. And it analyses both the demand and supply-side effects on output and employment.

Our ambition in this paper is more modest, basic and mainly didactic and pedagogical. We will focus on the introduction of a gender wage gap into a basic textbook neo-Kaleckian distribution and growth model, focusing on distribution, aggregate demand, growth and productivity effects. Since our simple model will be for a one-good economy, several features of developed or emerging capitalist economies which figure prominently in parts of the literature referred to above cannot directly be included. Thus, the model can be viewed to refer more to developed capitalist economies. However, the main purpose is analytical and it is meant to understand the channels of influence of changes in gender wage gaps on distribution, aggregate demand and growth in a systematic and stepwise approach, without claiming to be comprehensive even in the final model version. In Section 2, we will first examine the impact of closing the gender wage gap for a closed economy model, and then look at a model for an economy which is open for foreign trade (but not for international capital or labour movements) in Section

---

[4]See, for example, Hein (2012, 2014, Chapter 10).
[5]See, for example, Hein (2017) and Hein and Prante (2020).
[6]See Seguino (2019) for several arguments, why post-Keynesians should be concerned with more general stratification issues in macroeconomics, with gender being an important one among them. On the relevance and the contribution of stratification for the explanation of economic development and financial and economic crises, see, for example, Berik, van der Meulen Rodgers, and Seguino (2009) and Fukuda-Parr, Heintz, and Seguino (2013).
[7]See Onaran (2015) and Onaran, Oyvat, and Fotoupoulo (2019), and in particular Seguino (2020) for a more comprehensive review of the feminist macroeconomic literature.

3. In the last step, in Section 4, we will integrate endogenous productivity growth into the model. For each version of the one-good model, the effects of improving gender wage equality on distribution, equilibrium capacity utilisation and growth will be analysed. Section 5 will summarise and conclude.

2. The Closed Economy Model

2.1. Basic Structure

The closed economy version of our model builds on the basic neo-Kaleckian model in the tradition of Dutt (1984, 1987) and Rowthorn (1981), as presented in Hein (2014, Chapter 6), and it includes a gender wage gap into this model. In the basic version, we assume a closed economy without a government sector, which is composed of two classes, capitalists and workers. We now assume that workers are split into male workers (L_M) and female workers (L_F), whereas no gender division is assumed for the capitalist class. The labour force (L) thus consists of a male ($\theta = L_M/L$) and a female share ($1-\theta = L_F/L$):

$$L = \theta L + (1 - \theta)L \tag{1}$$

Male and female labour is generally in excess supply and poses no constraint to output. Capitalists own the means of production, hire male and female labour, organise the production process and decide about investment in and expansion of the capital stock. Capitalists receive profits, which they partly consume and partly save – buying assets issued by the corporate sector and thus the capitalists themselves or depositing parts of the profits with a banking sector, which is also owned by the capitalists. We do not model the financial sector here, but only assume, as usual in post-Keynesian distribution and growth models, that capitalists have access to (initial) finance, i.e. credit, generated by the financial sector 'out of nothing', for investment purposes. Therefore, investment in the capital stock is not constrained by saving at the macroeconomic level, although corporate saving, i.e. retained earnings, may have a positive impact on creditworthiness of firms and thus on their ability to finance investment expenditures at the microeconomic level. However, we will not consider this here.[8]

We assume that a homogenous output (Y) for consumption and investment purposes is produced combining direct male or female labour and a non-depreciating capital stock (K). We thus ignore overhead labour, costs of raw materials and intermediate products, as well as capital stock depreciations. We assume a fixed coefficient production technology without technical progress and set the capital-potential output ratio equal to one ($K/Y^P = 1$), such that the rate of capacity utilisation is given by the actual output-capital ratio ($u = Y/K$). Male and female workers operate the same technology and thus have the same labour productivity ($y = Y/L$):

$$\frac{Y}{L} = \frac{Y_M}{L_M} = \frac{Y_F}{L_F} = y = y_M = y_F \tag{2}$$

with Y_M and Y_F denoting male and female output, respectively, each produced in combination with the respective (fraction of the homogenous) capital stock. The assumption

---

[8]See Hein (2008, 2014, Chapter 9) for respective models.

of equality of male and female labour productivity allows us to focus on true gender wage gaps. Because of historically, socially and institutionally given discrimination of women, nominal wages for female work (w_F) will only be a fraction of nominal wages for male work (w_M):

$$w_F = \varepsilon w_M, \quad 0 < \varepsilon \leq 1 \tag{3}$$

Therefore, we have ε as a gender equality parameter and $(1-\varepsilon)$ for the gender wage gap. We will assume that this parameter is determined by gender conflict, history, institutions etc.., and we will treat this parameter as an exogenous variable, which can be affected by policies, and examine the macroeconomic effects of changes in this parameter. The assumption of equal male and female labour productivity but lower female wages indicates that our model refers to the gender wage gap adjusted for structural discrimination of women with respect to education, access to high skilled jobs, labour market segregation, etc., which are in the focus of most of the literature referred to in the introduction.[9]

Nominal income (pY), i.e. real income/output multiplied by the price level, in our model economy is distributed between male wages (W_M), female wages (W_F) and profits (Π):

$$pY = W_M + W_F + \Pi = w_M L_M + w_F L_F + rpK = w_M[\theta + \varepsilon(1 - \theta)]L + rpK \tag{4}$$

The rate of profit on the capital stock can be decomposed into the rate of capacity utilisation and the profit share ($h = \Pi/pY$):

$$r = \frac{\Pi}{pK} = \frac{\Pi}{pY} \frac{Y}{K} = hu \tag{5}$$

2.2. Pricing and Distribution

Income distribution, both between capital and labour and between male and female workers, can be derived starting from firms' mark-up pricing in incompletely competitive goods market. Following Kalecki (1954, Chapter 1), we assume that firms mark-up unit labour costs, consisting of male and female wage costs per unit of output, and the mark-up (m) is determined by the degree of price competition in the goods market and the relative strength of capital and labour in the labour market:

$$p = (1 + m) \frac{W_M + W_F}{Y} = (1 + m) \frac{w_M L_M + w_F L_F}{Y} = (1 + m) \frac{w_M[\theta + \varepsilon(1 - \theta)]}{y},$$
$$m > 0 \tag{6}$$

For the further analysis we assume the determinants of the mark-up to be constant for the sake of simplicity, in order to analyse the 'pure' effects of a change in the gender wage gap.

---

[9]These assumptions may raise the question, why, in our one-good economy, firms should hire male labour at all. However, it should be clear that this model is an extreme simplification of a more complex world determined by historical, social and institutional features. One of these features is a male dominated labour force

From equation (6) we get that profits are given by:

$$\Pi = m(w_M L_M + w_F L_F) = m w_M [\theta + \varepsilon(1 - \theta)]L \tag{7}$$

For the profit share in nominal income we thus obtain:

$$h = \frac{\Pi}{pY} = \frac{\Pi}{W_M + W_F + \Pi} = \frac{m w_M [\theta + \varepsilon(1 - \theta)]L}{(1 + m)w_M [\theta + \varepsilon(1 - \theta)]L} = \frac{m}{1 + m} \tag{8}$$

For the aggregate wage share (Ω) this means:

$$\Omega = 1 - h = \frac{W_M + W_F}{pY} = \frac{W_M + W_F}{W_M + W_F + \Pi} = \frac{w_M [\theta + \varepsilon(1 - \theta)]}{(1 + m)w_M [\theta + \varepsilon(1 - \theta)]} = \frac{1}{1 + m} \tag{9}$$

These are the well-known results from the very basic Kaleckian model without intermediate products, overhead labour and so on: Functional income distribution is only determined by the mark-up in firms' pricing (Hein 2014, Chapter 6). But now we also have to determine the male (Ω_M) and the female (Ω_F) share of wages in national income:

$$\Omega_M = \frac{W_M}{pY} = \frac{W_M}{W_M + W_F + \Pi} = \frac{w_M \theta}{(1 + m)w_M [\theta + \varepsilon(1 - \theta)]} = \Omega \frac{\theta}{\theta + \varepsilon(1 - \theta)} \tag{10}$$

$$\Omega_F = \frac{W_F}{pY} = \frac{W_F}{W_M + W_F + \Pi} = \frac{w_M \varepsilon(1 - \theta)}{(1 + m)w_M [\theta + \varepsilon(1 - \theta)]} = \Omega \frac{\varepsilon(1 - \theta)}{\theta + \varepsilon(1 - \theta)} \tag{12}$$

The wage shares of male and female workers therefore depend on the overall wage share and the respective gender shares in this overall wage share. These shares are affected by the share of male and female workers in the total labour force and by the gender wage equality parameter, and hence by the gender wage gap. An improvement towards gender wage equality and a reduction in the gender wage gap will have the following effects on income distribution:

$$\frac{\partial h}{\partial \varepsilon} = 0 \tag{8a}$$

$$\frac{\partial \Omega}{\partial \varepsilon} = 0 \tag{9a}$$

$$\frac{\partial \Omega_M}{\partial \varepsilon} = \frac{-\Omega \theta(1 - \theta)}{[\theta + \varepsilon(1 - \theta)]^2} = \frac{-\theta(1 - \theta)}{(1 + m)[\theta + \varepsilon(1 - \theta)]^2} < 0 \tag{10a}$$

$$\frac{\partial \Omega_F}{\partial \varepsilon} = \frac{\Omega \theta(1 - \theta)}{[\theta + \varepsilon(1 - \theta)]^2} = \frac{\theta(1 - \theta)}{(1 + m)[\theta + \varepsilon(1 - \theta)]^2} > 0 \tag{11a}$$

In this simple model, an improvement towards gender wage equality and a reduction of the gender wage gap will thus have no effect on the profit share and on the aggregate wage share, but it will improve the female wage share at the expense of the male wage share. An increase in the female nominal wage rate, keeping the male nominal wage rate constant, thus reducing the gap between them, will increase the price level, because we assume a constant mark-up and constant labour productivity. This increase in the price level, however, will be less than proportional since male nominal costs remain constant, such that the female real wage rate and the female wage share will rise, and it will make the male real wage rate and wage share fall accordingly. Of course, this basic model is open to assuming that lowering the gender wage gap is associated with an improvement of workers' bargaining power in the labour market and thus with a lower mark-up and a lower profit share, as Onaran, Oyvat, and Fotoupoulo (2019) have found for the UK. But it is not yet clear whether this can be generalised. Therefore, for analytical purposes we prefer to keep these channels distinct.

2.3. Distribution, Aggregate Demand and Growth

Aggregate demand in our model without a government and a foreign sector consists of investment and consumption demand. For the goods market equilibrium we thus have to look at investment and saving, i.e. income not consumed. For investment we assume the most basic neo-Kaleckian investment function,[10] according to which the firms' decisions to invest depend on animal spirits (α), i.e. the 'spontaneous urge to action rather than inaction' (Keynes 1936, 161), and on the rate of capacity utilisation. On the one hand, a high rate of capacity utilisation induces firms to increase productive potential by means of investment in the capital stock. On the other hand, a high rate of capacity utilisation has a positive effect on the rate of profit, for a given profit share (equation 5), and thus also on retained earnings, for a given retention ratio. This also improves the creditworthiness of the firm when it comes to obtaining external investment finance in the credit market, according to Kalecki's (1937) 'principle of increasing risk'. From these considerations, we get the following determination of the rate of capital accumulation (g), relating real investment (I) to the real capital stock:

$$g = \frac{I}{K} = \alpha + \beta u, \quad \alpha, \beta > 0 \tag{12}$$

Aggregate saving (S) consists of saving out of profit (S_Π), saving out of male workers' wages (S_{WM}) and saving out of female workers' wages (S_{WF}). Each saving aggregate is determined by the respective propensity to save and the respective income, with s_Π denoting the propensity to save out of profits, s_{WM} the propensity to save out of male wages and s_{WF} the propensity to save out of female wages. We therefore obtain for

---

[10]Different from the investment function in the neo-Kaleckian model used here, in the post-Kaleckian model proposed by Bhaduri and Marglin (1990) and Kurz (1990), there is also a direct positive effect of the profit share in the investment function. In the post-Kaleckian model, this slight change allows for wage- or profit-led demand and growth regimes for the closed economy, depending on model parameters, whereas in the neo-Kaleckian model used here, we only obtain wage-led regimes for the closed economy. In the neo-Kaleckian model, profit-led regimes only become possible for the open economy, as already shown by Blecker (1989) and as we will see in Section 3. Several estimations based on the post-Kaleckian model for OECD but also for emerging market economies have found that domestic demand is usually wage-led, and only through the inclusions of distribution effects on net exports some countries turn profit-led overall. See Hartwig (2014), Hein (2014, Chapter 7), Onaran and Galanis (2014) and Onaran and Obst (2016) for recent estimation results, and Blecker (2016) and Stockhammer (2017) for clarifying discussions. These empirical findings have induced us to choose the neo-Kaleckian model as the basis for our analysis. Giovanazzi (2018), following Braunstein, van Staveren, and Tavani (2011), has proposed a simple closed economy model including gender wage gaps into a basic post-Kaleckian model, however, abstracting from different saving propensities out of male and female wages and only focussing on distribution and productivity effects of narrowing the gender wage gap.

the saving rate, relating aggregate saving to the nominal capital stock:

$$\sigma = \frac{S}{pK} = \frac{S_\Pi + S_{WM} + S_{WF}}{pK} = (s_\Pi h + s_{WM}\Omega_M + s_{WF}\Omega_F)u,$$

$$0 \le s_{WM}, s_{WF} < s_\Pi \le 1$$
(13)

Since saving out of profits contains retained earnings of corporations, which cannot be consumed and are thus saved by definition, and since profits usually go to the high-income households, we assume the propensity to save out of profits to exceed each of the two propensities to save out of wages.[11] Whether the propensity to save out of female wages is higher or lower than the propensity to save out of male wages is an open question. On the one hand, female wages are lower than male wages and, according to Keynes's (1936, Chapter 8) absolute income hypothesis, we would expect a higher propensity to consume and thus a lower propensity to save out of female wages than out of male wages, as also expected by Onaran (2015). On the other hand, it has been found by Seguino and Sagrario Floro (2003) for semi-industrialised countries that higher relative income and more bargaining power of women increase aggregate saving rates, because women's income is more unstable and women's expenditures are dominated more by pre-cautionary motives. Interestingly, the estimations by Onaran, Oyvat, and Fotoupoulo (2019) for the UK support the notion that the propensity to save out of female wages is higher than out of male wages.[12] In our following analysis, we will therefore consider both cases, $s_{WM} > s_{WF}$ and $s_{WM} < s_{WF}$.

Plugging in the determination of the male and female wage shares from equations (10) and (11) into equation (13) we obtain:

$$\sigma = \left\{ h\left[s_\Pi - \frac{s_{WM}\theta + s_{WF}\varepsilon(1-\theta)}{\theta + \varepsilon(1-\theta)} \right] + \left[\frac{s_{WM}\theta + s_{WF}\varepsilon(1-\theta)}{\theta + \varepsilon(1-\theta)} \right] \right\} u$$
(14a)

The average propensity to save out of wages (s_W) is the weighted average of the propensity to save out of male and female wages, with weights given by the male and female share in wages:

$$s_W = \frac{S_W}{W} = \frac{S_{WM} + S_{WF}}{W_M + W_F} = \frac{s_{WM}\Omega_M pY + s_{WF}\Omega_F pY}{\Omega pY} = \frac{s_{WM}\theta + s_{WF}\varepsilon(1-\theta)}{\theta + \varepsilon(1-\theta)}$$
(15)

Using equation (15), the equation for the saving rate thus turns to:

$$\sigma = \{h[s_\Pi - s_W(\varepsilon)] + s_W(\varepsilon)\}u$$
(16)

[11]Since we assume the propensity to save out of male and female wages to be positive, it means that both types of workers accumulate financial assets and become co-owners of or creditors to the firms, and thus will also receive part of the profits generated in the firm sector. We will not follow this up, and therefore we have to be careful not to confuse the propensity to save of female and male workers with the propensity to save out of female and male wages. In essence, what we assume here is that male and female workers have two different propensities to save each: A higher one out of their profits and a lower one out of the wages they receive. This may be justified by the fact that profits to large parts are not paid out to households but are rather retained, increasing the value of the firms and thus also the wealth of the owners of the firms, who will be capitalists and also those workers who save. In a more elaborated model we should therefore also include consumption out of accumulated wealth. For the sake of simplicity we ignore this here and leave it for future modelling exercises.
[12]See also Seguino (2020) on the unclear results regarding different saving propensities of men and women.

The propensity to save out of wages is here endogenous with respect to the degree of gender wage equality and thus the gender wage gap:

$$\frac{\partial s_W}{\partial \varepsilon} = \frac{-(1-\theta)\theta(s_{WM} - s_{WF})}{[\theta + \varepsilon(1-\theta)]^2} \tag{15a}$$

An improvement towards gender wage equality and a decline in the gender wage gap will thus reduce the average propensity to save out of wages, if the propensity to save out of female wages falls short of the propensity to save out of male wages. It will raise the average propensity to save out of wages, if the propensity to save out of female wages is higher than out of male wages.

For the goods market equilibrium we need the equality of planned saving and invest-ment:

$$g = \sigma \tag{17}$$

For the stability of the goods market equilibrium, it is required that saving responds more elastically than investment towards a change in the endogenous variable, which is the rate of capacity utilisation:

$$\frac{\partial \sigma}{\partial u} - \frac{\partial g}{\partial u} > 0 \Rightarrow h(s_\Pi - s_W) + s_W - \beta > 0 \tag{18}$$

Aggregate demand adjusts to supply, and saving adjusts to investment, by means of changes in the rate of capacity utilisation. We receive the equilibrium rate of capacity uti-lisation (u*) plugging equations (12) and (16) into equation (17):

$$u^* = \frac{\alpha}{h(s_\Pi - s_W) + s_W - \beta} \tag{19}$$

Inserting this value into equations (12) and (5) we also obtain the equilibrium rates of capital accumulation and growth (g*), equal to the equilibrium saving rate (σ*), as well as the equilibrium rate of profit (r*):

$$g^* = \sigma^* = \frac{\alpha[h(s_\Pi - s_W) + s_W]}{h(s_\Pi - s_W) + s_W - \beta} \tag{20}$$

$$r^* = \frac{h\alpha}{h(s_\Pi - s_W) + s_W - \beta} \tag{21}$$

For this basic neo-Kaleckian model with positive saving out of wages it is well known that the paradox of saving applies, i.e. a higher propensity to save out of any type of income will lower all the endogenous variables, the rates of capacity utilisation, accumulation and growth, as well as the rate of profit (Hein 2014, Chapter 7.2.1). Furthermore, demand and growth in the economy are wage-led. A rise in the aggregate wage share, and thus a fall in the profit share, will lead to higher equilibrium rates of capacity utilisation, and accumu-lation/growth. The paradox of costs, i.e. a lower profit share generating a higher equilib-rium profit rate, which will emerge if there is no saving out of wages, may but will not necessarily apply in the model with positive saving out of wages.

For the improvement towards gender wage equality and a reduction in the gender wage gap, we obtain:

$$\frac{\partial u^*}{\partial \varepsilon} = \frac{\alpha(1-h)(1-\theta)\theta(s_{WM}-s_{WF})}{\{[h(s_\Pi - s_W) + s_W - \beta][\theta + \varepsilon(1-\theta)]\}^2} \tag{19a}$$

$$\frac{\partial g^*}{\partial \varepsilon} = \frac{\beta\alpha(1-h)(1-\theta)\theta(s_{WM}-s_{WF})}{\{[h(s_\Pi - s_W) + s_W - \beta][\theta + \varepsilon(1-\theta)]\}^2} \tag{20a}$$

$$\frac{\partial r^*}{\partial \varepsilon} = \frac{h\alpha(1-h)(1-\theta)\theta(s_{WM}-s_{WF})}{\{[h(s_\Pi - s_W) + s_W - \beta][\theta + \varepsilon(1-\theta)]\}^2} \tag{21a}$$

If the propensity to save out of female wages is lower than out of male wages, a reduction in the gender wage gap, and thus an increase in the female wage share at the expense of the male wage share, will be expansionary and lift the equilibrium rates of capacity utilisation, accumulation/growth and profit. The economy will thus be 'gender equality-led'. In the opposite case, however, if the propensity to save out of female wages exceeds the one out of male wages, a reduction in the gender wage gap will reduce the equilibrium rates of capacity utilisation, accumulation/growth and profit. The economy will thus be 'gender equality-burdened'. In the next section we will examine, if and how these results change in an economy which is open to foreign trade.

3. The Open Economy Model

3.1. Basic Structure

The open economy version of our model is based on the open economy analysis in Bhaduri and Marglin (1990) concerning the relationship between distribution, the real exchange rate, as an indicator of international price competitiveness, and demand and growth regimes, as well as on the analysis of the relationship between domestic redistribution and international competitiveness contained in Blecker (1989). Our modelling strategy follows Hein (2014, Chapter 7.3), but instead of a post-Kaleckian investment function we will make use of the neo-Kaleckian investment function from the previous section. We will include gender wage inequality and a gender wage gap into the model, following our analysis of the previous section.

We assume an economy without economic activity of the state, which is open to foreign trade, but not to international movements of capital and labour. The economy depends on imported inputs for production purposes and its output competes in international markets. We take the prices of imported inputs and of the competing foreign final output to be exogenously given. If they are changing, they are moving in step. The nominal exchange rate, here the relationship between domestic currency and foreign currency or the price of a unit of foreign currency in domestic currency, is determined by monetary policies and international financial markets and is also considered to be exogenous for our purposes. Foreign economic activity is also taken to be exogenously given.

3.2. Pricing, Distribution and International Competitiveness

We keep the assumptions regarding capital and labour inputs, the capital-potential output ratio and the labour productivity of male and female labour from the previous section. But now we also consider imported raw material and semi-finished product inputs and assume that firms mark-up unit variable costs, consisting of unit labour costs and unit semi-finished product and material costs. For the sake of simplicity, we assume that there are no domestically produced raw materials and semi-finished products in our advanced capitalist model economy. We denote raw material and semi-finished product inputs per unit of output by μ, the nominal exchange rate by e and the price of a unit of imported foreign goods in foreign currency by p_f. The pricing equation for domestically produced goods thus becomes:

$$p = (1+m)\left\{\frac{w_M[\theta + \varepsilon(1-\theta)]}{y} + p_f e\mu\right\}, \quad m > 0 \tag{22}$$

For further analysis, it is convenient, following Kalecki (1954, Chapter 1), to define a ratio between unit material and semi-finished product costs and unit labour costs, denoted by z:

$$z = \frac{p_f e\mu y}{w_M[\theta + \varepsilon(1-\theta)]} \tag{23}$$

Therefore, the price equation (22) can also be written as:

$$p = (1+m)\frac{w_M[\theta + \varepsilon(1-\theta)]}{y}(1+z) \tag{24}$$

The profit share in domestic value added, consisting of domestic profits, male and female wages, is given by:

$$h = \frac{\Pi}{W_M + W_F + \Pi} = \frac{(1+z)m}{1+(1+z)m} \tag{25}$$

The profit share in the open economy is hence determined by the mark-up and by the ratio of unit costs for imported material and semi-finished products to unit labour costs, consisting of male and female labour costs. The aggregate wage share is given by,

$$\Omega = 1 - h = \frac{W_M + W_F}{W_M + W_F + \Pi} = \frac{1}{1+(1+z)m} \tag{26}$$

and the male and female wage shares are determined by:

$$\Omega_M = \frac{W_M}{W_M + W_F + \Pi} = \Omega\frac{\theta}{\theta + \varepsilon(1-\theta)} = \frac{\theta}{[1+(1+z)m][\theta + \varepsilon(1-\theta)]} \tag{27}$$

$$\Omega_F = \frac{W_F}{W_M + W_F + \Pi} = \Omega\frac{\varepsilon(1-\theta)}{\theta + \varepsilon(1-\theta)} = \frac{\varepsilon(1-\theta)}{[1+(1+z)m][\theta + \varepsilon(1-\theta)]} \tag{28}$$

The ratio of unit material and semi-finished product costs to unit wage costs in equation

(23) is now affected by the gender wage equality parameter:

$$\frac{\partial z}{\partial \varepsilon} = \frac{-p_f e \mu y(1-\theta)}{w_M[\theta + \varepsilon(1-\theta)]^2} = \frac{-(1-\theta)z}{[\theta + \varepsilon(1-\theta)]} < 0 \tag{23a}$$

Therefore, any change in the gender wage gap will not only affect the distribution of wages between males and females, as in the closed economy case, it will also have an impact on the overall wage share and the profit share in the open economy case:

$$\frac{\partial h}{\partial \varepsilon} = \frac{-m(1-\theta)z}{[1 + (1+z)m]^2[\theta + \varepsilon(1-\theta)]} < 0 \tag{25a}$$

$$\frac{\partial \Omega}{\partial \varepsilon} = \frac{(1-\theta)mz}{[1 + (1+z)m]^2[\theta + \varepsilon(1-\theta)]} > 0 \tag{26a}$$

$$\frac{\partial \Omega_M}{\partial \varepsilon} = \frac{-(1-\theta)\theta(1+m)}{\{[1 + (1+z)m][\theta + \varepsilon(1-\theta)]\}^2} < 0 \tag{27a}$$

$$\frac{\partial \Omega_F}{\partial \varepsilon} = \frac{(1-\theta)\{\theta(1+m) + mz[\theta + \varepsilon(1-\theta)]\}}{\{[1 + (1+z)m][\theta + \varepsilon(1-\theta)]\}^2} > 0 \tag{28a}$$

An improvement of gender wage equality by narrowing the gender wage gap will improve the female wage share and reduce the male wage share for the same reasons as mentioned above for the closed economy. Furthermore, however, it will also raise the aggregate wage share and reduce the profit share in national income, because an increase in female wages, everything else constant, will lower the ratio of unit material and semi-finished product costs to unit labour costs.

Before we will be able to analyse the effects of gender wage inequality on aggregate demand and growth, we have to clarify the effects on international price competitiveness because the latter will affect exports and net exports. Following Bhaduri and Marglin (1990), we choose the real exchange rate (e^r) as an indicator for international competitiveness:

$$e^r = \frac{ep_f}{p} \tag{29}$$

An increase in the real exchange rate implies increasing international price competitiveness of domestic producers. From equation (29), it follows for the respective growth rates:

$$\hat{e}^r = \hat{e} + \hat{p}_f - \hat{p} \tag{30}$$

Therefore, higher price competitiveness can be caused by an increasing nominal exchange rate, hence a nominal depreciation of the domestic currency, increasing foreign prices or declining domestic prices. The effect of changes in profit and wage shares on international competitiveness will depend on the cause of distributional change, as has been analytically shown in Hein and Vogel (2008) and Hein (2014, Chapter 7.3). If, everything else constant, the profit share rises because of an increase in the mark-up, domestic prices will rise and the real exchange rate and international price competitiveness of domestic producers will fall. If, however, the profit share rises because of an increase in the ratio of unit material and intermediate product cost to unit labour costs, which may be driven by a fall in nominal wages, a rise in foreign prices or a rise in the nominal exchange rate, hence a nominal depreciation of the domestic currency, international price competitiveness of domestic producers will rise.

The reduction of the gender wage gap and a rise of the gender wage equality parameter have a uniquely negative effect on international price competitiveness, because it means a reduction in z, according to equation (23a). The effect of an increase in ε on the real exchange rate is:

$$\frac{\partial e^r}{\partial \varepsilon} = \frac{-(1-\theta)p_f e\mu y}{(1+m)w_M\{(1+z)[\theta + \varepsilon(1-\theta)]\}^2} = \frac{-(1-\theta)e^r}{(1+z)[\theta + \varepsilon(1-\theta)]} < 0 \qquad (29a)$$

The explanation is straightforward: With constant male nominal wages, constant labour productivity and constant mark-ups, a reduction in the gender wage gap means an increase in the female nominal wage rate. This will raise average unit wage costs and domestic prices, although less than proportional, such that female real wages and wage shares rise by more than male real wages and wage shares fall. Therefore, the profit share falls simultaneously with international price competitiveness of domestic producers. Again, we could assume here that a reduction in the gender wage gap by means of raising female wages is associated with a squeeze of the mark up, either because it goes along with an improvement of workers' general bargaining power, and/or because firms' attempt to maintain international price competitiveness, as Blecker (1989) and Blecker and Seguino (2002) have argued. This would then reinforce the reduction in the profit share, on the one hand, but dampen or even prevent the fall in international price competitiveness, on the other hand. However, in what follows we will not explicitly consider this when we examine the effects on aggregate demand and growth in the next section, in order to keep the analysis simple and tractable.

3.3. Distribution, Aggregate Demand and Growth

For the analysis of the effects of changes in the gender wage gap on aggregate demand, economic activity and capital accumulation, we start with the goods market equilibrium condition for an open economy without economic activity of the state: Planned saving has to be equal to planned nominal investment and nominal net exports (NX), the difference between nominal exports (pX) and nominal imports (ep_fM) of goods and services:

$$S = pI + pX - ep_fM = pI + NX \qquad (31)$$

Dividing equation (31) by the nominal capital stock, we get the following goods market equilibrium relationship between the saving rate, the accumulation rate and the net export rate (b = NX/pK):

$$\sigma = g + b \qquad (32)$$

We can use the saving function (16) and the accumulation function (12) from the closed economy model, and specify the net export function as follows:

$$b = \psi e^r(\varepsilon) - \varphi u + \zeta u_f, \qquad \psi, \varphi, \zeta > 0 \qquad (33)$$

The net export rate is positively affected by international price competitiveness of domestic producers, provided the Marshall-Lerner condition can be assumed to hold and the sum of the absolute values of the price elasticities of exports and imports exceeds unity. Under this condition, the real exchange rate will have a positive effect on net exports. However, net exports also depend on the relative developments of foreign and domestic demand. If domestic demand increases (decreases), ceteris paribus, net exports will decline (increase), because imports will rise (fall). Moreover, if foreign demand rises (falls), ceteris paribus, net exports will rise (fall). Net exports will thus depend on the real exchange rate, domestic capacity utilisation indicating domestic demand, and foreign capacity utilisation (u_f) representing foreign demand. The latter is considered to be exogenous for the purpose of our analysis. The coefficients on domestic and foreign utilisation are affected by the income elasticities of the demand for imports and exports.

Stability of the goods market equilibrium in equation (32) requires that saving responds more elastically towards a change in the endogenous variable, the rate of capacity utilisation, than investment and net exports do together:

$$\frac{\partial \sigma}{\partial u} - \frac{\partial g}{\partial u} - \frac{\partial b}{\partial u} > 0 \Rightarrow h(s_\Pi - s_W) + s_W - \beta + \varphi > 0 \tag{34}$$

Plugging equations (12), (16) and (33) into equation (32) and solving for capacity utilisation and then using equilibrium capacity utilisation to determine the equilibrium rates of capital accumulation, profit and net exports, yields the following results:

$$u^* = \frac{\alpha + \psi e^r + \zeta u_f}{h(s_\Pi - s_W) + s_W - \beta + \varphi} \tag{35}$$

$$g^* = \frac{\alpha[h(s_\Pi - s_W) + s_W + \varphi] + \beta[\psi e^r + \zeta u_f]}{h(s_\Pi - s_W) + s_W - \beta + \varphi} \tag{36}$$

$$r^* = \frac{h(\alpha + \psi e^r + \zeta u_f)}{h(s_\Pi - s_W) + s_W - \beta + \varphi} \tag{37}$$

$$b^* = \frac{(\psi e^r + \zeta u_f)[h(s_\Pi - s_W) + s_W - \beta] - \alpha\varphi}{h(s_\Pi - s_W) + s_W - \beta + \varphi} \tag{38}$$

For the effects of an improvement towards gender wage equality and a reduction in the gender wage gap, we obtain:

$$\frac{\partial u^*}{\partial \varepsilon} = \frac{\dfrac{\partial e^r}{\partial \varepsilon}\psi - u^*\left[\dfrac{\partial h}{\partial \varepsilon}(s_\Pi - s_W) + \dfrac{\partial s_W}{\partial \varepsilon}(1 - h)\right]}{h(s_\Pi - s_W) + s_W - \beta + \varphi} \tag{35a}$$

$$\frac{\partial g^*}{\partial \varepsilon} = \frac{\beta\left\{\frac{\partial e^r}{\partial \varepsilon}\psi - u^*\left[\frac{\partial h}{\partial \varepsilon}(s_\Pi - s_W) + \frac{\partial s_W}{\partial \varepsilon}(1-h)\right]\right\}}{h(s_\Pi - s_W) + s_W - \beta + \varphi} \tag{36a}$$

$$\frac{\partial r^*}{\partial \varepsilon} = \frac{h\left\langle\frac{\partial e^r}{\partial \varepsilon}\psi - u^*\left\{\frac{\partial h}{\partial \varepsilon}\left[s_\Pi - s_W - \frac{1}{h}(h(s_\Pi - s_W) + s_W - \beta + \varphi)\right] + \frac{\partial s_W}{\partial \varepsilon}(1-h)\right\}\right\rangle}{h(s_\Pi - s_W) + s_W - \beta + \varphi} \tag{37a}$$

$$\frac{\partial b^*}{\partial \varepsilon} = \frac{\frac{\partial e^r}{\partial \varepsilon}\psi[h(s_\Pi - s_W) + s_W - \beta] + \varphi u^*\left[\frac{\partial h}{\partial \varepsilon}(s_\Pi - s_W) + \frac{\partial s_W}{\partial \varepsilon}(1-h)\right]}{h(s_\Pi - s_W) + s_W - \beta + \varphi} \tag{38a}$$

Each of the equations (35a) – (38a) is written in a way that the different channels through which an improvement in gender wage equality affects the endogenous variables of the model are clearly visible. First, we have the channel via international price competitiveness of domestic producers ($\partial e^r/\partial \varepsilon$) which affects foreign demand for domestically produced goods and hence exports. Second, we have the channel via the profit share ($\partial h/\partial \varepsilon$) and third via gender wage distribution and the average propensity to consume out of wages ($\partial s_W/\partial \varepsilon$), which will each affect domestic demand. For the interpretation of our results, we have to remember that we assume the stability condition for the goods market equilibrium in (34) to hold, which means that the denominators in equations (35a) – (38a) are positive each. From equation (25a) we have $\partial h/\partial \varepsilon < 0$ and from equation (29a) we know that $\partial e^r/\partial \varepsilon < 0$. Furthermore, from equation (15a) we know that $\partial s_W/\partial \varepsilon < 0$, *if* $s_{WM} > s_{WF}$ and $\partial s_W/\partial \varepsilon > 0$, *if* $s_{WM} < s_{WF}$.

Let us start with the case in which the propensity to save out of female wages is lower than out of male wages, hence that $s_{WM} > s_{WF}$ and $\partial s_W/\partial \varepsilon < 0$. In this case, domestic demand will clearly rise whenever the gender wage gap is reduced, because the profit share falls and also the average propensity to save out of wages declines. However, the effect on foreign demand and exports will be negative, because of a declining real exchange rate. The effect on total demand, the rate of capacity utilisation and the rate of accumulation and growth will depend on the relative strengths of these effects. If the expansionary effect on domestic demand dominates the contractionary effect on foreign demand, the numerators in equations (35a) and (36a) will be positive, equilibrium capacity utilisation and accumulation/growth will rise and will hence be gender equality-led. As can clearly be seen in equations (35a) and (36a), this is the more (less) likely:

- the lower (higher) the price elasticity of exports indicated by ψ,
- the lower (higher) the effect of reducing the gender wage gap on the real exchange rate, $\partial e^r/\partial \varepsilon$,
- the higher (lower) the differential in the propensities to save out profits and out of aggregate wages, $(s_\Pi - s_W)$,

- the lower (higher) the profit share, h,
- and the stronger (weaker) the negative effects of an improvement of the gender wage equality are on the profit share, $\partial h/\partial \varepsilon$, and on the average propensity to save out of wages, $\partial s_W/\partial \varepsilon$.

If the contractionary effect of an improvement of gender wage equality on foreign demand dominates the expansionary effect on domestic demand, the numerator in equations (35a) and (36a) may turn negative, and the equilibrium rates of capacity utilisation and capital accumulation/growth will decline. The economy will thus be gender equality-burdened.

If the economy is gender equality-led, and the equilibrium rates of capacity utilisation and accumulation/growth rise in the face of a reduction in the gender wage gap, the profit rate is likely to improve, too, but not necessarily so, as can be seen in equation (37a). Furthermore, the net export rate will certainly fall, as can be seen in equation (38a). In the gender equality-burdened case, in which the equilibrium rates of capacity utilisation and accumulation/growth fall in the face of a reduction in the gender pay gap, the profit rate will also fall, and the net export rate may rise or fall, depending on the relative effects of decreasing exports (via the reduction in the real exchange rate) and decreasing imports (via the fall in domestic income and demand).

Turning to the case in which the propensity to save out of female wages is higher than out of male wages, hence $s_{WM} < s_{WF}$ and $\partial s_W/\partial \varepsilon > 0$, it is obvious that a gender equality-led demand and growth regime becomes less likely, although not impossible. The effect of lowering the gender wage gap on domestic demand may now already be negative, if the dampening effect via the increase in the average propensity to save out of wages exceeds the expansionary effect via the reduction in the profit share. In this case, the term $(\partial h/\partial \varepsilon)(s_\Pi - s_W) + (\partial s_W/\partial \varepsilon)(1 - h)$ in the numerators of equations (35a) and (36a) will turn positive, which will make the numerators negative and we will see lower equilibrium rates of capacity utilisation and capital accumulation. Demand and growth will be gender equality-burdened, and we will also see depressive effects on the equilibrium profit rate. The effect on the equilibrium net export rate may be positive or negative, as already mentioned above. A gender equality-led regime would need a very strong domestic demand effect via the change in the profit share, and very weak demand effects via the change in the average propensity to save out of wages and the change in the real exchange rate.

Although a gender equality-led regime is logically not impossible, if the propensity to save out of female wages is higher than out of male wages, it is less likely in this case. If the propensity to save out of female wages is lower than out of male wages, a gender equality-led regime is a very likely outcome, in particular if the depressive real appreciation-export effect is not too strong relative to the expansionary domestic demand effect.

4. The Open Economy Model with Productivity Growth

4.1. Basic Structure

Although the effect of closing gender wage gaps may not necessarily stimulate aggregate demand and demand-determined growth in the first place, we may expect positive effects on productivity growth and thus on long-run potential growth of the economy, as several authors have argued focusing on various channels (Braunstein, van Staveren, and Tavani 2011, 2020; Giovanazzi 2018; Seguino 2010, 2012, 2020; Onaran, Oyvat, and Fotoupoulo 2019). Therefore, we finally turn to this issue in our basic neo-Kaleckian modelling framework. Following a procedure initially proposed by Setterfield and Cornwall (2002), then applied by Naastepad (2006), Hein and Tarassow (2010) and Hartwig (2013, 2014), as well as in Hein (2014, Chapter 8),[13] we will first amend the open economy demand and growth model from the previous section by exogenous productivity growth. This will yield the 'demand growth regime'. Then we will introduce productivity growth as a function of exogenous demand growth and income distribution, in particular the gender wage gap, which will yield the 'productivity growth regime'. Finally, in the third step, we will examine the interaction of the demand growth and the productivity growth regimes and explore the effects of closing gender wage gaps on the 'long-run overall growth regime'.

As will be seen below, we will focus on the effects of distribution, and of gender wage inequality in particular, on the demand growth and productivity growth regimes, and on their interaction. For this purpose, we will ignore potential direct effects of technical change and productivity growth on distribution, both between labour and capital and between male and female workers.[14] For the demand effects of technical change and productivity growth, we will focus on investment in the capital stock. We will abstract from potential effects of technical change on consumption, i.e. an effect on the propensity to consume and thus to save through the innovation of new products, for example. We will also ignore potential effects of technical change on exports, i.e. product innovation which might affect the income elasticity of demand for exports. Finally, regarding the type of technical change, we assume that it is labour saving and capital embodied, and hence 'Harrod-neutral'. Technical progress is hence associated with rising labour productivity. And since we keep the assumption that productivity of male and female labour is the same, it also means that they grow at the same rate. The capital-labour ratio $[k = K/(L_M + L_F)]$ increases at the same rate as male and female labour productivity does, and the capital-potential output ratio therefore remains constant, and for simplicity we continue assuming that it is equal to one $(K/Y^P = 1)$. For the technical material and intermediate product-output ratio (μ) we also assume that this is not affected by technical progress and thus remains constant, too.

For our model from the previous section these assumptions imply that technical change has no direct effect on the mark-up and on the ratio of unit material and intermediate product costs to unit wage costs (z) (equation (23)). This also implies that the male nominal wage rate (w_M), as well as the female wage rate $(w_F = \varepsilon w_M)$ rise at the same rate as labour productivity, we thus have productivity-oriented wage increases, such that neither distribution nor the domestic price level is affected by technical

---

[13]However, in Hein (2014, Chapter 8), as well as in Naastepad (2006), Hein and Tarassow (2010) and Hartwig (2013, 2014), a post-Kaleckian model has been used, and, of course, gender wage inequality has not been of any concern.

[14]See Naastepad (2006) and Hartwig (2013, 2014) for models in which productivity growth negatively affects the wage share. Giovanazzi (2018) has proposed a model in a similar vein, in which a reduction in the gender wage gap promotes productivity growth and reduces the overall wage share. See Hein (2014, Chapter 8) for a critical assessments of such approaches and the underlying assumption – basically that real wage growth does not keep pace with labour productivity growth, which means some implicit long-run productivity illusion of workers, apart from the deterioration of their bargaining power which would be reflected in a change in the mark-up.

change, ceteris paribus. As productivity growth does not affect the domestic price level, and we rule out, somewhat unrealistically, an improvement of the income elasticity of exports by means of technical progress, then also the real exchange rate (e^r) and exports are not directly affected by domestic technical change.

With these assumptions, we can keep for the model in the current section the equations (25)-(28) determining income distribution, equation (29) for the real exchange rate and international price competitiveness of domestic producers, as well as the saving function in equation (16) and the net export function in equation (33).

4.2. Demand Growth Regime with Exogenous Productivity Growth

For the determination of the demand growth regime, we use the saving function in equation (16), the net export function in equation (33), the equilibrium condition (32) and the goods market equilibrium stability condition (34). Technical progress, which for the time being is assumed to be exogenous, only affects investment in our simple model. Since technical progress is embodied in the capital stock, it will stimulate investment. Firms have to invest in new machines and equipment in order to gain from productivity growth, which is made available by new technical knowledge. This effect on investment will be the more pronounced the more fundamental technical change is: The invention of new basic technologies will have a stronger effect on real investment than marginal changes in technologies already in existence. With these considerations, we can extend the investment function (12) by a term indicating the positive effect of (potential) productivity growth ($\hat{y}$):

$$g = \alpha + \beta u + \omega \hat{y}, \quad \beta, \omega > 0 \tag{39}$$

With this new investment function, our equilibrium rates of capacity utilisation and capital accumulation become:

$$u^* = \frac{\alpha + \omega \hat{y} + \psi e^r + \zeta u_f}{h(s_\Pi - s_W) + s_W - \beta + \varphi} \tag{40}$$

$$g^* = \frac{(\alpha + \omega \hat{y})[h(s_\Pi - s_W) + s_W + \varphi] + \beta(\psi e^r + \zeta u_f)}{h(s_\Pi - s_W) + s_W - \beta + \varphi} \tag{41}$$

Since productivity growth is still considered to be exogenous, the effects of changes in the gender wage gap are the same as analysed in the previous section:

$$\frac{\partial u^*}{\partial \varepsilon} = \frac{\frac{\partial e^r}{\partial \varepsilon} \psi - u^* \left[\frac{\partial h}{\partial \varepsilon}(s_\Pi - s_W) + \frac{\partial s_W}{\partial \varepsilon}(1 - h) \right]}{h(s_\Pi - s_W) + s_W - \beta + \varphi} \tag{40a}$$

$$\frac{\partial g^*}{\partial \varepsilon} = \frac{\beta \left\{ \frac{\partial e^r}{\partial \varepsilon} \psi - u^* \left[\frac{\partial h}{\partial \varepsilon}(s_\Pi - s_W) + \frac{\partial s_W}{\partial \varepsilon}(1 - h) \right] \right\}}{h(s_\Pi - s_W) + s_W - \beta + \varphi} \tag{41a}$$

Considering only stable goods market equilibria, the demand growth regime may be gender equality-led or -burdened, depending on the parameters, as explained in the previous section.

4.3. Productivity Growth Regime with Exogenous Capital Accumulation

Our productivity growth regime is based on Kaldor's (1957, 1961) technical progress function, according to which productivity growth is positively affected by the growth of capital intensity, because technical progress is capital embodied.[15] By means of investing in the capital stock, firms turn potential technical progress (developed in the R&D departments) into actual productivity growth. Apart from capital accumulation, we will consider a second determinant of productivity growth, which has been taken into account in recent theoretical and empirical work based on Kaleckian models. Making use of an idea proposed by Marx (1867) and Hicks (1932), we introduce a wage-push variable into the productivity growth equation. An increase in wages and pressure towards a rising wage share and falling profit share, associated with narrowing the gender wage gap, will accelerate firms' efforts to improve productivity growth in order to prevent the profit share from falling, for example through the acceleration of the diffusion of innovations (Dutt 2006). Taking into account both determinants yields the following equation for labour productivity growth:

$$\hat{y} = \eta(\varepsilon) + \rho g - \gamma h(\varepsilon), \quad \eta, \rho, \gamma > 0 \tag{42}$$

Independently of capital stock growth and functional income distribution, productivity growth is also affected by several institutional circumstances, like government technology and education policies, and also by 'learning by doing' effects. Here we can include another effect of improving gender wage equality on productivity growth, which has been explored by Braunstein, van Staveren, and Tavani (2011, 2020) and highlighted by Onaran, Oyvat, and Fotoupoulo (2019) and Seguino (2020) in the context of gender (in)equality effects on social reproduction. Since female expenditures seem to focus more on the education of children, for example, narrowing the gender wage gap will raise long-run productivity growth through enhanced human capacities.

Summing up, the productivity growth regime in our model is always gender equality-led. Not yet taking into account the effects on demand growth, a lower gender wage gap will be associated with higher productivity growth because of the associated wage-push effects, on the one hand, and the social reproduction and human capacities effect, on the other hand:

$$\frac{\partial \hat{y}}{\partial \varepsilon} = \frac{\partial \eta}{\partial \varepsilon} - \gamma \frac{\partial h}{\partial \varepsilon} > 0 \tag{42a}$$

4.3. Overall Long-run Growth Regime

In order to include the interaction between the demand growth regime and the productivity growth regime, we plug equation (42) into (41) and receive the long-run overall

---

[15]Another possibility would have been Kaldor's (1966) application of Verdoorn's law, according to which the growth rate of labour productivity in industrial production is positively associated with the growth rate of output. This can be explained by static and dynamic economies of scale: The expansion of aggregate demand, sales and hence the market allows for increasing rationalisation and mechanisation and favourably affects technical progress and productivity growth. See Hein (2014, Chapter 8) for the introduction of this possibility and a review of the empirical estimations of such a productivity growth equation.

equilibrium rate of capital accumulation:

$$g^{**} = \frac{[\alpha + \omega(\eta - \gamma h)][h(s_\Pi - s_W) + s_W + \varphi] + \beta[\psi e^r + \zeta u_f]}{(1 - \omega\rho)[h(s_\Pi - s_W) + s_W + \varphi] - \beta} \qquad (43)$$

Inserting equation (41) into (42) provides the long-run equilibrium rate of labour productivity growth:

$$\hat{y}^{**} = \frac{(\alpha\rho + \eta - \gamma h)[h(s_\Pi - s_W) + s_W + \varphi] + \beta[\psi e^r + \zeta u_f - \eta + \gamma h]}{(1 - \omega\rho)[h(s_\Pi - s_W) + s_W + \varphi] - \beta} \qquad (44)$$

Graphically, this long-run endogenous overall growth equilibrium can be seen in Figure 1, which presents equilibrium capital accumulation of the demand growth regime from equation (41) as a function of productivity growth, and productivity growth from equation (42) as a function of capital accumulation. The existence and the stability of the overall growth equilibrium require that the slope of the graph for the capital accumulation equation exceeds the slope of the graph representing the productivity growth equation. Assuming the goods market stability condition (34) to hold, for the existence of positive long-run overall equilibrium values of the rates of capital accumulation and productivity growth in equations (43) and (44), and for the stability of this equilibrium, we also need:

$$\omega\rho < 1 \qquad (45)$$

Since the derivatives of the long-run overall equilibrium values in equations (43) and (44) with respect to the gender wage equality parameter turn quite cumbersome, we provide a graphical analysis of the long-run overall growth equilibrium effects of a reduction in the gender wage gap. Figure 2 shows the case in which the demand growth regime is gender equality-led. A reduction in the gender wage gap shifts the curve of the equilibrium rate

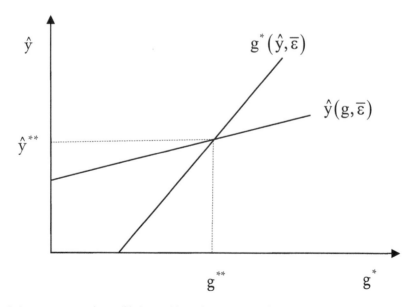

Figure 1. Long-run growth equilibrium with endogenous productivity growth.

of capital accumulation (g*) to the right. Without considering the human capacities and the wage push effects, each associated with narrowing the gender wage gap, the economy would thus move from equilibrium A to equilibrium B, i.e. a higher rate of capital accumulation and a higher rate of productivity growth because of higher capital accumulation. Including the human capacities and wage push effects on productivity growth, however, also shifts the productivity growth function to the left, so that the economy will end up in equilibrium C, with much higher rates of capital accumulation and productivity growth.

Whereas the effect of reducing the gender wage gap in the case of a gender equality-led demand growth regime is uniquely positive, this is no longer the case if the demand growth regime is gender equality-burdened, as can be seen in Figure 3(a–c). With only a weakly negative effect on the demand growth regime but a strong positive effect through the human capacities and wage push channels on the productivity growth regime, the effect on the long-run overall growth regime might still be expansionary (Figure 3(a)). However, with strongly negative effects on the demand growth regime and only weakly positive effects on the productivity regime, the effect of closing the gender wage gap on the long-run overall growth regime will be contractionary (Figure 3(c)). Finally, with intermediate effects on both sub-regimes, the effect of narrowing gender wage gaps on the long-run overall regime might be mixed or intermediate: Whereas the effect on the accumulation rate in the long-run equilibrium is negative, the effect on the productivity growth rate may nonetheless be positive (Figure 3(b)).

Table 1 summarises the different responses and shows the different long-run overall growth regimes which may emerge. Since the partial effect of improving gender wage equality on the productivity regime is always positive, the overall long-run equilibrium growth effects will then depend on the type of the demand growth regime, i.e. gender equality-led or -burdened. The effect of closing the gender wage gap on the demand growth regime can be decomposed into domestic and foreign demand effects, which depend on those factors analysed in Section 3.3: the differential in the propensities to

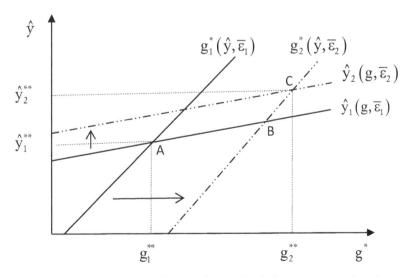

Figure 2. Decreasing gender wage gap in a gender equality-led demand growth regime.

a) expansionary long-run overall regime

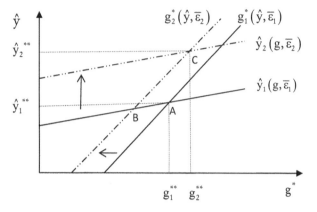

b) Intermediate long-run overall regime

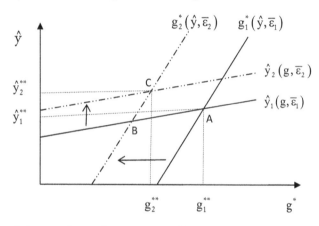

c) Contractionary long-run overall regime

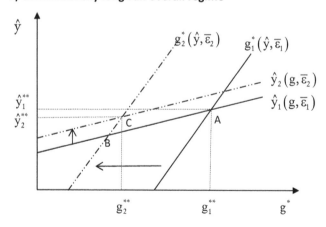

Figure 3. Decreasing gender wage gap in a gender equality-burdened demand growth regime. (a) expansionary long-run overall regime; (b) Intermediate long-run overall regime and (c) Contractionary long-run overall regime.

Table 1. Effects of a decline in the gender wage gap ($d\varepsilon > 0$) on the long-run overall growth regime.

	Gender equality-led demand growth regime ($\partial g^*/\partial\varepsilon) > 0$		Gender equality-burdened demand growth regime ($\partial g^*/\partial\varepsilon) < 0$	
$\partial g^{**}/\partial\varepsilon$	+	+	−	−
$\partial \hat{y}^{**}/\partial\varepsilon$	+	+	+	−
Overall	Expansionary	expansionary	intermediate	contractionary

save out of female and male wages, the differential in the propensities to save out profits and out of aggregate wages, the strengths of the effects of an improvement of the gender wage equality on the profit share and on the average propensity to save out of wages, the price elasticity of exports, and the effects of reducing the gender wage gap on the real exchange rate.

5. Conclusions

We have introduced a gender wage gap, adjusted for structural discrimination of women with respect to education, access to high skilled jobs and labour market segregation, into basic one-good textbook versions of the neo-Kaleckian distribution and growth model for advanced capitalist economies. For these model economies, we have examined the effects of improving gender wage equality on income distribution, aggregate demand, capacity utilisation, capital accumulation and productivity growth.

In a stepwise process, gradually raising the complexity of the models in order to understand some of the channels of influence of improving gender wage gaps and the related effects on distribution and the macro-economy, we have started with a closed economy model. Here, narrowing the gender wage gap will not affect income distribution between profits and wages, but only improve the female wage share at the expense of the male wage share if those factors determining the mark-up in firms' pricing, like the overall bargaining power of labour or the degree of competition of firms in the goods market remain, constant. Under these conditions, if the propensity to save out of female wages falls short of the propensity to save out of male wages, aggregate demand and growth will be gender equality-led, and if the propensity to save out of female wages is higher than out of male wages, the demand and growth regime will be gender equality-burdened.

In the open economy model, narrowing the gender wage gap will also affect profit and aggregate wage shares, even with mark-ups in pricing remaining constant. The female wage share will rise more than the male wage share falls, raising the aggregate wage share and lowering the profit share accordingly. This will be associated with a loss in international price competitiveness of domestic producers, which will have a negative impact on foreign demand. If the propensity to save out of female wages is lower than out of male wages, reducing the gender wage gap will have an unambiguously expansionary effect on domestic demand, and if the effect on net exports is small, the total regime will be gender equality-led. Even if the propensity to save out of female wages is higher than out of male wages, and the effect on net exports remains weak, a gender equality-led regime is still possible, because of the rise in the aggregate wage share and the fall in the profit share. However, with high positive differentials between female and male propensities to save out of wages and stronger net export effects, we will rather see a gender equality-burdened regime.

In the final model, we have included endogenous productivity growth driven by capital stock growth, human capacities and wage-push effects. We have found that with a gender equality-led demand growth regime, the overall equilibrium growth regime will be expansionary: Reducing the gender wage gap will improve long-run demand growth and productivity growth. With a gender equality-burdened demand growth regime, the overall equilibrium growth regime may still be expansionary, if improving gender wage equality generates strong productivity growth effects. If this is not the case, we will see intermediate or contractionary regimes. In the latter, reducing the gender wage gap will generate lower demand and productivity growth.

Similar to more complex models designed for developing and emerging economies, which contain different sectors, segregated labour markets and balance-of-payments constraints, for example, we have shown with our much simpler model that the effects of improving gender wage equality on distribution, aggregate demand and growth are not unique but depend on specific institutional and behavioural features. These have been clearly identified for the different variants of the model – without claiming to be comprehensive.

Acknowledgements

This paper has benefitted from discussions with Carmen Giovanazzi on her Master thesis (Giovanazzi 2018). For helpful comments I would also like to thank Ryan Woodgate and two anonymous referees. Remaining errors are mine, of course.

Disclosure Statement

No potential conflict of interest was reported by the author(s).

References

Berik, G., Y. van der Meulen Rodgers, and S. Seguino. 2009. 'Feminist Economics of Inequality, Development, and Growth.' *Feminist Economics* 15 (3): 1–33.

Bhaduri, A., and S. Marglin. 1990. 'Unemployment and the Real Wage: The Economic Basis for Contesting Political Ideologies.' *Cambridge Journal of Economics* 14: 375–393.

Blecker, R. A. 1989. 'International Competition, Income Distribution and Economic Growth.' *Cambridge Journal of Economics* 13: 395–412.

Blecker, R. A. 2016. 'Wage-led Versus Profit-led Demand Regimes: The Long and the Short of it.' *Review of Keynesian Economics* 4 (3): 373–390.

Blecker, R. A., and S. Seguino. 2002. 'Macroeconomic Effects of Reducing Gender Wage Inequality in an Export-Oriented, Semi-Industrialized Economy.' *Review of Development Economics* 6: 103–119.

Blecker, R. A., and M. Setterfield. 2019. *Heterodox Macroeconomics: Models of Demand, Distribution and Growth.* Cheltenham: Edward Elgar.

Braunstein, E., R. Bouhia, and S. Seguino. 2020. 'Social Reproduction, Gender Equality and Economic Growth.' *Cambridge Journal of Economics* 44 (1): 126–156.

Braunstein, E., I. van Staveren, and D. Tavani. 2011. 'Embedding Care and Unpaid Work in Macroeconomic Modeling: A Structuralist Approach.' *Feminist Economics* 17 (4): 5–31.

Dutt, A. K. 1984. 'Stagnation, Income Distribution and Monopoly Power.' *Cambridge Journal of Economics* 8: 25–40.

Dutt, A. K. 1987. 'Alternative Closures Again: A Comment on "Growth, Distribution and Inflation".' *Cambridge Journal of Economics* 11: 75–82.

Dutt, A. K. 2006. 'Aggregate Demand, Aggregate Supply and Economic Growth.' *International Review of Applied Economics* 20: 319–336.

Fukuda-Parr, S., J. Heintz, and S. Seguino. 2013. 'Critical Perspectives on Financial and Economic Crises: Heterodox Macroeconomics Meets Feminist Economics.' *Feminist Economics* 19 (3): 4–31.

Giovanazzi, C. 2018. *'Macroeconomic Effects of Gender Inequality – A Structuralist Approach.'* (Master Thesis). Master International Economics and Master Economic Policies in the Age of Globalisation, Berlin School of Economics and Law and University Paris 13.

Hartwig, J. 2013. 'Distribution and Growth in Demand and Productivity in Switzerland (1950–2010).' *Applied Economics Letters* 20: 938–944.

Hartwig, J. 2014. 'Testing the Bhaduri–Marglin Model with OECD Panel Data.' *International Review of Applied Economics* 28 (4): 419–435.

Hein, E. 2008. *Money, Distribution Conflict and Capital Accumulation. Contributions to 'Monetary Analysis'.* Basingstoke: Palgrave Macmillan.

Hein, E. 2012. *The Macroeconomics of Finance-Dominated Capitalism – and its Crisis.* Cheltenham: Edward Elgar.

Hein, E. 2014. *Distribution and Growth after Keynes: A Post-Keynesian Guide.* Cheltenham: Edward Elgar.

Hein, E. 2017. 'Post-Keynesian Macroeconomics Since the mid-1990s – Main Developments.' *European Journal of Economics and Economic Policies: Intervention* 14 (2): 131–172.

Hein, E., and F. J. Prante. 2020. 'Functional Distribution and Wage Inequality in Recent Kaleckian Growth Models.' In *Economic Growth and Macroeconomic Stabilization Policies in Post-Keynesian Economics,* edited by H. Bougrine, and L.-P. Rochon. Cheltenham: Edward Elgar.

Hein, E., and A. Tarassow. 2010. 'Distribution, Aggregate Demand and Productivity Growth – Theory and Empirical Results for Six OECD Countries Based on a Post-Kaleckian Model.' *Cambridge Journal of Economics* 34: 727–754.

Hein, E., and L. Vogel. 2008. 'Distribution and Growth Reconsidered – Empirical Results for six OECD Countries.' *Cambridge Journal of Economics* 32: 479–511.

Hicks, J. 1932. *The Theory of Wages.* London: Macmillan.

Kaldor, N. 1957. 'A Model of Economic Growth.' *The Economic Journal* 67: 591–624.

Kaldor, N. 1961. 'Capital Accumulation and Economic Growth.' In *The Theory of Capital,* edited by F. A. Lutz, and D. C. Hague. London: Macmillan.

Kaldor, N. 1966. *Causes of the Slow Rate of Economic Growth in the United Kingdom.* Cambridge, UK: Cambridge University Press.

Kalecki, M. 1937. 'The Principle of Increasing Risk.' *Economica* 4: 440–447.

Kalecki, M. 1954. *Theory of Economic Dynamics.* London: George Allen and Unwin.

Keynes, J. M. 1936. *The General Theory of Employment, Interest, and Money, The Collected Writings of J.M. Keynes, Vol. VII.* London, Basingstoke: Macmillan. 1973.

Kurz, H. D. 1990. 'Technical Change, Growth and Distribution: A Steady-State Approach to "Unsteady" Growth.' In *Capital, Distribution and Effective Demand,* edited by H. D. Kurz. Cambridge, UK: Polity Press.

Lavoie, M. 1995a. 'The Kaleckian Model of Growth and Distribution and its neo-Ricardian and neo-Marxian Critiques.' *Cambridge Journal of Economics* 19 (6): 789–818.

Lavoie, M. 1995b. 'Interest Rates in Post-Keynesian Models of Growth and Distribution.' *Metroeconomica* 46: 146–177.

Lavoie, M. 1996. 'Unproductive Outlays and Capital Accumulation with Target-Return Pricing.' *Review of Social Economy* 54 (3): 303–322.

Lavoie, M. 2009. *'Cadrisme* Within a Post-Keynesian Model of Growth and Distribution.' *Review of Political Economy* 21 (3): 371–393.

Lavoie, M. 2014. *Post-Keynesian Economics: New Foundations.* Cheltenham: Edward Elgar.

Marx, K. 1867. *Das Kapital. Kritik der politischen Ökonomie, Erster Band: Der Produktionsprozeß des Kapitals, 4th edition 1890*, edited by F. Engels. Reprinted as Marx-Engels-Werke, Volume 23, Berlin: Dietz Verlag 1962. English translation: *Capital. A Critique of Political Economy, Volume 1: The Process of Capitalist Production*. New York: International Publisher.

Naastepad, C. W. M. 2006. 'Technology, Demand and Distribution: A Cumulative Growth Model with an Application to the Dutch Productivity Growth Slowdown.' *Cambridge Journal of Economics* 30: 403–434.

Onaran, Ö. 2015. 'The Role of Gender Equality in an Equality-led Sustainable Development Strategy.' Greenwich Papers in Political Economy, No. GPERC26, Greenwich Political Economy Research Centre.

Onaran, Ö, and G. Galanis. 2014. 'Income Distribution and Growth: A Global Model.' *Environment and Planning A: Economy and Space* 46: 2489–2513.

Onaran, Ö, and T. Obst. 2016. 'Wage-led Growth in the EU15 Member-States: The Effects of Income Distribution on Growth, Investment, Trade Balance and Inflation.' *Cambridge Journal of Economics* 40 (6): 1517–1551.

Onaran, Ö, C. Oyvat, and F. Fotoupoulo. 2019. 'The Effects of Gender Inequality, Wages, Wealth Concentration and Fiscal Policy on Macroeconomic Performance.' Greenwich Papers in Political Economy, No. GPERC71, University of Greenwich, Institute of Political Economy, Governance, Finance and Accountability.

Rowthorn, R. E. 1981. 'Demand, Real Wages and Economic Growth.' *Thames Papers in Political Economy* Autumn: 1–39.

Seguino, S. 2010. 'Gender, Distribution, and Balance of Payments Constrained Growth in Developing Countries.' *Review of Political Economy* 22: 373–404.

Seguino, S. 2012. 'Macroeconomics, Human Development, and Distribution.' *Journal of Human Development and Capabilities: A Multi-Disciplinary Journal for People-Centered Development* 13 (1): 59–81.

Seguino, S. 2019. 'Feminist and Stratification Theories' Lessons from the Crisis and Their Relevance for Post-Keynesian Theory.' *European Journal of Economics and Economic Policies: Intervention* 16 (2): 193–207.

Seguino, S. 2020. 'Engendering Macroeconomic Theory and Policy.' *Feminist Economics* 26 (2): 27–61.

Seguino, S., and E. Braunstein. 2019. 'The Costs of Exclusion: Gender Job Segregation, Structural Change and the Labour Share of Income.' *Development and Change* 50 (4): 976–1008.

Seguino, S., and M. Sagrario Floro. 2003. 'Does Gender Have an Effect on Aggregate Saving? An Empirical Analysis.' *International Review of Applied Economics* 17 (2): 147–166.

Setterfield, M., and J. Cornwall. 2002. 'A neo-Kaldorian Perspective on the Rise and the Decline of the Golden Age.' In *The Economics of Demand-led Growth. Challenging the Supply-Side Vision of the Long Run*, edited by M. Setterfield. Cheltenham: Edward Elgar.

Stockhammer, E. 2017. 'Wage-led Versus Profit-led Demand: What Have we Learned? A Kaleckian-Minskyan View.' *Review of Keynesian Economics* 5 (1): 25–42.

Index

For Product Safety Concerns and Information please contact our
EU representative GPSR@taylorandfrancis.com Taylor & Francis
Verlag GmbH, Kaufingerstraße 24, 80331 München, Germany